Elochukwu E. Uzukwu (Ed.)

Mission for Diversity

Interreligious Studies

edited by

Prof. Dr. Frans Wijsen
and
Dr. Jorge E. Castillo Guerra

This series is published by the
Centre for World Christianity
and Interreligious Studies
at Radboud University Nijmegen

Volume 8

LIT

Mission for Diversity

Exploring Christian Mission in the Contemporary World

edited by

Elochukwu E. Uzukwu

LIT

Bibliographic information published by the Deutsche Nationalbibliothek
The Deutsche Nationalbibliothek lists this publication in the Deutsche Nationalbibliografie; detailed bibliographic data are available in the Internet at http://dnb.d-nb.de.

ISBN 978-3-643-90641-0

A catalogue record for this book is available from the British Library

Klosbachstr. 107
CH-8032 Zürich
Tel. +41 (0) 44-251 75 05 Fax +41 (0) 44-251 75 06
E-Mail: zuerich@lit-verlag.ch http://www.lit-verlag.ch

Distribution:

In the UK: Global Book Marketing, e-mail: mo@centralbooks.com
In North America: International Specialized Book Services, e-mail: orders@isbs.com
In Germany: LIT Verlag Fresnostr. 2, D-48159 Münster
Tel. +49 (0) 2 51-620 32 22, Fax +49 (0) 2 51-922 60 99, E-mail: vertrieb@lit-verlag.de

In Austria: Medienlogistik Pichler-ÖBZ, e-mail: mlo@medien-logistik.at
e-books are available at www.litwebshop.de

Contents

Foreword

As a fellow Spiritan who had the privilege of working closely with Fr. Pierre Schouver while he was Superior General of the Spiritan Congregation, and as one who now succeeds him in that leadership capacity, I am very pleased to present this collection of essays and studies, compiled and published under the auspices of the Endowed Chair in Mission at Duquesne University which bears Pierre Schouver's name.

The Spiritan Congregation, which today serves in over 60 countries worldwide and comprises members from the continents of Africa, Asia, Europe, Australia, North and South America, owes much of its current missionary vision and dynamism to Pierre Schouver who led the Congregation from 1992 to 2004, a critical period in the evolution of missionary theology and of the Congregation to which he belonged. Immersed in the spirit of the Second Vatican Council which took place while he was a student in Rome, imbued by his profound grasp of the creative missionary intuitions of the founders of the Spiritan Congregation, and shaped by his own personal experience as a missionary in the Central African Republic, Schouver promoted a vision of mission that stressed the primacy of the role of the Spirit of God, attentiveness to the signs of the times, a willingness and a courage to launch out anew into the unknown even with limited means, the mutual enrichment of intercultural encounter and the importance of credible personal and community witness on the part of missionaries who must first live and embody the Gospel they are called to bring to others.

As the editor Elochukwu Uzukwu points out in his introduction, this understanding of mission called for a critical and creative appropriation and a re-evaluation of its history on the part of the Congregation, for a process of genuine conversion in seeking to discern and respond to the call of the Spirit in the rapidly changing circumstances of the contemporary world. As the Congregation itself evolved significantly in its international and intercultural composition over Schouver's period in office, this process of reflection and re-examination led inter alia to a growing realization that the diversity of its membership is integral to Spiritan mission today: "Conflict, racialism and the cult of the individual are all too prevalent in the world of today. By coming together from so many different places and cultures, we are saying to our brothers and sisters that the unity of the human race is not an impossible dream" (Maynooth General Chapter, 1998). Diversity is a "response to the call of the Holy Spirit to all of us, to witness to a new quality of human solidarity, surpassing individualism, ethnocentrism and nationalism" (Torre D'Aguilha General Chapter, 2004).

Pierre himself embodied the humility essential to missionary activity in any era: a profound awareness of one's own limitations, a perennial willingness to listen and to learn, a joyful openness to the other in his or her otherness, the certainty of enrichment in diversity and mutual encounter. In reflecting on the experience of the past he once pointed out with typical perspicacity that the greatest obstacle to Spirit-led missionary activity was not our human mistakes but our pretensions.

Uzukwu, the current holder of the Father Pierre Schouver C.S.Sp. Endowed Chair in Mission, has done a very valuable service for contemporary mission in compiling the present collection of essays and special studies emerging from diverse locations and cultural groups and written by scholars who do theology from a multidisciplinary perspective. With contributors from Asian, African, Caribbean, European and North American perspectives on topics ranging from a methodology for mission in the contemporary world, the impact of Vatican II on Church and mission, mission and dialogue, and specific issues related to mission and ministry, the collection will appeal to a wide audience. Pierre Schouver would have read this collective work with great interest as it reflects his fundamental intuition that mission is essentially a pilgrimage together to discover the action of the Spirit in our midst.

John Fogarty, C.S.Sp.
Superior General
February 2, 2015

Introduction: Setting the Stage – Prospects and Challenges from the South

1 Proclaiming the Gospel Today – Dynamics and Challenges of Location

Elochukwu UZUKWU

Pierre Schouver: Insight into Spiritan and World Mission

The will to embrace change, diversity and difference, to commit to the unknown and to launch into deep and uncharted waters, trusting in and guided by the sure and unerring hand of the Holy Spirit, is the way Father Pierre Schouver read the Spiritan mission commitment, located within the worldwide mission of the Church.

The Congregation of the Holy Spirit (the Spiritans), diverse in membership and composition, missions today in a very complex multicultural world. Father Schouver was Superior General of this group of about 3000 priests, brothers and lay associates for 12 years (1992-2004), a period that witnessed a radical shift in the demographics of world Spiritan membership and ministry. For example, at the end of his first mandate, May 1 1998, Pierre Schouver stated, "Since 1992, 414 [candidates] have joined the Institute, of whom 321 are from Africa"[1].

Within this small group of Catholic missionaries, the Church, fervent in the Spirit, is grappling with the profundity of its very nature-mission and is courageously facing the imponderable in the praxis of mediating/displaying worldwide human inter-relationship. This is the heartbeat of mission today: mission is true only when it is a participation in the mission of the relational Triune God.

The Triune God, an excited Pierre Schouver learned, is the energy behind the opening of "new frontiers to be crossed" by Spiritan missionaries! The frontiers embody diversity and difference. The frontiers call for creative imagination and exchange through hospitality and collaboration! The challenging "new frontiers to be crossed" call for the praxis of synesthesia (the culture of hearing or feeling with all the senses at the same time) enabling the full encounter of the other in her otherness.[2]

---

1 Pentecost Message, 1998.

2 See the suggestive phenomenological reflection of David Abram, *The spell of the sensuous: perception and language in a more-than-human world*, 1st ed. (New York: Pantheon Books, 1996).

The rapid tilt of the demographics of Spiritan membership in a way recaptures the worldwide southward shift of Christianity. Prompted by this, Schouver took a second and creative look at the miracle or surprise of Pentecost:

> In Christian times the Gospel left the shores of Europe to go to what then appeared to be the ends of the earth. But this picture is turned on its head when we look at the missionary appointments of the present generation of Spiritans; a Nigerian leaves for Papua, an Australian for Kenya; a Mauritian goes to Pakistan, a Zairian to Brazil, a Brazilian to Senegal.[3]

Schouver did not say this to confound the oft-quoted line of Hillaire Belloc, "the faith is *Europe and Europe* is the faith." However, he was insistent that the urgency of the new Pentecost must be lived in the Congregation. It is a call for radical change, another name for striving towards perfection. He borrowed the saying of John Henry Newman, "To live is to *change*, and to be perfect is to *have changed often*." In his report to the 18th General Chapter of the Spiritan Congregation, Dublin, Ireland (1998) Schouver challenged the members of the Congregation of the Holy Spirit to have their feet firmly planted in the real and ever changing earth of human habitation and be ready to adapt without betraying the Gospel: "Our Congregation is not a separate planet." This insight is rooted in the vision of Francis Mary Paul Libermann, the second founder of the Spiritans:

> The trouble with the clergy in recent times, is that they have got stuck in the ideas of the past. The world moves on, and our enemies have adapted their armoury to the spirit of the age while we are left way behind! Without abandoning the spirit of the Gospel, we must get up to date, do good and combat evil in the world as it is today.[4]

Pierre Schouver was guiding Spiritans in the renewed Spirit of the founders (Poullart des Places and Francis Libermann) and in the spirit of renewal inaugurated by Vatican II. Schouver was a graduate student in Rome when Vatican II was in session. He imbibed the spirit of the council that understood mission as woven into the life of the Church that is "in Christ like a sacrament or as a sign and instrument both of a very closely knit union with God and of the unity of the whole human race."[5] In the view of Schouver, all missionary congregations, and in particular Spiritan missionaries, must appreciate the profound impact and import of Vatican II on the self-awareness of the Church that gets a mission that it does

---

3 Pentecost Message 1996.

4 Congregation of the Holy Spirit, Superior General's Report, XVIII General Chapter, Maynooth, Ireland, 12 July -08 August 1998. Document CG98-17E, 1.0.1. The quote comes from Fr. Libermann in 1848. N.D. 151.

5 Vatican II, Lumen Gentium, 1.

not own. The mission that is constitutive of the church's very nature flows from the fount-like love of the Trinitarian God—from the Father through the Son, and in the Holy Spirit.[6] Spiritan mission, in the mind of Vatican II, is located within the wider mission of the Catholic Church. As the Vatican II Professor of Theology at Catholic Theological Union, Robert Schreiter, puts it: for Vatican II

> Mission became, therefore, more than an extending of the perimeters of the church, it was to be something motivating the very heart of the church, not because some command had been laid upon the faithful, but because by being missionary the church was drawn into the life of the Trinity itself.[7]

Spiritan insight into this insertion of the Church into the life of the Triune God creates the enabling passion to witness to the life of the Trinity (mission) anywhere and anytime; especially in those locations where the Church has difficulty finding laborers. In the time of Libermann (the second founder of the Spiritans), the focus was *l'œuvre des noirs*: the work among Blacks enslaved and oppressed worldwide. With the strengthening of the membership of the Congregation by continental Africans, Schouver and his council thought it was the right time to implement the decision of the General Chapter of Itaici, Brazil (1994), to reopen Spiritan mission to Asia.

Spiritans were in India between 1862 and 1888. They withdrew in 1888 to focus their attention on Africa. The new move towards Asia after 1994 was going to generate controversy: "How could we take on the challenge of mission in South-East Asia with such small means at our disposal?"[8] Does the "new initiative in Asia" not mean, "lessening our efforts in Africa", especially with "the cry of refugees?"[9] He had to explain in his measured and humble style that mission to East Asia does not compromise the focus on Africa. Secondly, the protagonist of mission is the Holy Spirit in whom we trust! To engage in mission today, one must endorse the overriding spirituality of waiting for the moment of the Holy Spirit. Schouver explained to the Enlarged General Council of Spiritans in 2001 (Duquesne University, Pittsburgh): "We cannot give the Spirit to ourselves so this is why we need sources of inspiration." The moment dictates receiving

---

6 Vatican II, Ad Gentes, 2.

7 Cited in Stephen B Bevans and Roger P. Schroeder. *Constants in Context – a Theology of Mission for Today*. New York: Orbis, 2004. 249-250; Robert J. Schreiter, "Changes in Roman Catholic Attitudes toward Proselytism and Mission" in Scherer, James A., and Stephen B. Bevans, eds. *New Directions in Mission and Evangelization*. Vol. 2. *Theological Foundations* (Maryknoll: Orbis, 1992), 113-125, p. 117

8 Christmas Message 1996.

9 Pentecost Message 1997

this inspiration—God is doing among us in our world what we need to discover. Borrowing from the "Testament" of the saintly Abbé Pierre, founder of Emmaus movement in France, Schouver chimed, "Emmaus [read Spiritan mission] is not so much what we have done as what has happened to us." Spiritan missionaries trusting in and guided by the Holy Spirit should always be ready to learn.[10] The 1998 Spiritan General Chapter in Maynooth affirmed the Holy Spirit as guide: "The very name 'Spiritan' means that we are people dedicated to following the ways of the Spirit; our spirituality must therefore be based on discernment, availability and practical union with God. Mary is a model to be followed" (Maynooth 3.1.).[11]

It is in the power of the new Pentecost, embracing the spirituality of learning from what has happened to us (thanks to the Spirit) rather than what we are doing, that we present this collective work, *Mission for Diversity: Exploring Christian Mission in the Contemporary World.*

Mission for Diversity is a collection of essays and special studies that emerge from diverse locations and diverse cultural groups. The contributors to the collection are well-known experts, scholars who do theology from a multidisciplinary perspective. The collection is made up of edited papers presented under the auspices of Father Pierre Schouver C.S.Sp. Endowed Chair in Mission, Duquesne University. Contributors come from the Vatican (Pontifical Council for Justice and Peace), Colleges in the USA, Europe, Asia and Africa. The tone of the essays shows how theology is done; how mission theology should be done as an interdisciplinary and intercultural conversation.

Before presenting the different foci of the collection, I underline two key points that embody Schouver's missiological insight that impacted the Congregation of the Holy Spirit in particular and that is a major contribution to worldwide mission in general. Contributors to this collection perhaps reecho these points. First, Schouver led the Spiritans, a missionary congregation, into a critical and creative appropriation or reevaluation of their history. Second, Schouver insisted that Spiritans and missionaries must strive to abandon the territorial, colonial-imperial image of mission, and always live in the Church (local-universal), and everywhere honor the church as sacrament, in the image of the relational Triune God.

---

[10] Congregation of the Holy Spirit, Superior General's Report, XVIII General Chapter, Maynooth, Ireland, 12 July -08 August 1998. Document CG98-17E, 4.1.1.

[11] Schouver, EGC (Enlarged General Council) Pittsburgh 2001, p. 3

Schouver and Ressourcement: Rejuvenating Spiritan Mission History and Focus

Pierre Schouver dreamed of Spiritans as a group that will constantly reexamine their history and tradition, for ongoing missiological revitalization. The self-review is not to nostalgically direct "our gaze back on the past," but rather to "sharpen our vision as we seek to know where the Spirit is leading us in our time."[12] At the beginning of the *Spiritan Jubilee Year* (2nd February 2002)—celebrating the 300 years of the foundation of Spiritans (1703-2003)—Schouver noting the difficulties of the times, nevertheless drew attention to Spiritan buoyancy in the Spirit captured by the logo of the Jubilee Year, a boat with the sails "filled with the breath of the Spirit." The truth of the matter is that the journey is fraught with uncertainties. The present situation is filled with crises (including pedophilia). As Spiritans, we find ourselves in a "world of quickening change, cultural diversity, complexity and specialization;" "we feel at times that we are losing our footing." However, we draw inspiration from our founders, never discouraged while "waiting confidently for God's moment to arrive."[13] Consequently, *ressourcement*—or going back to the sources, a kind of self-examination, laying bare one's self before the profound resources of one's tradition—not only strengthens us but also profoundly challenges us as a Congregation in the Jubilee Year.[14] "We are not leaving for a cruise among archives; if we look back to the past, it is to prepare ourselves, with the power of the Spirit, to set out into the deep for a long journey ahead." This keeps us focused on the big dream, the "essentials of our vocation: ... solidarity with the poor ... spiritual renewal ... greater friendship and fraternal sharing in the life of our Congregation which is ever more international and inter-cultural."[15]

---

[12] Pentecost Message 1993.

[13] Quoting from Libermann, *Notes et Documents*, 6:3-8.

[14] This paraphrases Congar's citation of Charles Péguy who first used the term *ressourcement* in this sense in 1904: "Nothing is as anxiously [sic] beautiful as the sight of a people who lift themselves up again through an interior movement, a return to the sources (*ressourcement*) of their ancient pride, by means of a new release of the instincts of their race". Yves Congar, *True and false reform in the church*, Rev. ed. (Collegeville, Minn.: Liturgical Press, 2011). 39n35

[15] Pierre Schouver, *Spiritan Jubilee Year*

Schouver: Spiritan Mission as Frontline Mission in new Local Churches

The second point is that Spiritan mission, as frontline mission, is mission directed to those places where the Church has the greatest need, at the heart of new local churches or young churches. Through reading carefully the meaning of Church as sacrament, and understanding mission in the Trinitarian perspective, Schouver insists that the missionary never loses sight of the fact that being "sent" essentially means always receiving a "call" ("*l'envoyé demeure toujours l'appelé*").[16] One is called to be attentive to what the Spirit is doing and what the Spirit commands in a particular context: the Spirit precedes the missionary.[17] Consequently, according to Schouver, relationship in the young churches is never conceived in terms of mother-daughter church. Or else, one is stuck to the unacceptable colonial-imperial and conquering image of mission; the "sending Church" vs. the "receiving Church"—viewing the new/young churches as material for mission. Rather as respondents to the Word of God in the Spirit, the young churches in their freedom and otherness are fully churches, local churches, as the home churches of origin of Spiritan missionaries.[18] Schouver references the symbolic but radical dimensions of Pope Paul VI's visit to Bombay (1964) and his intervention at the United Nations (1965) as missionary initiatives that did two crucial things. First, the Pope was struggling to clarify the meaning and role of the Church in the world, and the way the Church in the contemporary world is realizing its mission to carry the Gospel to all nations. Second, the Pope in India was trying to reevaluate the full meaning of catholicity, and the complex relationship between Christianity, the religions and other faith traditions. The visit to India brought home to Paul VI the truth of the oneness of the Church of Rome and India, a catholic unity that must not be confused with uniformity.[19] This sense of catholicity that is lived in diversity is the burning question of missiology and ecclesiology today. Schouver's insight inspires this collective work, *Mission for Diversity.*

16 Pierre Schouver, *L'Église et la mission*, Croire et comprendre (Paris: Le Centurion, 1975). 118.

17 "Western missionaries did not introduce God to Africa – rather, it was God who brought them to Africa, as carriers of news about Jesus Christ." (John S Mbiti), John S. Mbiti, *Bible and theology in African Christianity* (Nairobi: Oxford University Press, 1986);. 11

18 Schouver, *L'Église et la mission*. 118.

19 Ibid. 66-67 ; 111.

Foci of this Collective Work

The array of competent scholars, contributors to this collective work, helps us clarify some of these issues relevant today for mission, the churches, and the religions. The keynote address of Cardinal Peter Turkson, President of the Pontifical Council for Justice and Peace, points to the possible new world that justice and peace mediate. Then the collection addresses methodological questions of mission in a diverse world, providing clues to the understanding of mission studies as intercultural studies. The interest on interculturality and the appreciation of the limits of speaking from a particular perspective or location without being solipsistic, characteristic of postmodernity, reflect the strength and weakness of each study presented in this collection. None of the studies claims to be definitive.

The methodological option of mission theology as *intercultural studies,* that *Mission for Diversity* endorses, opens a window to move missiology beyond the colonial Western level of discourse: the "hermeneutics of globality" enables greater awareness of and respect for paradox and resilience—the marks of "catholicity" (Schreiter). The uncomfortable relationship between mission and the coloniality of power is challenged by transparent missiological studies that embraces decolonial thinking and privileges knowledges produced from the wounded margin (Boodoo). Similarly, the American missiologist, as religious critic and cultural analyst, surveys with caution/suspicion the worldwide democratic movements and contestations of American inspiration. These evoke for many American Christians the politico-theological missionary identity of the nation on an errand in the wilderness, the city on a hill, and a light to the nations. The theologian, as critic and cultural analyst, scrutinizes with iconoclastic rigor any missiological interventions in a world of mass alienation and oppression (Anderson). Thanks to Vatican II and its impact on the Church and world, the development of resilient theological and missiological language, attentive to location and interculturality, is generating fertile and more humane conversation within the world Church.

The essays presented in this collection applaud *Vatican II* as inspiration for the study of worldwide mission as intercultural conversation, and as providing new insight into the relationship of the Church to the world. Vatican II enabled Catholicism (and the Christian Church) to re-appropriate its worldwide spread, its pristine legacy of diversity, and its testimony to catholicity. Indeed it opened the window to appreciate God's self-disclosure as universal in intent; and it throws a fresh light on the relationships between Christians and neighbors of other faiths. For example, the reception of Vatican II in Asia is enabling the Church-community to be truly a Church of the people, dialoguing continuously with peoples of other faiths (Wilfred).

Studies of specific documents of the Council like the *Constitution on the Liturgy* (Driscoll) and the *Declaration on Interreligious Dialogue* (McCabe, Phan) strongly display the powerful impact of Vatican II. Furthermore, some studies reach back to draw attention to the worldwide value of papal documents that effectively reframed the Church's attitude to world peace: a presumption against war as the path to justice—such as John XXIII's *Peace on Earth,* that influenced Vatican II and subsequent positions of the popes on peacebuilding, "pacifism" and conscientious objections to war (Himes). In addition, the synod of Bishops that was established in response to the wishes of the Council Fathers generated post-synodal documents that are a reception of the Council, and would have been impossible without Vatican II (Magesa; Okoye). Nevertheless, like Pierre Schouver, some contributors are quick to point out that Vatican II has to be critically received or appropriated; note must be taken of the limitations of its positions on mission, the local church and the religions. That is why it may be correct to say that Vatican II is appreciated for what it subsequently offered in terms of theological and practical insights and possibilities (Magesa).

Of particular salience to location and the respect of diversity and difference are the contributions that speak from the Asian, African and the Middle Eastern perspectives. Mission in Asia reinvents itself through focusing on the Kingdom: the experience of the local church leads it to set aside the focus on mission to the nations (*ad gentes*). Rather, mission is understood as among the nations (*inter gentes*) and with the nations (*cum gentibus*). Instead of engaging in dialogue as an instrument of mission, one embraces interfaith dialogue as mission. Christians work for God's reign of justice, peace and reconciliation only in collaboration with others (Phan). This collaboration with peoples immersed in their cultural and sociopolitical contexts informs the witness of the African local churches, attentive to the local practices of marriage and building the family in dialogue with the novelty of the Christian Gospel (Bujo and Ngong). The Middle Eastern Christian communities that strive to respond creatively to their context dominated by sectarian identities present another unique point of view. The Christian Churches united with the Roman Church abandon the image of a minority under pressure from the Arab Muslim environment and in need of protection by the West. They affirm that they are communities fully integrated within the region. They boldly embrace the concept of a "church of Islam," or a "church with Islam." This understanding of mission goes beyond the sectarian divisions to embrace the vision of *Nostra Aetate*, by articulating mutuality with Islam based on a new interpretation of pastoral experience and the unique location of Middle Eastern churches (Andraos). Finally, the missional challenge of the local Churches of USA rests in reinventing the Church-sacrament of unity through breaking the unfortunate divide between laity and clergy to reimagine collaborative ministry. The lay ecclesial ministers exercise real prophetic-priestly ministry, navigating between the margin and the center of ministerial functions in the Church (O'Brien).

Mission for Diversity, a collective work put together under the auspices of the Pierre Schouver Chair in Mission, echoes Schouver and the Spiritan founders and hones on what the Spirit is doing in God's world today. *Mission for Diversity* insists that mission today is more about listening with all the senses to hear/feel/see what the Spirit is saying and doing precisely in what is happening around us and in our world rather than what we as church are achieving in the world.

References

Abram, David. *The Spell of the Sensuous: Perception and Language in a More-Than-Human World*. 1st ed. New York: Pantheon Books, 1996.

Congar, Yves. *True and False Reform in the Church*. Rev. ed. Collegeville, Minn.: Liturgical Press, 2011.

Mbiti, John S. *Bible and Theology in African Christianity*. Nairobi: Oxford University Press, 1986.

Schouver, Pierre. *L'église Et La Mission*. Croire Et Comprendre. Paris: Le Centurion, 1975.

2 The Second Vatican Council and the Challenges of Justice and Peace in Africa

Cardinal Peter K. A. TURKSON

I do thank President Charles Dougherty and the entire Duquesne University community for inviting me to participate in this important symposium on the Second Vatican Council and Africa. I am also most thankful for the gracious honor bestowed on me in the awarding of a doctoral degree *honoris causa*. I happily embrace the motto of Duquesne, *"Spiritus est qui vivificat"—"It is the Spirit that gives life"*. Moreover, I am very grateful to the Spiritan community for their important ministry in Africa and throughout the world. Their dedicated commitment to the poor and marginalized responds to the need for justice, witnesses to the Gospel, and nourishes the hope for peace around the globe.

In my presentation, an experience of the Church in Africa and a document of Vatican II will serve as introduction. Then, in broad strokes, I consider Africa's problems and challenges, the Church's orientation towards society from *Gaudium et Spes,* and then I conclude with education which offers everyone the tools to be active co-creators of justice and peace.

Vatican II and Africa, *Gaudium et Spes* and Peace

If you mention Vatican II to an adult Catholic, chances are that the first image that will come to mind involves the Pope, Saint John XXIII. When he broached the idea of an Ecumenical Council only three months into his pontificate, he reportedly opened a window and said, "I want to throw open the windows of the Church so that we can see out and the people can see in."[1] Let us imagine the Holy Father looking out his window at Africa in 1962 and then again fifty years later—what change would he notice? To answer the question, although statistics do not usually have a place in a theological essay, I will use them to share an important experience and indeed a reality of the Church in Africa.[2]

When the Council opened in 1962, there were 29 million Catholics out of the total population of 283 million. In 2010, nearly fifty years since Vatican II, there

1 http://www.newworldencyclopedia.org/entry/John_XXIII

2 Thanks to Drs. Brian Grim and Juan Carlos Esparza Ochoa of the Pew Foundation and Dr. Peter Crossing of Global Christianity for assembling and interpreting the data.

were 186 million Catholics out of a total population of one billion. So Africa's population is about four times larger today, while the Catholic population in Africa is about seven times larger. Africa was about 10% Catholic in 1962; now it is nearly 19% Catholic.[3]

When one takes a glance at the clergy, the number of Bishops grew from fewer than 400 in 1962 to 700 in 2012. A larger increase has occurred among priests, whose numbers rose over two and a half times—from 15,000 to 40,000. The number of religious Sisters increased to the same degree, from 26,000 to 68,000, while the religious Brothers stayed approximately the same at 9,000.[4]

What these numbers convey is that the Church in Africa—implanted in the very cruel and unjust context of colonialism, yet magnificently nurtured with the tireless and indeed heroic ministry of the missionaries—is now a Church of Vatican II, beginning with the facts of population. Most of us have come into the Church since Vatican II. Ours is an experience of a Church "vibrant with vitality" in the ringing words of Pope John XXIII when convoking the Council.[5]

Nearly 40 years later, marking the Great Jubilee, Saint John Paul II exclaimed:

> What a treasure there is … in the guidelines offered to us by the Second Vatican Council! … With the passing of the years, *the Council documents have lost nothing of their value or brilliance*. They need to be read correctly, to be widely known and taken to heart as important and normative texts of the Magisterium, within the Church's Tradition.

The Holy Father went on to point to the Council as "*the great grace bestowed on the Church in the twentieth century:* there we find a sure compass by which to take our bearings in the century now beginning."[6]

For the purposes of this essay, the most important document is *Gaudium et Spes.*[7] It is a Pastoral Constitution which, along with the Doctrinal Constitutions, bears the highest level of formal authority of any Church document—even greater

---

3 For the entire presentation, many thanks to Dr. Brian J. Grim for preparing the data. Principal source: Todd M. Johnson and Brian J. Grim, eds., *World Religion Database,* Brill, 2012.

4 Based on rough estimates by the World Christian Database and the Association for Religion Data Archives, both using the *Annuario Pontificio.* See also Melissa J. Wilde, study of pre-Vatican-II, http://www.thearda.com/Archive/Files/Analysis/VATICAN/VATICAN_VAR13_1.asp#I-REGION; Melissa J. Wilde *Vatican II: A Sociological Analysis of Religious Change*. Princeton: Princeton University Press, 2007.

5 Walter M. Abbott, ed., *The Documents of Vatican II,* 1966, p. 705.

6 John Paul II, *Novo Millennio Ineunte* (6 January 2001), § 57.

7 http://www.vatican.va/archive/hist_councils/ii_vatican_council/documents/vat-ii_const_19651207_gaudium-et-spes_en.html

than an encyclical. The first part is mainly doctrinal; the second part makes pastoral application to various urgent problem-areas of contemporary life.

On the topic of peace, the Council Fathers offer four enduring insights and guiding principles in the context of human nature, social and economic life, and the human family from married couples to the world community. First, peace is intimately related to justice. Second, the challenge of obtaining peace is an unending process. Third, peace requires the deepest respect for human dignity amid human diversity. Fourth, all Christians are called to be peace builders. Peacemaking is a constitutive element of our Christian vocation.

Peace has also been an ongoing concern of the Church in Africa. The Second Special Assembly of the Synod of Bishops for Africa took place in Rome in 2009 with the theme "The Church in Africa in service of reconciliation, justice and peace." From my personal experience as *Relator*, the Second Synod grappled extensively and unflinchingly with the realities of Africa today. To these I will now turn, using the post-synodal exhortation *Africae Munus*[8] for some of my references, but our horizon throughout is peace with our Lord's promise always in mind, "Peace I leave with you, my peace I give to you" (Jn 14:27).

Challenges of Reconciliation, Justice, and Peace

Pope Benedict XVI delivered *Africae Munus* in Benin on 19 November 2011. Soon after, in January 2012, West African Bishops met in Yamoussoukro (Cote d'Ivoire) on the topic "The Church, God's family in West Africa in service to reconciliation, justice, and peace."

This frequent return to the theme of justice and peace in the meetings of the Church leadership is undoubtedly a sign of the great commitment of Africans to implement the teachings of the Second Vatican Council, so that people can live in peace on this rich continent.

Africa today has a tremendous hunger and thirst for peace and justice. *Africae Munus* confirms this emergency in these terms: "Millions of migrants, displaced persons and refugees are searching for a homeland and a peaceful country in Africa or elsewhere."[9] The emigration of Africans is the consequence of profoundly bad governance in which the rights of citizens are constantly undermined by dictatorships, unjust laws, wars and conflicts. In fact, the size of such an exodus, which affects virtually all the countries of Africa, reveals the extent of the

8 http://www.vatican.va/holy_father/benedict_xvi/apost_exhortations/documents/hf_ben-xvi_exh_20111119_africae-munus_en.html

9 *Africae Munus,* § 84.

hidden poverty caused by deficiencies in public administration. As a consequence, "Thousands of people have tried and continue trying to cross deserts and seas, searching for an oasis of peace and prosperity, better education and greater freedom. Unfortunately, many refugees and displaced persons encounter all kinds of violence and exploitation, even prison, and all too often, death."[10]

Migration is not a magical solution. Africans often meet difficulties both within Africa and on other continents. They are often seen as threats to peace and tranquility, and some states have responded with repressive legislation to prevent the entry of Africans. This is particularly true of Europe and the U.S.A. The inhabitants and authorities in many countries "regard migrants as a burden and view them with suspicion, seeing them only as a source of danger, insecurity and threat. This perception provokes reactions of intolerance, xenophobia and racism." Because of restrictions and their precarious situation, further exacerbated by the economic crisis, migrants regularly do "low-paid work that is often illegal, humiliating or degrading."[11]

Thus, though God has given Africa tremendous natural resources, his children there are often poor and exploited migrants. This contradiction challenges all Africans—especially their rulers and authorities, who are often involved in this impoverishment. Such unjust exploitation may not only be caused by native rulers; outside groups may also contribute to the injustice. In August 2012, the police shooting of workers seeking to gain a pay increase in a platinum mine in South Africa—with 30 people dead and over 27 injured—is a prime example. "Given the chronic poverty of its people, who suffer the effects of exploitation and embezzlement of funds both locally and abroad, the opulence of certain groups shocks the human conscience. Organized for the creation of wealth in their homelands, and not infrequently with the complicity of those in power in Africa, these groups too often ensure their own prosperity at the expense of the well-being of the local population".[12]

Unfortunately, in the Africa of today, "some business men and women, governments and financial groups are involved in programs of exploitation which pollute the environment and cause unprecedented desertification. Serious damage is done to nature, to the forests, to flora and fauna, and countless species risk extinction. All of this threatens the entire ecosystem and consequently the survival of humanity."[13]

---

10 *ibid.*

11 *ibid.*

12 *Africae Munus,* § 79.

13 *Africae Munus,* § 80.

The mass migration caused by war, injustice, poverty, insecurity and persecution of Christians in some parts of the continent gives rise to great indignation. The lack of justice and peace resulting in this migration within and outside the continent thus becomes a multi-dimensional drama which seriously affects the human capital of Africa. The outcome: the destabilization and destruction of countries and families.[14]

The Church's Mission of Reconciliation, Justice, and Peace

The connection between justice and peace is so close as to constitute an interdependence. *Gaudium et Spes* puts it this way: "Peace is not merely the absence of war; nor can it be reduced solely to the maintenance of a balance of power between enemies; nor is it brought about by dictatorship. Instead, it is rightly and appropriately called an enterprise of justice."[15] As mentioned earlier, this is the first major insight of this great document. *Justice is the necessary foundation of peace*. Justice "prompts us to give the other what is 'his', what is due to him by reason of his being or his acting."[16] The Latin 'suum,' or 'his,' denotes a citizen's right to flourish as a human being and to live decently according to his/her needs. Peace is threatened when the 'suum' of the citizen is constantly undermined. The 'suum' of the citizen must be the result of a fair sharing of the common good or public affairs.

The second major point of *Gaudium et Spes* is that *obtaining peace is an unending process.* To build justice and peace, the common good must be distributed with the proper rules, continually updated, that guarantee fairness. Its compass is eternal, but navigation requires constant adjustment: "The common good of humanity finds its ultimate meaning in the eternal law. But since the concrete demands of this common good are constantly changing as time goes on, peace is never attained once and for all, but must be built up ceaselessly."[17] And the Council Fathers warn that human frailty is an unavoidable factor in this effort: "Moreover, since the human will is unsteady and wounded by sin, the achievement of peace requires a constant mastering of passions and the vigilance of lawful authority."[18]

Third, peace requires not only justice, fairness and unending effort. It also requires *respect for human dignity amid human diversity.* Peace "cannot be obtained

---

14 cf. *Africae Munus,* § 84.

15 *Gaudium et Spes*, § 78.

16 Benedict XVI, *Caritas in Veritate,* § 6

17 *Gaudium et Spes*, § 78.

18 *ibid*.

unless personal well-being is safeguarded and men freely and trustingly share with one another the riches of their inner spirits and their talents. A firm determination to respect other women and men, other peoples and their dignity, as well as the studied practice of brotherhood is absolutely necessary for the establishment of peace. Hence peace is likewise the fruit of love, which goes beyond what justice can provide."[19] Applying these principles, the Council Fathers decry every form of slavery. The diversity of the human family does not justify differential application of fundamental human rights: "every type of discrimination, whether social or cultural, whether based on sex, race, color, social condition, language or religion, is to be overcome and eradicated as contrary to God's intent."[20]

Diversity in the ownership of goods between people is consistent with the natural order, since even though they have equal dignity, people are not all the same in terms of their physical capacities and the diversity of their intellectual and moral needs. These differences, however, must be just. They must not infringe on what belongs to one person or another by reason of his being, status and needs. Indeed, peace is threatened when inequalities are huge, disproportionate and shocking. The common public good—which is for the joy of all—must be distributed according to the rules that respect the divine order. In this regard, the Council teaches that "excessive economic and social differences between the members of the one human family or population groups cause scandal, and militate against social justice, equity, the dignity of the human person, as well as social and international peace."[21] Needless to say, this harmful inequality has occurred in developing countries when multinational corporations extract resources on a mammoth scale, but provide benefits to only a small portion of the population while the majority suffer the miseries of poverty, hunger and disease. Unfortunately, local government functionaries sometimes join in the exploitation, using their positions to embezzle public resources and further oppress the poor.

Before I turn to the fourth and final key point about peace, I want to talk about what the Council Fathers did to implement their vision of peace. They strongly recommended to the Holy Father that he establish an office or body within the universal Church so that "both the justice and love of Christ toward the poor might be developed everywhere." Just over a year later, in January 1967, Pope Paul VI established this body, which now bears the name "*Pontifical Council for Justice and Peace.*" Its role, in the words of *Gaudium et Spes*, is "to stimulate the Catholic community to promote progress in needy regions and social justice on

[19] *ibid.*

[20] *Gaudium et Spes*, § 29.

[21] *ibid.*

the international scene," in accordance with the Gospel and the *Social Teaching of the Church*.[22]

In simple terms, the Church asks this Council to promote the active engagement of Christians for *justice and peace* in the world. They should be inspired by Christian faith and by the charity or love of Christ. In his encyclical *Caritas in Veritate*, Benedict XVI states the overall vision this way: "Man's earthly activity, when inspired and sustained by charity, contributes to the building of the universal *city of God* which is the goal of the history of the human family."[23] In the case of Africa, such building depends most heavily upon *education*.

The Promotion of Education for Peace and Justice

Corruption and exploitation are not conducive to a peace based on justice, which is unfortunately very difficult to achieve in Africa. The continent is rich in resources but many of its people live in extreme poverty, illiteracy and ignorance. Africa's challenges are immense. The one main solution to the many and complex challenges is education. Education needs to foster the ability to respect other people and to properly manage the wealth of the nation for the common good of the community. Leaders are needed who can clarify the duties and ensure the rights of everyone. Though wealth or natural resources may contribute to the development of a continent, it is insufficient without leaders and rulers who are not merely educated but well-educated, who administer honestly and give to each his own. "An undisciplined king will ruin his people" (Sir 10:3).

Thus, the development of human resources is vital. This ensures the emergence of men and women who are well trained in regard to public affairs and human values; men and women able to apply skills and creativity to ensure that the inhabitants of their countries can enjoy their rights, exercise their duties, and live with dignity. This education should apply to all vocations, not only to public office holders. It must comply with all temperaments, differences in responsibilities, duties, gender, culture and traditions. It must also embrace fraternal relations with other peoples in order to foster true unity and peace. Children and young people should be helped to harmoniously develop their physical, moral and intellectual lives. They must also be helped to gradually acquire a mature sense of responsi-

22 *Gaudium et Spes*, § 90; cf. John Paul II, *Pastor Bonus* (1988), art. 142.

23 *Caritas in Veritate*, 7.

bility with respect to improving their personal lives and those of the community and nation.[24]

Africa at present lacks responsible and educated leaders who seek the welfare of their citizens. But "a city will grow through the understanding of its rulers" (Sir 10:3). Education must help Africans become aware of their great potential and stimulate their talents. It should prepare future leaders and public authorities who will seek the interests of all citizens according to justice with just laws.

During his 2011 trip to the continent, Pope Benedict XVI said of rulers and policy makers who neglect or even despise human dignity in Africa: "Many conflicts have originated in man's blindness, in his will to power and in political and economic interests which mock the dignity of people and of nature. Human beings aspire to liberty; then to live in dignity; they want good schools and food for their children, dignified hospitals to take care of the sick; they want to be respected; they demand transparent governance which does not confuse private and public interests; and above all they desire peace and justice."[25]

In the face of difficulties that worsen by the day, all of the various religious leaders—indeed, all good leaders—have the duty to form the consciences of their people. Thanks to their teachings, which should be based on natural values and sacred knowledge, the people should be enabled to create justice and peace. For its part, the Catholic Church instructs all its pastors and ministers of the Word to employ the Catechism in ways that are suitable for all ages, in order to breathe life into the faith of the faithful—an active and industrious faith. Catechetical instruction enlightens and strengthens the faith. It nourishes the life of the faithful according to Christian principles, especially love, which always seeks the welfare of others. Thus, "All scripture is inspired by God and profitable for teaching, for reproof, for correction, and for training in righteousness, that the man of God may be complete, equipped for every good work" (2 Tim 3: 16-17).

In addition to catechetical instruction, schools play a particular role in the formation of young people. As an instrument of education, with special care, and thanks to competent teachers, the Catholic school forms the intellectual faculties with particular regard to human and Christian values. It develops "the ability to judge rightly, to hand on the cultural legacy of previous generations, to foster a sense of values, to prepare for professional life. Between pupils of different talents and backgrounds it promotes friendly relations and fosters a spirit of mutual un-

---

24 This paragraph is based on Vatican II's Declaration on Christian Education, *Gravissimum Educationis* (1965), § 1.

25 Benedict XVI, *Address* to Government Members, Representatives of State Institutions, Diplomatic Corps and Major Religions, 19 November 2011.

derstanding; and it establishes as it were a center whose work and progress must be shared together by families, teachers, associations of various types that foster cultural, civic, and religious life, as well as by civil society and the entire human community."[26]

Today, Africa is full of schools, universities and Catholic institutions. Although science and technology are important, in these institutions priority should be put upon the subjects that prepare people to be more fully human and humane. Students must be educated on the great virtues of loyalty, honesty, humility, justice and, above all, transparency in the management of public affairs. Africa today has a great thirst for these virtues. It has a great desire to observe the actions of its leaders and to build justice and peace. Education at all levels must be in accordance with the common good, in accordance with generosity and love for the country. It must promote the knowledge that justice and peace are directly threatened when rulers access power and manage public affairs as if they were their own private property, through coup d'état or election-fixing or unjust electoral laws.

In addition, "Great care must be taken about civic and political formation, which is of the utmost necessity today for the population as a whole, and especially for youth, so that all citizens can play their part in the life of the political community."[27] Actual or potential politicians must be formed who are prepared to practice without regard for their own interest and material advantages. They must act with integrity and wisdom against injustice and oppression, absolutism and intolerance and "dedicate themselves to the service of all with sincerity and fairness, indeed, with the charity and fortitude demanded by political life."[28]

Conclusion: all Christians to be peace builders

Before reflecting on education, I spoke about three of the four insights of *Gaudium et Spes* on the subject of peace. First, peace is intimately related to justice. Second, the challenge of obtaining peace is an unending process. Third, peace requires the deepest respect for human dignity amid human diversity. For the fourth key point in *Gaudium et Spes,* the Council Fathers call on *all Christians to be peace builders*. Peacemaking is a constitutive element of our Christian vocation. What I have explained is how complex the twinned challenges of peace and justice are in present-day Africa. The special focus on education is to enable Africa overcome the obstacles and build a better and holier life for all Africans.

[26] *Gravissimum Educationis*, 5.

[27] *Gaudium et Spes,* § 75.

[28] *ibid*.

But this call, this vocation, does not stand apart, in time or location. In spite of epochal differences—such as between pre-colonial, colonial and post-colonial conditions affecting African political organization, society and economy—and differences of natural environment, Africa is not a separate case in God's eyes, in the Church's eyes. In December 2005, Pope Benedict noted a wonderful interplay of continuity and innovation when he reflected on the Second Vatican Council.[29] The Church adheres to constant truths and principles, which it strives to apply appropriately, and thus in different ways, to the particular conditions of different situations. He applied the expression *dynamic of fidelity* to this blend of continuity of principles with innovation in application. What I am suggesting is that, if we see this *dynamic of fidelity* linking our concerns for and work in Africa with our concerns and work elsewhere, and if we discern the deep, constant principles that underlie the changing practices over time, then we will truly understand our solidarity within the Church and with the world.

In the 50 years since the Second Vatican Council, the Church has repeatedly emphasized that the root causes of violence are frequently located in the abuse of human dignity, in the failure to recognize that resources exist for the common good, and in social systems and institutions which limit rather than enhance human freedom and development. The Church has called for the implementation of social justice across all arenas of social and cultural life. It has called for the creation of legal systems which respect human dignity and human freedom. It has challenged the wealthy and developed nations and persons to recognize their bond with those who are less fortunate and suffer from poverty and dislocation. There can be no peace without justice and there can be no justice without love for the truth.

At the beginning of 1968, as a means of putting the Council's teaching into action, Pope Paul VI established the World Day of Prayer to be celebrated on the 1st of January each year. His first message, addressed not just to Catholics but to the whole world, proposed that "this commemoration be repeated as a hope and as a promise at the beginning of the calendar" each year.[30] The drafting of the annual message soon became the responsibility of our Pontifical Council for Justice and Peace.

The Message for the World Day of Peace at the beginning of 2013 was the

---

[29] Benedict XVI, *Address* to the Roman Curia, 22 December 2005. http://w2.vatican.va/content/benedict-xvi/en/speeches/2005/december/documents/hf_ben_xvi_spe_20051222_roman-curia.html

[30] Paul VI, *Message Proclaiming a "Day of Peace"*, 8 December 1967.

46th. With its title "Blessed are the peacemakers,"[31] it referred to many of the unjust and violent situations of our world, including those in Africa which we have considered in this essay. The Holy Father encouraged everyone, not just Catholics and fellow-believers, to take the initiative in building a broader, deeper, more enduring peace. With the help of God's grace, may such an all-encompassing *shalom* also be the fruit of these conferences marking the 50th anniversary of the Second Vatican Council.

[31] http://www.vatican.va/holy_father/benedict_xvi/messages/peace/documents/hf_ben-xvi_mes_20121208_xlvi-world-day-peace_en.html

Part I:

Posing the Hermeneutical Question: Mission, Interculturality, Coloniality and Theological Method

3 The Role of Intercultural Hermeneutics in the Understanding of Mission Studies as Intercultural Studies

Robert SCHREITER, C.PP.S.

In recent years the terminology used to describe the academic discipline of the study of mission in the United States and in Northern Europe has been taking an interesting turn. Missiology has been re-branding itself as "intercultural studies," "intercultural relations," or "World Christianity." This phenomenon has taken place across the ecumenical spectrum, from conservative Protestant to Roman Catholic institutions. There are three reasons most frequently adduced for this change from missiology to intercultural studies.

The first is to escape the colonial connotations of the term "mission." Christian mission is seen to be laden with an opprobrious past through its connection with the imperialist expansion of European powers. That connection continues to be dissected in post- and decolonial[1] studies in universities. While a closer reading of history shows that missionaries were not always perfectly aligned with imperial forces (and sided on occasion with those being colonized in acts of resistance), the fact that there was such collusion cannot be denied. To be sure, the use of the term "mission" to describe the Church's activity derives from a secular use of mission as the sending forth of groups for economic or military purposes, first surfacing in Portugal in the fifteenth century.[2] (*Missio* of course also had a theological meaning, referring to the sending of the Son and the Holy Spirit into the world. This sense of the *missio Dei* enters here in the twentieth century.) When the examination of this history of collusion is paired with an anti-religious bias, missiology is simply derided and dismissed. The move to alternative terminology is an attempt to acknowledge this imperialist past and refocus the field of study. Turning toward the work in inculturation and the contextualization of theology in the Global South seemed to provide a remedy by focusing on culture.

The second reason for the turn to new terminology is related to the first. In European universities, missiology as an academic discipline was becoming increasingly marginalized in faculties of theology. Since its inception in the nineteenth

1 I am understanding *postcolonial* here as those studies deriving especially from Francophone influence, and focusing on the colonizing process in Africa and Asia; and *decolonial* as those studies focusing on Latin America.

2 Paul Kollman, "At the Origins of Mission and Missiology: A Study in the Dynamics of Religious Language," *Journal of the American Academy of Religion* 79(2011), 425-458.

century, it was often paired with studies in ecumenism and comparative religion. It had been largely taught by church historians who themselves had overseas mission experience. Today there is a greater likelihood that missiologists have some training in the social sciences and linguistics. The hope in Europe has been that the shift to the intercultural will make the study of Christian mission more palatable in the theological faculty and the university as a whole.

The third reason came from ecclesiastical considerations. "Mission" connotes for many an asymmetrical relationship between the "sending" churches of the Global North and the "receiving" churches of the Global South. The substitution of the term "intercultural" would put the churches on a more equal footing.

I have been critical of this move from missiology to intercultural studies—not because I am against intercultural studies (far from it!), but because the matter has not been fully reflected upon by those who advocate this change.[3] Unless missiology as intercultural studies adds to the knowledge of the intercultural field, it will continue to occupy a marginalized place as an academic discipline and a form of theology. Indeed, if it fails to contribute in some measure to intercultural studies, it will marginalize the theologies of the local churches of the Global South even further.

In this presentation, I want to explore some possible contributions that missiology might be able to make to intercultural studies. I would like to suggest two here. The first is how Christian faith shapes local and regional contexts in light of the changing field of international relations. Since the early 1990s it has become increasingly evident that the secularization hypothesis that dominated twentieth-century sociological thought did not fit much of the world outside Europe, North America, and Australia. There has actually been a resurgence of religion in much of the world. In the field of international relations the role of religion continues to be under-theorized. The secularization narrative continues to hold sway: religion should be a private matter kept out of the public forum. When religion is present in the public forum, it most likely will foment violence. Religion, on this view, is a primitive notion that is destined to fade away or it is an irrational force that dis-

3 Robert Schreiter, "Verbreitung der Wahrheit oder Interkulturelle Theologie? Was meinen wir, wenn wir heute von Mission sprechen?" *Interkulturelle Theologie* 36(2010), 13-31; idem, "Missiology's Future between the Intercultural and the Interreligious," in Stephen Bevans (ed.), *Mission and Culture: The Louis B. Luzbetak Lectures* (Maryknoll, NY: Orbis Books, 2012), 275-290.

rupts the public forum. Among younger scholars of international relations, these old premises are beginning to be rethought.[4]

To be sure, religion can be invoked to justify armed violence; more often, however, it is reached for to legitimate violence rather than put forward the actual motives—greed for power, grabbing natural resources, settling old disputes and the like.[5] Missiology could do the world and the study of theology a great service by examining how Christian faith shapes intercultural interaction at local, regional, and global levels. This would enhance more general work in peacebuilding, something the Church itself is turning to more and more. Indeed the churches are a major source of peacebuilding actions—they constitute fully 97% of the efforts made in this direction in Colombia, for example.

The second place where missiology as intercultural studies could make a significant contribution would be in the area of intercultural hermeneutics. I understand intercultural hermeneutics here as the study of how understanding (and misunderstanding) occur across one or more cultural boundaries. In a world where local environments are becoming increasingly multiethnic—now that a majority of the world's population live in large cities, and one in every thirty-five people on the planet is in migration—how meaning is communicated and (mis)understood across those cultural boundaries becomes an increasingly important task.

I would like to take up these two areas here to explore how missiology might be renewed and, at the same time, contribute to wider understandings of intercultural interaction. I do this first by imagining a renewed missiology as intercultural studies, and then turn to potential contributions to intercultural hermeneutics.

A Renewed Missiology as Intercultural Studies

What might a renewed missiology as intercultural studies look like? It goes without saying that it must be more than applying intercultural approaches to the study of mission. It will have to be able to make contributions to intercultural studies at an analytic or methodological level. I would suggest it might do this in four ways.

4 Timothy Samuel Shah, Alfred Stepan, Monica Duffy Toft (eds.), *Rethinking Religion and World Affairs* (New York: Oxford University Press, 2012).

5 See for example Marc Engelhardt, *Heiliger Krieg, Heiliger Profit. Afrika als neues Schlachtfeld des internationalen Terrorismus* (Berlin: Christoph Links Verlag, 2014).

A Critical Re-appropriation of Missiology's Past

First, this renewed missiology has to *reappropriate critically its own past*. Missiology cannot simply wipe its hands clean of how it guided missionary practices in a previous era, and declare that it wants to start afresh. Missiologists cannot simply disown and abandon their past without some critical engagement of it. The missiological record is hardly one of unadulterated wrongdoing. The good and the bad need to be sorted through, both to assure that the negative consequences are indeed eliminated as much as possible, and to build upon positive elements that can help integrate sometime "mission lands" into the contemporary world community.

The use of postcolonial theory has been to this point the principal tool to deal with the consequences of colonialism and imperialism in the history of mission. There an agenda has already been established, involving (1) a critique of the ideologies upon which earlier mission theory was built (such as the *mission civilisatrice* and other religions as idolatrous), (2) a critique of the continuing consequences of colonialism, (3) combating the injustices enshrined in colonial structures, and (4) examining how colonial ideologies and structures are perpetuated in globalization's economic and social policies.

Postcolonial theory has been a very effective tool of analysis in this regard. Missiology could contribute to this enterprise by critiquing some of the blind spots in postcolonial theory as well. There are, for example, some conundrums at the heart of postcolonial theorizing, such as the troubling social location of so many major postcolonial theorists dwelling in elite research universities of the "metropolis" (i.e., the West); or the use of attenuated concepts such as "strategic essentialism" (Gayatri Chakravorty Spivak) that permits essentialism as a tool for some, but not for others. Another question is to what extent postcolonial theory (since Edward Said) is simply Western postmodernism imposed upon a non-Western area of study. These points are raised not to discredit postcolonial theory, but rather to press it toward more precision.

Put another way, missiology's critical appropriation of its past must use tools that are now available, but also must contribute to their development and refinement. In exposing strategies that destroyed aspects of cultural and social systems, it must also at the same time look at the positive consequences, such as the introduction of literacy and some forms of education that allowed oral cultures to better engage literate ones. Studying these dynamics might also illumine the spread of the so-called "axial religions" in the centuries before the Common Era, and Christianity and Islam in subsequent centuries.

A Re-Mapping Beyond the "Exotic" and the "Other"

A renewed missiology as intercultural studies has to re-conceive its cartography, its ways of mapping the world. Missionaries provided great service by describing customs, and constructing grammars and dictionaries of hitherto unrecorded languages. But dividing the world into an "us" (the West) and "them" (the Rest) no longer fits the world reality. One of the effects of globalization, in its compressing of time and of space, is that the "other" is less far away than it used to be. Our mental maps of humankind are in drastic need of being reshaped. The Western gaze on the "Other" needs to be dismantled and repositioned, if we are to achieve a more accurate view of the human condition.

This is not a call for some misty-eyed communitarian utopian vision, but for an analytic approach that can recognize difference, yet find less coercive modes of engaging difference in non-violent and more inclusive ways. This begins, I think, with attending to how we use the language of the "universal." De-colonial theorists in the Americas, such as Walter Mignolo, Edouard Glissant, and Nestor García Canclini have joined others in Europe in noting the oppressive weight of the language of universalism inherited from the Enlightenment.[6] The "universal" coincided with the "Enlightened European", and everyone else was but a partial, fragmented, or incomplete representation of it. Is a "just universalism" possible?[7]

One possibility, as yet largely unexplored, is to think in terms of "global" and "globality" and the "local." The global is always admittedly from a perspective, that is, from the site of the viewer to as far as the viewer's horizon reaches. It is never all-encompassing. This is evident in the growth of the use of the term "global" (at least in English) from the sixteenth century. The "local" as its counterpart shows a similar flexibility—it expands or contracts according to the viewer.[8] Likewise, when the global falls short on its promises, the local reasserts itself in a critical manner over against the universalizing pretenses of the global (as one sees in current debates about the future of the European Union). Global-local may be a way of perceiving a new mapping of the world inasmuch as the starting point of

---

6 Walter Mignolo, *The Darker Side of the Renaissance: Literacy, Territoriality and Colonization* (Ann Arbor, MI: University of Michigan Press, 1995); Edouard Glissant, *Poetique de la relation* (Paris: Gallimard, 1990); Nestor García Canclini, *Hybrid Cultures: Strategies for Entering and Leaving Modernity* (Minneapolis: University of Minnesota Press, 1995).

7 On this see the proceedings of the 10th International Congress for Intercultural Philosophy: Raul Fornet-Betancourt, Franz Gmainer-Pranzl, and Hans Schelkshorn (eds.), *Auf dem Weg zu einer gerechten Universalität* (Aachen: Wissenschaftsverlag Mainz, 2013).

8 Harry Redner, *Beyond Civilization: Society, Culture and the Individual in the Age of Globalization* (New Brunswick, NJ: Transaction Publishers, 2013).

each can be from anywhere, and they can exercise a critical correlation between themselves, correcting each other as to promises made.

The Intercultural as Critical Cultural Reflection

The third element in a renewed missiology as intercultural studies is what is meant by "cultural" and "intercultural." Much of missiological analysis has rested upon the so-called "modern" concept of culture—culture as the unity of language, custom and territory. This model, which grew out of a reaction in the Romantic Era to Classical universalism and normativity, was well suited to investigating small-scale, relatively enclosed cultures. With the majority of the world's population now living in megacities, however, the modern concept of culture has lost some of its analytic usefulness. In those settings, language as a distinctive feature encounters other languages (and sometimes a creolized language that mediates between languages). Customs become attenuated, as kinship lineages have broken down, and village life can only be partially replicated in urban spaces. Territory has been largely ceded altogether.

The postmodern concept of culture has been found more useful in these settings. Indeed the forces of globalization have changed the conditions even of rural areas, thanks to technologies of communication and to migration. A postmodern concept of culture views culture as a kind of force-field where identities are negotiated out of the diverse resources that are at hand. Such a concept is keenly attuned to the dynamics of power that limit the choice of possibilities and press people in certain directions.

What does this mean for the study of culture and intercultural encounter in a renewed missiology? Two things come immediately to mind. First of all culture, as previously understood, cannot be studied in isolation from the social, political, economic and ecological currents that shape the production, articulation and reproduction of culture. Thus cultural analysis that focuses exclusively on issues of identity (as did much of first-generation contextual theologies) will be seen as inadequate. The full range of social forces at play has to be taken into account. To cite but one instance: Western reified categories of "religion" will need to be reconsidered. The boundaries between religion and culture are extremely porous. This becomes especially important for studying interreligious encounter that is now part and parcel of missiology, as well as for what kind of agency religion is given in complex social settings such as those of violent conflict.

The second thing that the study of culture and intercultural encounter raises for a renewed missiology is the meaning of "inter" in intercultural encounter. The "inter-zone" as a site in itself has been a matter of much interest in intercultural encounter, especially for how power is exercised there.[9] Missiology cannot pretend that this is some neutral zone of interaction, for this "inter-zone" is a central moment for missiology. An example would be the practice of mission as reconciliation. Reconciling activity takes place in such an inter-zone—between perpetrator and victim, between present and past time.[10]

A Reflexive Praxis for the Church

The fourth and final element of a renewed missiology is that it must be a reflexive praxis of and for the Church. It is not just critical reflection on one part of the Church's activity. It needs to proceed from an understanding of the Church as being missionary in its very nature. It must situate the Church's activity theologically in the *missio Dei*, the action of the Trinitarian God in the world. What this implies is that as it engages in critical reflection on the Church's activity, it must be able to articulate an explicit theology of mission, and measure the Church's action against that theology. As an academic discipline, missiology's critical reflection on the Church's missionary praxis shows how a major actor on the world stage understands itself and its role in world affairs today. Examples of this may be found in the self-understanding of some of the world-wise Christian organizations such as the World Council of Churches, the Lutheran World Federation, the World Communion of Reformed Churches, and the Lausanne Covenant as they face the challenges of the present time.

Here one might call attention to the "missiology" of Pope Francis, articulated in his Apostolic Exhortation *Evangelii gaudium* and even more pointedly in his many symbolic gestures that embody his teaching. His emphasis on the Church "going forth" rather than one preoccupied with itself or concerned only for its own privileges and prerogatives—a Church of and for the poor—bespeaks a missiology that intends to engage the critical issues of our time.

Missiology's Potential Contribution to Intercultural Hermeneutics

I turn here to the second major area where missiology might make a contribution to intercultural studies; namely, in the area of intercultural hermeneutics. Intercul-

[9] See for example Homi Bhabha discussion of "third space" in *The Location of Culture* (London: Routledge, 1994), 37.

[10] Robert Schreiter and Knud Joergensen (eds) *Mission as Ministry of Reconciliation* (Oxford: Regnum Books, 2013).

tural hermeneutics has been explored in a number of different disciplines, especially in the social sciences (intercultural communication) and in philosophy. In missiology and theology, it has been explored especially in contextual theologies and in inculturation[11], in studies in interreligious dialogue,[12] as well as in the new discipline of comparative theology.[13] Here I would like especially to draw upon literature from intercultural philosophy to help frame some missiological issues.

In looking at the intercultural philosophy literature, one can discern two distinct approaches that have been articulated, and a third one that is in the process of emerging. I would designate them as a hermeneutics of commonalities, a hermeneutics of difference, and a hermeneutics of globality.

A Hermeneutics of Commonality

The first approach or framework is a hermeneutics of commonality. In crossing cultural boundaries, this hermeneutics seeks out commonalities in the world of its interlocutors. These commonalities then serve as the basis for intercultural dialogue. Two of the most prominent names in intercultural philosophy have been the Indian-German philosopher Ram Adhar Mall and the Austrian philosopher Martin Wimmer.[14] In differing ways, both have sought out commonalities upon which to build: Mall, with his concept of an "analogical hermeneutics"; and Wimmer, with his concept of a "polylogue."

Such a hermeneutics tracks agreements or "rough parity" on issues in different cultures. It compares well with what has been called a "hermeneutics of generosity" as it has been espoused by followers of Hans-Georg Gadamer. An intercultural hermeneutics of commonalities will be essential for reaching consensus agreements among nations on issues that no single country can address

[11] For an overview of the hermeneutical issues as they have been developed in contextual theologies, see Volker Küster, *Einführung in die kontextuelle Theologie* (Göttingen: Vandenhoeck & Ruprecht, 2011).

[12] See for example Raimun Panikkar's *The Intrareligious Dialogue* (Mahwah, NJ: Paulist Press, 1999).

[13] For an introduction to comparative theology, see Francis X. Clooney, *Comparative Theology: Deep Learning across Religious Borders* (Chichester: Wiley-Blackwell, 2010), and his edited collection, *The New Comparative Theology: Interreligious Insights for the Next Generation* (London: T. & T. Clark, 2010).

[14] For Mall, see his *Philosophie im Vergleich der Kulturen* (Darmstadt: Wissenschaftliche Buchgesellschaft, 1996) and *Interkulturelle Logik* (Paderborn: mentis, 2009. Of interest here also is his *Gadamers Hermeneutik interkulturell gelesen* (Nordhausen: Bautz, 2005). For Wimmer, see his *Interkulturelle Philosophie* (Vienna: Passagen, 1990), 2 vols.; *Perspektiven interkulturellen Philosophierens* (Vienna: Wiener Universitäts Verlag, 2012).

or resolve: climate change is perhaps the greatest example here.[15] The work on various fronts to develop a global ethic is a proving ground for the elaboration of such an intercultural hermeneutics of commonalities. This finding of paths toward consensus—and the sociolinguistic and cultural rules that shapes those paths—will grow in importance in the coming decades. It will be especially attractive to societies that have a strong collectivist or sociocentric impetus.

Inasmuch as interreligious dialogue is a central focus of current missiology, this hermeneutics of commonality becomes important for deepening the capacities for dialogue as well as working toward common action as an outcome.

Through the years, the hermeneutics of interreligious dialogue—and now, an intercultural hermeneutics of generosity—has grown more sophisticated, as it has come to respond to potential pitfalls. It distinguishes itself from a hermeneutics of "sameness" that can result in homogenizing similarities and creating a hegemonic rather than a dialogical relationship between the two entities. The universalism of Western Enlightenment thinking, already touched upon above, is something it has sought to avoid. Indeed, navigating its way between universalism and commonality is one of its most important challenges and tasks. It also seeks to distance itself from a rationalist and idealist mode of philosophy that does not pay sufficient attention to context and social location. These are not easy tasks to undertake and sustain. But given the ethical necessity of finding ways to come together around common issues such as peacebuilding and climate change, this mode of intercultural hermeneutics has become vital to our planet's future. The religious or interreligious mediation of such issues means that missiology, with its experience in intercultural interaction, needs to participate in this process and to deepen its methodological and analytic acumen to address such issues.

A Hermeneutics of Difference

The second form of intercultural hermeneutics focuses on *differences* in meaning between two or more cultures. If the first form of intercultural hermeneutics is at home in a "hermeneutics of generosity" then this second form finds its place in a "hermeneutics of suspicion."

A hermeneutics of difference derives from a number of sources. One of the most important has been the rise of "standpoint" philosophies highlighting social features that had been ignored in traditional hermeneutics, such as gender, race,

15 For a review of developments in interreligious dialogue in this regard see Catherine Cornille, *The (Im)Possibility of Interreligious Dialogue* (New York: Crossroad, 2008).

and class. In doing this it was a reaction to the homogenizing and hegemonic character of the Western hermeneutics of the first half of the twentieth century, which attempted to marginalize, suppress, or even erase differences that complicated master narratives. As such, it opened up discourse to voices not heard before, and gave new agency to women, to oppressed and silenced peoples, and to minorities of all types.

A second source has been coming to terms with otherness or alterity. A growing awareness that there were features of the Other that could not be reduced to a oneness prompted great difficulties for a philosophical mindset that was monologic in nature. It continues to haunt this kind of thinking, namely, how to conceive of a unity that does not require uniformity.

A third source has been engaging the plurality and diversity that otherness implies. Here both modern and postmodern attempts can be found: modernity, as it were, continuing to seek a unity; postmodernity, on the other hand, acknowledging and even celebrating diversity and fragmentation.

Pursuit of a hermeneutics of difference has enriched the scope and texture of intercultural hermeneutics immensely. Indeed it is hard to imagine what going back to a previous state of some four decades ago might be. Important has been how difference can no longer mean variation in peripheral dimensions of experience or discourse; difference can shift the framework of experience and discourse itself.

An example can be found in shifts in the frameworks for interreligious dialogue. Christians have typically worked from a soteriological framework, since the question of salvation in Christ was the prime motivator for entering interreligious dialogue. Engaging the deeper differences of other religious traditions has led to moving from solely soteriological concerns to an attitude of greater openness.[16]

In the theologies of inculturation mentioned above, a hermeneutics of difference has played an enormous role in their development. In the early stages, inculturation often meant asserting cultural difference as a basis of identity for colonized and marginalized groups. In a later stage, inculturation was seized upon for renewal of societies in the secularized Christian-majority countries of the Global North and for the reconstruction of post-communist societies of Central and Eastern Europe. Today, it has taken on a third dimension of critically building culturally diverse societies.[17]

---

[16] Marianne Moyaert, "Recent Developments in the Theology of Interreligious Dialogue: From Soteriological Openness to Hermeneutical Openness," *Modern Theology* 38(2012), 26-41.

[17] I have explored this in greater detail in "Mission in der Spannung von universalem Anspruch und

As with any hermeneutical framework, a hermeneutics of difference has its limitations. There are two such limitations that stand out especially. First of all, if difference becomes the principal defining characteristic in intercultural hermeneutics, one can end up with a world of "others" that do not share sufficient characteristics to permit dialogue and exchange. Anselm Min has explored this, especially by engaging postmodern thinking about difference. In such an extreme setting, solidarity that permits interaction of any kind becomes an extrinsic "add-on" that may or may not compromise difference.[18] When there is near incommensurability, how can there be intercultural interaction?

Second, Latin American thinkers such as Cuban philosopher Raul Fornet-Betancourt have noted that the emphasis on difference and fragmentation can lead to an abdication of ethical responsibility: because I am different, how can I take any responsibility for the other, or the other for me? He points to the political and ethical problems this raises for an intercultural hermeneutic.[19] The kind of solipsism that can grow out of this, coupled with the hegemonic power the West still enjoys, makes this kind of postmodern thinking potentially quite destructive of intercultural inter-action and discourse.

One finds a hermeneutics of difference already fairly well developed in the attempts to narrate the underside of history, to listen for the silences within text, and to develop a variety of identity theologies. Such a hermeneutics of difference will continue to be necessary in a world filled with injustice and oppression. The importance of identity theologies may begin to fade (as is already becoming evident in the second—and in the case of feminism, third—generation). But the relative location of difference in any cultural discourse, as well as its salience within the culture, necessitates continuing attention to difference. But this hermeneutics, too, must attend to its own limits. If a hermeneutics of commonalities can drift into relativism, an overemphasis on difference can lead to solipsism, making communication impossible.

---

partikularem Kontext," in Markus Luber (ed.), *Kontextualität des Evangeliums. Weltkirchliche Herausforderungen der Missionstheologie* (Regensburg: Verlag Friederich Pustet, 2012), 53-67.

18 Anselm Kyongsuk Min, *The Solidarity of Others in a Divided World: A Postmodern Theology after Postmodernism* (New York: T. & T. Clark International, 2004).

19 See Fornet-Betancourt's and other Latin Americans' reflection on this in Orlando Espín, *Grace and Humanness: Theological Reflections Because of Culture* (Maryknoll, NY: Orbis Books, 2007), 19-21.

A Hermeneutics of Globality

I turn now to a potential third framework for intercultural hermeneutics. As a third form, it seeks to acknowledge both the strengths and the weaknesses of a hermeneutics of commonality and a hermeneutics of difference. However, this third framework should not be seen as a sublation of the previous two. It is still "potential" in the sense that a lot of work needs to be done on it. I call this third form a hermeneutics of globality.

In *The New Catholicity*, I spoke of "integrated" and "globalized" concepts of culture.[20] "Integrated" concepts of culture coincided largely with "modern" concepts of culture. But it reaches beyond them by taking the paradoxes and ambivalences of globalization (rather than some form of late modernity) as their frame of reference. Globalization, I believe, changes the context for the monological framing of a hermeneutics of commonality and the late-modern context of a hermeneutics of difference (in either its postmodern or postcolonial forms). Globalization carries deep ambivalences which cannot be overcome by dialectical thinking; they need to be confronted with paradox as a mode of engagement.

Here I have found Latin American thinking of greatest value. I have already mentioned the Cuban philosopher Raul Fornet-Betancourt, who brings a decided ethic and a political reading to postmodern thinking and to the consequences of globalization.[21] In arguing for what he calls "interculturality" instead of "inculturation," he outlines a mode of dialogue that seeks to overcome hegemonic holds on the discourse by erstwhile colonizers. In significant ways, his proposal looks like what Habermas called "communicative action," but with a more conscious and explicit gesture toward the ethical and political implications. Another source that I have found helpful has been the decolonial writing of the Argentinian philosopher Walter Mignolo, already mentioned above.[22]

I would like to summarize under four headings the elements that I think go into an intercultural hermeneutics of globality.

The first heading is: *the frame of reference is globality*. I am proposing this term over "universality" or "commonality." Globality evokes the globalization that

---

[20] Robert Schreiter, *The New Catholicity: Theology between the Global and the Local* (Maryknoll, NY: Orbis Books, 1997), 46-61.

[21] See among his recent work *Interculturalidad, critica y liberación* (Aachen: Mainz Verlag, 2012) and *Interkulturalität und Religion* (Aachen: Mainz Verlag, 2012).

[22] Besides the literature already mentioned above, see his *The Darker Side of Western Modernity: Global Futures, Decolonial Options (Latin American and Otherwise)* (Durham, NC: Duke University Press, 2011); *Local Histories/Global Designs* (Princeton, NJ: Princetion University Press, 2012).

is our inevitable (at least for now) context for any cultural endeavor. Globality suggests a broad spread of certain phenomena, even as that spread is uneven and can evoke very opposing reactions. This is evident, for example, in the way religion has come to be seen in the public forum; the ethnification of cultural identities that did not exist previously in that form; and reactions expressive of the asymmetries of power. Globality reflects too what has happened to worldwide communication in so many (but not all) parts of the world, and the unexpected agency it has given to oppressed people. The very unevenness of globality mirrors better the diversity that remains even under the most persistent homogenizing forces that globalization may bring to bear on distinct locales.

The theological counterpart to globality is "catholicity," itself a potentially comprehensive but also uneven and at times oppressive reality. Catholicity holds together from a theological point of view both local integrity and the interactive nature of global communion.

The second heading for this intercultural hermeneutical proposal is: *paradox*. Methodologically paradox is a call to embrace the ambivalences and interconnectedness of seeming opposites in order to articulate meaning in intercultural encounter. It is the methodological acknowledgement of diversity and complexity. Much thinking in globalization has been a reversion to dialectic, itself a useful tool of analysis. But the binaries that dialectic implies can stand in the way of what Fornet-Betancourt would call a genuine interculturality.

Closely related to paradox is the third heading of this proposal: *resilience*. Much attention has been paid to resistance as an important form of agency for the oppressed and subjugated in postmodern and postcolonial theory. Resistance has been a very fruitful way of exploring the dynamics of the subaltern and the colonized. I am not suggesting discarding resistance in a consideration of an intercultural hermeneutic, but rather adding another concept that has been gaining ground on a number of fronts; namely, resilience. Resilience is another form of agency whereby a population maintains its integrity in face of adversity, and how that population adapts to maintain that integrity over time. It has become an important category in biology and ecological studies, and is gaining ground in social psychology and in theology.[23] Important in human populations is the use of ritual for gaining resilience. One important ritual involves narrating the founding myths of a community to seek out ways of discovering how adversity was dealt with effectively in the past. As an example, take the murder of six Sikhs in their gurdwara

---

23 For the theological arena, see Clemens Sedmak, *Innerlichkeit und Kraft. Eine Studie über epistemische Resilienz* (Freiburg: Herder, 2013).

in Oak Creek, Wisconsin in 2012. To respond to this, the Sikh community, whose narratives carry many stories of persecution, read aloud their holiest Scripture, the *Guru Granth Sahib*—a ritual that takes two full days. In so doing they reaffirmed their identity, values and ideals as Sikhs in the face of the attack upon their community. One could imagine the series of readings that make up the Catholic Easter Vigil serving the same purpose for Christians.

Work on resilience is still continuing apace. A hermeneutics of globality needs to take the crafting of resilience into account for the sake of the duress that so many communities experience.

The fourth heading is: *aesthetics*. Here I am not suggesting an aesthetics that advocates withdrawal from critical thinking and ethical commitment, but one suggested by the work of Alejandro García-Rivera, who developed an aesthetics that grows out of communities of the marginalized and the wounded.[24] Art—and an aesthetics that articulates it in a verbal medium—is one of the principal ways we give expression to paradox and the complexities and contradictions of existence in a globalized world. In such a world, this is especially important for those who experience the ambivalences of globalization most acutely.[25]

These four headings suggest an outline for the development of the next phase of intercultural hermeneutics, keeping an eye both on the efforts that have been made thus far to define a hermeneutics of globality, as well as the immediate issues pressing now upon us.

Conclusion

In sum, a renewed missiology as intercultural studies and the three kinds of intercultural hermeneutics discussed here can contribute immensely to the life of the Church in its mission of cooperating with the *missio Dei* in the world. For the world itself, tracking new turns in the process of globalization, emerging forms of neo-colonialism, and the continuing impact of migration will help create a more just and peaceable world. As societies around the world become more multiethnic, especially in their urban manifestations and through migration, tools will have to be developed and further enhanced for more effective human interaction. Secular forms of intercultural hermeneutics have, to this point, discounted the importance

---

[24] Alejandro García-Rivera, *The Community of the Beautiful* (Collegeville, MN: Liturgical Press, 1999) and *A Wounded Innocence: Sketches for a Theology of Art* (Collegeville, MN: 2003).

[25] See the aesthetical writing of film maker Antonio Sison on Third Cinema, *World Cinema, Theology and the Human: Humanity in Deep Focus* (New York: Routledge, 2012).

of religion in the social equation. Missiology would seem to be an ideal location for improving our capacities in this regard.

But the tools of intercultural hermeneutics are not intended only for communication between Global North and Global South. The New Evangelization—first proposed by Pope John Paul II and now embraced also by the current pope—could well be served with these same intercultural hermeneutical approaches. To this point I have not seen much on the New Evangelization that looks at how societies in North America and Europe are changing. There seems rather to be a certain conviction that the Church already knows what is wrong with a de-Christianized society and knows how to present the Gospel anew in those settings. If former Catholics were a distinct Christian denomination in the United States, they would be the second largest one after Roman Catholicism itself. Why is this happening? Simply to rail against secularism, consumerism, relativism and the like will not be convincing to such an audience. The Church must be in a position to listen again to the cultures it is trying to re-evangelize. Smug formulas will likely have grown outdated. And the hermeneutics through which it reads the reality of a multiethnic city will require that the Church will look again at itself, and see where it needs to repent and be transformed by God's grace. If missiology as intercultural studies can help the Church create a better diagnostic of the world it is trying to address in the New Evangelization, it will more than attain its rightful position among the theological disciplines.

The inauguration of a new chair in missiology is an apt time to think about the state of missiology, especially in its current turn to intercultural studies. My hope is that the Pierre Schouver Chair will be a place where missiology is done critically, faithfully and prophetically.

4 Mimetic Reflections: The Religious Critic between the Church and Empire

Victor ANDERSON

Introduction

These are not only difficult times for any articulation or marshalling of democratic ideals arising from the U.S. much less talking about Christian missions emanating from the U.S. This is especially the case as we are witnessing what some see as a radicalizing of democratic energies and contestations in Arab countries such as Iraq and Syria and Northern African states such as Tunisia, Egypt, and Libya. Simultaneously such democratic movements and contestations evoke for many Americans renewed confirmation of the U.S.'s politico-theological missionary identity once narrated as an errand in the wilderness, the city on a hill, and a light to the nations. This is a powerful meta-narrative of historical self-understanding and self-determination. And it is deeply embedded in formations of the spirit of American empire and a globalizing U.S. neoliberal establishmentarianism.

Several recent articles have foregrounded the challenges that this historical moment pose for U.S. Christian missions. For example, professor of evangelism and missions, Philip L. Wickeri, writes:

> Many believe that the international Christian mission has been tainted by its association with colonization and imperialism in the past that world mission belongs to a bygone era. At the same time, there are more American Protestant missionaries serving overseas than at any time in history, but they are largely related to more conservative, evangelical churches and parachurch organizations. Critics charge that missionaries from the United States contribute to the "clashes of civilizations" especially in the Islamic world and the nations of the former Soviet Union. Supporters argue that American churches still have a vital role to play in fulfilling the Great Commission, addressing situations of human need, and pressing for greater religious freedom in countries with serious human right problems.[1]

Indeed, these challenges are great. And these mimetic reflections explore, from the point of view of a religious critic and cultural analyst, the cultural dynamics

[1] Philip L. Wickeri, "Christian Mission Impossible: The Global Role of U.S. Denominations." www.TheThoughtfulChristian.com. 2006. 1

underlying the concerns expressed in Wickeri's critical judgments regarding U.S. Christian missions.

Religious criticism or self-reflexivity affirms creative possibilities for the fulfillment of our political, social, and spiritual strivings.[2] Moreover, it imagines and performs a rigorous iconoclasm regarding the ideation of the Great Commission, which is often reflected by supporters of American Christian missions. The religious critic operates from a self-reflexive position, which in my case, as an American and Christian. In this essay, I analyze discursive formations of U.S. colonizing power, sovereignty, and imperial reach as they are wedded in formations of U. S. Christian missionary discourses, which together produce and reproduce binary subject positions between colonials/colonizers and subalterns of their making. From this mimetic knotting, I isolate a number of challenges to any consideration that U.S. Christian missions can free itself from the history of mimetic desire and rivalry whose violence make up the subalterns of the spirit of American empire. While my reflections are rather iconoclastic, focusing on the dark union between church and empire, I remain pessimistically open to possibilities for hope and human flourishing beyond this unholy union, that is, beyond the spirit of American empire. I share this hope with religious critics Cornel West, Néstor Míguez, Jeorg Rieger, and Jung Mo Sung.

In *Democracy Matters: Winning The Fight Against Imperialism*, Cornel West schematizes the spirit of American empire by three dogmas of free-market fundamentalism, aggressive militarism, and escalating authoritarianism. The first dogma locates empire in the "unregulated and unfettered market as idol and fetish," says West. "This glorification of the market has led to a callous corporate–dominated political economy in which business leaders are to be worshiped... and the most powerful corporations are delegated magical powers of salvation.... Free-market fundamentalism—just as dangerous as the religious fundamentalisms of our day—trivializes the concerns of public interest".[3] The second dogma is aggressive militarism. "This dogma posits military might as *salvific* in a world in which he who has the most and biggest weapons is the most moral and masculine, hence worthy of policing others".[4] The third dogma is escalating authoritarian-

[2] Victor Anderson, *Beyond Ontological Blackness: An Essay on Religious and Cultural Criticism*. New York, NY: Continuum, 1995. See also VictorAnderson "Black Scholarly Aesthetics and the Religious Critic: Black Experience as Manifolds of Manifestations and Powers of Presentations. *American Journal of Theology and Philosophy*. Vol. 33, No. 2, May 2012.

[3] Cornel West, *Democracy Matters: Winning The Fight Against Imperialism*. New York, NY: The Penguin Press, 2004. 3-4

[4] Ibid. 5.

ism, which marks American empire by "understandable paranoia toward potential terrorists, our traditional fear of too many liberties, and our deep distrust of one another".[5] In a word, West asserts, "American empire struts across the globe like a behemoth. We have built up uncontested military might, undeniable cultural power, and transactional corporate and financial hegemony," while acknowledging "a huge trade deficit, budget deficit, and intensifying class, racial, religious, and ideological warfare at home".[6] According to West, "the three dogmas of free-market fundamentalism, aggressive militarism, and escalating authoritarianism are snuffing out the democratic impulses that are so vital for deepening the spread of democracy in the world".[7] One notes in West's powerful critique of American empire languages of salvation, power, idols, and fetishism. In West's critique of American empire, these religious languages mimetically conspire to deconstruct US imperial reach and the legitimating power of US Christian missions.

In their book *Beyond the Spirit of Empire*, liberation theologians Néstor Míguez, Joerg Rieger, and Jung Mo Sung offer a powerful theological critique of the spirit of American empire.[8] In comparison to West, they acknowledge presenting a rather mitigated critique of what they call the spirit of American empire. In light of West's analysis, for them, the neoliberal politics of the Bush administration has taken a somewhat weakening turn with the election of Barack Obama's promises to dismantle U.S. military conflicts, closure of the U.S prison at Guantanamo Bay, Cuba, greater push for radicalizing democratic energies in many Arab states, even state intervention into private markets due to failing national economies of so called developed countries, but also a growing awareness that our planetary resources, once deemed infinite, just may be too limited for sustaining neoliberal economic demands of consumption and commodities.[9] Although acknowledging these mitigating factors regarding American empire, Miguez, Rieger, and Sung nevertheless propose:

> Since we consider the whole world of financial capitalism as a confluence of the imperial vocation, we wonder why there is a particular incarnation of the wandering spirit of Empire in this context. We are interested in the Spirit of Empire: that is, in seeing what moves this conglomeration of forces that generates this particular form with its propensity for total domination, what spurs the underlying motivations of imperial

---

5 Ibid. 6.
6 Ibid. 9.
7 Ibid. 8.
8 Néstor Míguez, Jorge Rieger, and Jung Mo Sung, *Beyond the Spirit of Empire*. London, UK: SCM Press2009.
9 Ibid. ix.

> companies, and what creates this intangible and secret ruse of forms of power that seek to circumvent all controls, which constantly increase in excessiveness. Reflecting on the weakness of Empire must not allow us to forget that the thrust of Empire can reappear in new guises, and this insight obliges us to think closely about the opportunity to overcome this understanding of power with a political ethics that enables other ways of organizing politics and the political.[10]

My reflections analyze the manner in which the technologies of empire, which are based on a neoliberal globalization of capitalism, are mimetically embedded and derived from a prior ethos of Christian colonized and colonizing operations of sovereignty. I suggest that this mimesis of colonizing sovereignty (the imperial reach of England) and anti-establishment sovereignty (the sovereignty of the people) on which the spirit of American empire is founded is joined to capitalist formations of economic power that today manifest a U.S. neoliberal establishmentarianism. Moreover, I read this contemporary state of U.S. Christian missions as a mimetic repetition of prior mission narratives of the founding of the American empire. Deconstructing this history of mimetic missionary effects by the production of counter-histories has not been very effective. For as René Girard has insisted, whose theory of mimetic desire and rivalry I draw on throughout this easy, what is required of the religious critic is nothing short of a complete renunciation of all mimetic desire and rivalries that are oriented toward violence[11] and the death dealing effects of the U.S.'s imperial reach through its neoliberal establishmentarianism, which is constitutive of the spirit of American empire. For some, such a renunciation is required if, in the end, U.S. Christian missions is to be a vital force of salvation for the world's poor most impacted by economic globalization. West, Míguez, Rieger, and Sung agree. Míguez, Rieger, and Sung articulate this call for radical renunciation well. They "look for a better political vision than the imperial one, and continue searching for that which reaches beyond Empire".[12] Such is also the hope of a religious critic such as West who remains committed to the languages of prophetic faith and gospel. I move forward by analyzing the mimetic relations of desire and rivalry that bind colonized/colonial and missionary powers, sovereignty and reach by a violent history of effects, resulting in an ever proliferation of alterity of church and empire's global subalterns.

---

[10] Ibid. x.

[11] René Girard, *The René Girard Reader*, James G. Williams, ed. New York, NY: The Crossroad Publishing Company, 2003.

[12] Míguez, Rieger, and Sung, *Beyond the Spirit of Empire*.xi.

Mimesis of Colonizing Sovereignty

There is a current and pervasive discourse going on in much of continental and postcolonial discourses concerning sovereignty, imperialism, and empire. However, as Míguez, Rieger, and Sung have noted above translatability of U.S. formations of empire to this larger continental discourse is not easy without considerable nuances and disclaimers. The difficulties stem from the U.S. emergence in the seventeenth and eighteenth centuries as anti-establishmentarian colonies of England. The dynastic relation between European political and ecclesial sovereignties was joined in ways that were not historically enjoyed in a New England colonial and Puritan ethos that was politically and religiously anti-establishmentarian. This was an ethos at once resistant to an earthly sovereign and beholden to divine sovereignty.

This meta-narrative of anti-establishmentarianism enters into the spirit of American empire as a strange note of difference, which was well noted by Tocqueville, says philosopher Lucy Hartley.[13] According to Hartley, Tocqueville "proceeds to investigate the internal function of the democratic nation, tracing the principle of the 'sovereignty of the people' as embodied at every level of society by townships and municipal bodies, the legislative and executive power of the state, and finally the federal constitution".[14] Tocqueville takes note of what sociologist Max Weber much later would undertake in his *Protestant Ethic and the Spirit of Capitalism* (1905).[15] It is the manner in which American anti-establishmentarianism embraced the Protestant ethic and the spirit of capitalism in the formation of American empire. Tocqueville's remarks are illustrative. In *Democracy in America*, he writes: "The American republics of the present day are like companies of adventurers to explore in common the waste lands of the New World, and busied in a flourishing of trade. The passions that agitate the Americans most deeply are not their political but their commercial passions".[16]

This missionary spirit of American empire—adventurous, borderless, enterprising, and entrepreneurial—circulates throughout U. S. politico-theological imaginaries. Resistant to every threat of absolutism, whether political or ecclesial, the American anti-establishmentarian spirit operates on a imaginary plane of egalitarian sovereignty of the people that is leery of empire's imperial reach

[13] Lucy Hartley, "War and Peace, or Governmentality as the Ruin of Democracy," in *Foucault in an Age of Terror: Essays on the Biopolitics and the Defense of Society*. Stephen Morton and Stephen Bygrave, eds. New York, NY: Palgrave Macmillan, 2008.

[14] Ibid. 142.

[15] Max Weber, *The Protestant Ethic and the Spirit of Capitalism*. New York: Scribner, 1948.

[16] Cited by Hartley, "War and Peace, or Governmentality as the Ruin of Democracy," 143.

(in this case England and Europe), anti-protectionist in foreign trade, and non-interventionist in international affairs. Nevertheless, U.S. mimetic desire and rivalry of and with European sovereignty's imperial reach, which stretched across the globe by annexing as accumulative capital raw materials of lands and peoples from the fifteenth century well into the early twentieth century, joins the spirit of American empire with the larger colonizing discourse of European sovereignty. Economist Jeffry A. Frieman describes this global economic integration as the golden age of global capitalism. He says "as the economies of Europe, America and Japan were celebrating market forces, they were using forces of a different kind—artillery, gunboats, infantry—to subordinate hundreds of millions of new colonial subjects in Africa, Asia, and Latin America".[17] Through mimetic desire and rivalry, the spirit of American empire becomes a liberal capitalist establishment now joined both in the glories of European sovereignty in global markets and the violence and alterity that comes with this colonizing power.

Mimesis ought not to be taken as signifying imitation alone. There is imitation, but much more is involved. Mimesis produces a surplus of effects says Michael Potolsky, including patterns of dissimilitude, mimicry, doubling, repetition, emulation, and more.[18] In my mimetic reflections, the spirit of American empire—its power and imperial reach through economic, military, and missionizing colonizing discourses—is approached from what philosopher, Robert Sokolowski describes as identity in manifolds. Taking the historical event of the Normandy invasion in the Second World War as a point of departure, Sokolowski explains:

> This event was experienced in one way by those who participated in it, in another way by those same people when they remember it, in another way by those who read about it as it was reported in the newspapers, in another way by those who write and those who read books about it later on, in another way by those who join in a memorial celebration on the Normandy beaches, in another way by those who see movies and television shows made about it. The same event was also anticipated by those who were planning to do it, and those who, on the other side, were planning to resist it. There are undoubtedly still other ways in which one and same event can be intended and made present, and the identity of the event is sustained through them all".[19]

Within identity in manifolds, the spirit of American empire represents in power

---

[17] Jeffry A Friedman, *Global Capitalism: its Fall and Rise in the Twentieth Century.* New York, NY: W.W. Norton & Company, Inc., 2006. 26.

[18] Michael Potolsky, *Mimesis.* New York, NY: Routledge, 2005. 1.

[19] Robert Sokolowski. *Introduction to Phenomenology.* New York, NY: Cambridge University Press, 2000. 28-29.

and privilege, conflict and exchange, and alterity, a mimesis, a mirroring, repetition, and representation of European sovereignty and empire. It (re)presents England's imperial arms stretched to North American settlements. And although anti-establishment, the colonized simultaneously share an imperial identity as Englishmen and women. However, as defenders of an anti-establishmentarian sovereignty, that is, the sovereignty of the people, they are marked by their own alterity or difference to English and European dynastic sovereignty. Moreover, this mimesis of identity in manifolds provided colonials the privilege and power of a self-defining sovereignty in relation to their conflicts and exchanges with England and Europe in treaties, trade, markets, commerce, and the trafficking of raw goods and cheap labor.

A mimetic inversion occurs. The colonized paradoxically create subalterns of their own making of indigenous peoples and enslaved Africans, both reduced to mere flesh and accumulative capital. In this mimetic doubling of New England otherness (Englishmen and women by extension of England's imperial reach and Europe's other by colonial distinction), New England colonials reproduced a spirit of empire through a repetition of colonizing sovereignty over their subalterns, making of them an unlimited stock of accumulative capital, constituting them human property by dividing shares and making real-estate of lands annexed and fenced, and subjecting them to disciplinary tactics of the biopolitics of colonizing sovereignty.

French social theorist Michel Foucault describes these tactics under biopolitics, which he introduced in his lectures and writing in the 1970s. Biopolitics disciplines and regulates subaltern bodies not only through colonizing sovereignty but also through a variety of tactics of control and management. The latter he describes as governmentality. Foucault spoke of biopolitics along two poles: the anatomo-politics of the body and the regulatory politics over populations. First, anatomo-politics of the human body renders the body a machine through technologies for "disciplining, the optimization of its capabilities, the extortion of its forces, the parallel increase of its usefulness and its docility, the integration into a system of efficient and economic controls".[20] Second, the regulatory biopolitics over populations produces a "species body" that is policed by regulatory controls: "The body imbued with the mechanics of life and serving as the basis of the biological processes; propagation, births and mortality, the level of health, life expectancy and longevity, with all the conditions that can cause these to vary".[21] In

[20] Michel Foucault, *The History of Sexuality: An Introduction Volume I*. Translated by Robert Hurley. New York, NY: Vintage Books, 1990. 139.

[21] Ibid.

sum, "the discipline of the body and the regulations of the population constituted the two poles around which the organization of power over life was deployed," says Foucault.[22]

Foucault's analysis is helpful for seeing connections between mimetic relations of colonizing sovereignty, the capitalist formation of privilege and power, conflict and exchange, and alterity and difference, and the manner in which these forces operate and circulate throughout the spirit of American empire. This spirit of American empire, at once missionary and colonizing sovereignty, annexed lands and controlled subalterns as accumulative capital and both were disciplined and regulated by laws of laissez-faire economic schemes. These schemes endured quite well and virtually unchecked without direct intervention of state, church, or juridical power until the Civil War. With the maturing of the U.S. economic rise in world economies, its stabilizing national identity with the Spanish American war, and its late arrival into the global sphere of world conflicts, due to its economic, industrial and technological powers demonstrated in the two World Wars, the spirit of American empire—both missionary and colonizing— invented itself as a world power representing the integration of a global capitalist sovereignty. These discursive formations of privilege, power, conflict, exchange, alterity in the spirit of American empire mimetically enter into the desires of and in rivalry with a militant evangelical Christianity. Together, they legitimate the global imperial reach of the U.S. and the biopolitics and governmental technologies of state that discipline and regulate a world of subalterns of their own making. *This mimesis of colonizing power poses great challenges today for articulating any missiological interventions in a world of mass alienation and oppression spawned by the spirit of American empire and its neoliberal capitalist establishmentarianism.*

Mimesis of Missionary Sovereignty

As suggested above, simultaneous with the U.S. imperial reach of power and privilege through colonizing sovereignty was a mimesis of supreme sovereignty operating in a militant Christianity that mirrored the ecclesial arm of European sovereignty and empire in the formation of the modern nation state. Here, U.S. colonized and colonizing sovereignty justified themselves in ideologies of progress, civilization, and a world commonwealth rooted in missionary ideations. Consider American religious historian Sydney Ahlstrom's discussion of the Massachusetts Bay Company: "The trading company thus became a commonwealth,

[22] Ibid.

though it was far from being a 'democracy' in the modern sense".[23] Moreover, American religious historian Winthrop S. Hudson describes the biopolitics of American empire's missionary vision:

> God had "sifted a whole nation" in order to plant his "choice grain" in the American wilderness, but his purpose was more far-ranging than merely to enable them to escape the inhibitions they had suffered at home. They were not fleeing persecution; they were executing a flank attack upon forces of unrighteousness everywhere. Their role, John Winthrop had reminded them, was to be "a city on a hill" to demonstrate before "the eyes of the world" what the result would be when a whole people were brought into covenant with God. As part of God's program of instruction, they were to provide the nations with a working model of a godly society, and by the contagion of their example were to be God's instruments in effecting the release from bondage of all mankind.[24]

However, these missionary ideations could neither be divorced from deployments of governmental technologies of state and church power nor the biopolitics of global capitalism that annexed and controlled the subalterns of American empire. As Hudson recalls, there existed "[t]wo segments of the population, which were unable to share the eager expectations of the dominant majority".[25]

> The native Americans quickly became strangers in the land with no heady vision of the future to sustain them. To evangelize the Indians and make them joint-heirs of the promise had been one of the motives of colonization, and there was intermittent missionary activity. For the most part, however, Indians were treated as an alien presence to be pushed back beyond the forward-moving end of "civilization." In similar fashion captives brought from Africa as slaves were outsiders who had little reason to view the future as pregnant with the possibility of all things being made new.[26]

Although a founding narrative, this missionary myth of the errand in the wilderness pervades the spirit of American empire. For as Wickeri suggests, even today, this machinery of sovereignty and empire is reinforced by an evangelical, post-denominational, and neo-Pentecostal missionary militarism throughout Africa, Asia, and Latin America. It is a Christian establishment deeply settled in a Constantinian myth of the U.S. as God's new Christendom, that is, a nation joined by God and civilization in the formations of global economic sovereignty and empire.

---

23 Sydney E. Ahlstrom, *A Religious History of the American People*. New Haven,, CT: Yale University Press, New Haven, CT. 1972. 147.

24 Winthrop S. Hudson, *Religion in America.* New York, NY: Charles Scribner's Sons, 1981. 20.

25 Ibid. 22.

26 Ibid.

Contemporary Christianities face considerable difficulties identifying, articulating, and executing a missionary scheme untangled from this mimesis of church and empire. Doing so would require renunciation of the missionizing narratives embedded in the founding of American empire. However, any renunciation of these narratives also means risking erasure of the U.S. Christian settlement with civilization (missions) and church with empire (global capitalism). Such a mimetic renunciation appears most difficult given the knotted relations between the biopolitics and tactics of state disciplinary and regulatory operations of power over the subalterns of U.S. making and U.S. Christian missionary power. Through colonizing power, Christian colonials attached English monies, sponsorships, and martial powers to support their errand into the lands of wild humans, called savages, and the cultivation of those lands by importation of African slaves. What was home to subalterns became wilderness to the colonials. Wilderness was for the wanderers, and like Canaan, it was mimetically open and not closed, borderless and unmapped. Renunciation of this mimesis of boundary-less wandering, and adventure is not possible without self-interrogation and self-renunciation of the privilege, power, exchange, alterity afforded by the spirit of American empire.

My mimetic reflections thus far have been intentionally mixing metaphors, metaphors that are rooted in geography and biblical narratives. Theologian Willie J. Jennings has shown quite persuasively that such a joining of metaphors provides a consistent narrative of the U.S. evangelical imaginary of contact and conquest and conflict and exchange.[27] Contact and conquest (empire) entail cultural logics of conflict and exchange. The spirit of American empire is structurally mediated by the conflict and exchange provided by Christian missions, which produces and reproduces the *subalterns* of American empire's missionizing and economic power. Such conflicts and exchanges are manifolds of the spirit of American empire with narratives of progress, civilization, and national wealth.

These narratives of conflict and exchange signify the denigration of indigenous, colonized, and enslaved peoples to nothingness, to wilderness, and borderlessness. Ironically, most counter-narratives or counter-knowledges produced by subalterns themselves, which were and are produced under the sway of American empire, sadly mirror the mimetic desires of and rivalry for empire's power, for such counter-knowledges are embedded in or are mimetic effects of empire's own perpetual recoiling as counter narratives of sovereignty. *Tragically, the mimetic desire and rivalry among subalterns of empire's sovereignty all too often end up*

[27] Willie James Jennings, *The Christian Imagination: Theology and the Origins of Race.* New Haven, CT: Yale University Press, 2010.

replicating deeper levels of otherness among themselves, and this proliferation of otherness among subalterns of American empire poses still greater challenges for reconciling U.S. Christian missions and the spirit of American empire.

Mimetic Alterity and Violence

The spirit of American empire is at once missionary (evangelical) and imperial (expansionist). In articulations of its missionary identity, the spirit of American empire is constituted by a mimetic repetition where power reproduces power, which produces and reproduces alterity and otherness. Here, evangelical missionizing power operates within the borderlessness of U.S. Multinational Corporations and the neo-liberal free market morality that legitimates their cooperation of powers. As subalterns engage these powers, which through biopolitics and tactics of governmentality in transnational governments, the combined powers of church and empire operate to assure that real control of indigenous lands and peoples, vast mineral resources, and labor allocations and realignments benefit the comparative advantage the Multinational Corporations (MNCs), International Financial Institutions (IFIs), NGOs, and states over the defused competing rights and claims of indigenous peoples, tribes, and ethnicities.

This mimesis of alterity and violence is articulated persuasively in Sawyer and Gomez. In case studies of indigenous peoples in Australia, Bolivia, Canada, Chad, Cameron, India, Nigeria, Peru, and the Philippines, researchers wanted to study the impact of *Transnational Governmentality and Resources Extraction* in these countries in conjunction with MNCs, IFIs and states to address United Nations concerns over the impact of resource extraction of gold, minerals, and hydrocarbons on indigenous peoples. In the creation of "consultative platforms that would provide indigenous groups with an avenue to participate in decisions that affect their way of life," new institutions were created that "afford indigenous peoples the power to veto, sanction or reformulate projects recommended by the government, International agencies or MNCs that were detrimental to their way of life".[28]

Despite mandates, charters, and legislations designed to assert and protect the rights of indigenous peoples, the majority, nevertheless, find themselves increasingly "subjected to discrimination, exploitation, dispossession and racism".[29]

[28] Suzana Sawyer and Terrence Gomez, *Transnational Governmentality And Resource Extraction: Indigenous Peoples, Multinational Corporations, Multilateral Institutions and the State*. Identities, Conflict and Cohesion, Program Paper 13. Geneva, Switzerland: United Nations Research Institute for Social Development, September 2008. iii.

[29] Ibid.

Moreover, "public-private partnership eventually led to institutional capture, undermining the neutrality of the state and its capacity to protect indigenous communities".[30] Not discounting efforts of states and NGOs to intervene in these countries' development, neoliberal biopolitics and governmentality in and through MNCs, IFIs, and states effectively creates *subalterns* among indigenous peoples in class, caste, and ethnic tiers, say Altman, Tauli-Corpuz and Rovillos, and Urteaga-Crovetto. Urteaga-Crovetto's case study of the Peruvian Camisea gas project is illustrative of conclusion drawn by other researchers.

> Obtaining property deeds has both allowed the Machiguenga to legally protect their ancestral territory and, together with natural gas extractive activity, has radically transformed indigenous cultural, social political and economic reality. The Machiguenga—who until the early 1980s were a semi-nomadic population migrating seasonally among dispersed settlements—became, with state land titling policy, settled through the establishment of state-recognized permanent nuclear settlements. It is with these native communities that the Camisea gas consortium negotiated its terms of engagement with indigenous peoples. But far from being the foundation of a deeply rooted social structure, these newly created settlements lacked indigenous organization and could easily be manipulated. Different negotiations with the gas consortium obtained different outcomes, which in turn led to division within and among communities. This, together with the powerful influence of the evangelical and Catholic missions, created a situation in which, as Urteaga-Crovetto notes 'most Machiguenga understand progress as synonymous with material consumption.' These special, cultural and ideological transformations have largely aided the Camisea project and further augmented poverty, inequity and the exploitation of indigenous people.[31]

The above case study shows how it is possible for indigenous peoples, already *"Other,"* to mimetically create subalterns among own communities.

Sawyer and Gomez explain that with juridical power, "rights, in practice are embedded in complex legal, political and economic structures (forged frequently with corporate influence) that delineate who exactly counts as indigenous and what they might claim".[32] Furthermore, "identity-based rights necessitate first defining who officially will be recognized as right-bearing subjects, and second, what they will have rights over."[33] For instance, "those individuals legally recognize as deservingly indigenous may have surface rights to land, but beyond that they may or may not have rights to a range of mechanisms that provide degrees

[30] Ibid.

[31] Cited in Sawyer and Gomez, *Transnational Governmentality*, 2.

[32] Ibid. 3.

[33] Ibid.

of leverage for negotiating with resource extraction firms."[34] Sawyer and Gomez conclude, "consequently, the rigid delineation of land in the name of precise individuals deemed authentically indigenous and worthy by the state often leads to conflicts within and between indigenous communities over authenticity, history, authority, and exclusion. And perhaps most insidiously, it can become a perverse mechanism through which the state and multinational corporations codify, fix, and control the goals and aspiration of what were fluid and mobile collectivities."[35]

Under U.S. neoliberal establishmentarianism in colonizing power, relief comes to the subalterns through the governance of education, health, labor, housing, and multilateral MNCs, IFIs, and NGOs, and state projects oriented toward economic and ecological sustainability. All such projects are intended to lift the world's poorest, while simultaneously, reinforcing power through alienating strategies of class, tribal, and caste differences, conflicts over lands, jobs, economic ownership of trade, manufacturing, as well as right and control over legitimating structures provided by law, religion and governance. *Legitimating this mimesis of alterity and otherness among subalterns of empire is a mobilization of evangelical, post-denominational and neo-Pentecostal Christianities that are simultaneously militant, missionary, democratic, and protected by Cornel West's three dogmas of empire: free-market fundamentalism, an aggressive U.S. militarism, and an escalating authoritarianism. This mimesis of alterity and otherness presents a still further challenge for critical reflections on U.S. Christian missions and the spirit of American empire.*

On the Possibility of Mimetic Renunciation

Religious criticism is a form of cultural analysis that attempts to disclose the emancipatory aspects of persons and groups, which they have a right to expect from the democratic impact on cultures. As a mode of cultural analysis, religious criticism can be enlightening yet iconoclastic when it exposes and rejects totalizing discourses of empire, sovereignty, global capitalism, and U. S. Christian missions, which conspire to render vacuous multitudes suffering the biopolitics and governmentality of MNCs, IFIs, NGOs, and states. As cultural analysis, religious criticism can be emancipatory and utopian when it sees beyond debilitating and oppressive structures possibilities for human flourishing and fulfillment. It requires an iconoclastic rigor and utopian hope.[36] The religious critic seeks to in-

[34] Ibid.

[35] Ibid.

[36] Anderson, *Beyond Ontological Blackness:* 38.

tervene into the many ways that conflicts between faith and power become sites of human violence and brutalities. He/she may describe such conflicts and exchanges as demonic. However, the critic also envisions the possibility that human betterment can be found when our conflicts over and exchanges with culture, power, and governmentality become creative of human good and fulfillment. The religious critic analyzes and promotes critical intervention into the ways that culture and life, faith and power contribute to the furtherance of basic human need for social, moral, spiritual, economic, political, and cultural fulfillment.

However, the religious critic is not content with describing only the dark sides of our cultural forms and relations, although in my mimetic reflections above, I foreground the dark sides and effects, indeed, the manner in which Christian evangelical missiology and its colonizing sovereignty join mimetically in the maintenance of U.S. global capitalistic neoliberal establishmentarianism. I wanted to show how a mimetic inversion occurs among the colonized of European sovereignty become through mimetic desire and rivalry a colonizing power. The effect was the creation of subalterns of their own making in indigenous Americans and African slaves. I also wanted to see connections between this mimesis of colonizing and Christian missions united in the global mobilization of capitalist annexation of lands and peoples as raw materials to feed European and American demands for consumption of goods and labor well into the twentieth century. Moreover, legitimating this union of sovereignty and imperial reach by American missions is the formation of a neoliberal establishmentarianism. Finally, at the end of each section, I suggested problems that these cultural moves create for contemporary U.S. Christian missions and alterity.

Now I am left asking whether U.S. Christian missions have enough internal resources for self-interrogation and self-renunciation of its power and privilege to intervene in the collusion of evangelical, post-denominational, and neo-Pentecostal missionizing power with forces of transnational governmentality, MNCs, IFIs, NGOs, and state juridical power, in countries most negatively impacted by U.S. global economic reach and whose existence are described by Sawyer and Gomez as "just living." I ask whether the hopes of West, Míguez, Rieger, and Jung, derived from the resources of faith and Christian practices, are strong enough to untangle U.S. Christian missions from the spirit of American empire and its imperial global reach.

Given my worries, religious criticism seems to call for complete renunciation of all mimetic desire between missions and empire and renunciation of mimetic rivalry oriented toward violence. In their vision of a *laocratic* messianism over the spirit of empire, Míguez, Reiger and Sung appear to call for such a radical mimetic renunciation.

> Beginning with the cross and resurrection of Jesus, the new era has begun. In this way, the new *laos* of God incarnates not a nation but a multitude, a 'popular' people, a new experience of humanity without exclusions. Thus, messianism expresses the anti-imperial, the surprise that upsets history, the necessity of maintaining the meaning of the public, so that the voice of the *laos* shows the limits of power, returns meaning to the political, puts into play the hope of the excluded, and redeems the human in the creature, and with it, the whole dimension of creation.[37]

This is a tall order for mimetic renunciation, namely, a radical reversal of all mimetic desire and rivalry. However, Girard acknowledges the dangers that follow such a radical renunciation. He contends that mimetic desire lies at the root of every mimetic rivalry where the consequence is violence and that the gospel of Jesus renounces this history of violence. However, whether all mimetic desire must be renounced, Girard explains:

> As to whether I am advocating "renunciation" of mimetic desire, yes and no. Not the renunciation of mimetic desire itself, because what Jesus advocates is mimetic desire. Imitate me, and imitate the Father through me, he says, so it's twice mimetic. Jesus seems to say that the only way to avoid violence is to imitate me, and imitate the Father. So the idea that mimetic desire itself is bad makes no sense. It's true, however, that occasionally I say "mimetic desire" when I really mean only the type of mimetic desire that generates mimetic rivalry, and in turn, is generated by it.[38]

For Girard, therefore, mimetic desire that generates rivalry produces violence, which is occasioned by "human failure to walk away from mimetic rivalry" and violence.[39] According to Girard, then, mimetic desire is dangerously oriented toward mimetic rivalry and violence. It is the rivalry of the copy toward the model, the type toward its antitype, or the truly real toward appearances; it is the rivalry of sovereignties, of powers, of imperial reach between the church and empire. Like West, Míguez, Rieger, and Sung, Girard encourages Christians to imitate Jesus and his kingdom.

However, for Christian missions embedded in the spirit of American empire and its neoliberal capitalist establishmentarianism, such a radical mimetic renunciation will risk self-erasure. What it requires is self-renunciation of power and privilege, of conflict and exchanges, and alterity, which are the gains of American

[37] Míguez, Rieger and Sung, *Beyond the Spirit of Empire*.202.

[38] Girard *The René Girard Reader*. 63.

[39] Ibid. 215.

Christian mission's mimetic desire of and rivalry with European sovereignty and its imperial global reach. Such a mimetic renunciation with empire means a radical renunciation of American missionary founding narratives and identity born of mimetic rivalry and violence. Attempts to free U.S. mainline Christianities from these prior narratives and identity have been relatively unsuccessful in creating a counter-history to this missionary history and its scandalous gospel of reach, privilege, power, conflict, exchange, and alterity. Through mimetic desire and rivalry, the narratives recoil into just so many repetitions of dissimilitude and mimetic otherness operating today on a global scale.

Conclusion

The picture I have presented displays a deep pessimism for any effective reversal or mimetic renunciation of the spirit of American empire's missionary power from U.S. colonizing sovereignty and neoliberal global capitalist establishmentarianism. However, I am not overwhelmed by the demands of such a mimetic renunciation however difficult the demands are to achieve. Rather, I am most aware of just how challenging any conversations today must be over how Christian missions can be creative forces of human betterment. Still as a religious critic I hold firmly to the saving power embedded in the languages of faith and self-reflexively affirm the creative possibilities in which faith translates into action and action moves us all toward fulfillment of our political, social, economic, and spiritual strivings. West articulates this position well even as he acknowledges what he calls a "Constantinian captivity of much of the Christian movement."

> My philosophy of democracy is deeply shaped by that particular Jew named Jesus who put the love of God and neighbor at the core of his vision of justice and his deeds of compassion. His vision of a just future consoles those who cry and his deeds of compassion comfort those who shed tears. His loving gift of ministry, grace, and death under the rule of nihilistic imperial elites enacts divine compassion and justice in human flesh. The ultimate Christian paradox of God crucified in history under the Roman empire is that the love and justice that appear so weak may be strong, that seem so foolish may be wise, and that strike imperial elites as easily disposable may be inescapably indispensable. The prophetic tradition is fueled by a righteous indignation at injustice—a moral urgency to address the cries and tears of oppressed peoples. Despite the Constantinian captivity of much of the Christian movement here and abroad, the prophetic tradition has a deep legacy of providing extraordinary strength of commitment and vision that helps us to care in a palpable way about the injustices we see around us.[40]

[40] West, *Democracy Matters: Winning The Fight Agianst Imperialism.* 214.

As a religious critic, standing between the church and empire, my pessimism runs deep even as I find agreement with West, Míguez, Reiger, and Sung in calling for a radical renunciation of Christian mission's mimetic desire and rivalry with empire. I find Wickeri's challenge most persuasive: "Globalization, according to *New York Times* columnist Thomas Friedman, divides the world into a fast world and a slow world. Empire seeks to incorporate both worlds of its own orbit. Churches can either ride the cocktails of Empire or resist the dehumanizing forces of globalization, but we cannot do both. How transnational Christian committees such as our own relate to the powers that seek to structure and order the international community will affect our churches decades to come."[41]

Counting on decades to come, there is great urgency for U.S. Christians to take seriously religious critics' call for a radical renunciation of the mimesis of American empire. Also counting on decades to come, there is time for a prophetic and priestly renewal in U.S. Christian missions for the mimetic desire to follow the patterns of Christ's orientation toward power, privilege, conflict, exchange, and alterity beyond the spirit of American empire. Such possibilities strike even me, this iconoclastic religious critic, with hope and promise for the cultural, moral and spiritual fulfillment of the global subalterns of our own making.

Works Cited

Anderson, Victor. *Beyond Ontological Blackness: An Essay on Religious and Cultural Criticism*. New York, NY: Continuum, 1995.

Anderson, Victor, "Black Scholarly Aesthetics and the Religious Critic: Black Experience as Manifolds of Manifestations and Powers of Presentations. *American Journal of Theology and Philosophy*. Vol. 33, No. 2. May 2012.

Ahlstrom, Sydney E. *A Religious History of The American People*. New Haven,, CT: Yale University Press, New Haven, CT., 1972.

Foucault, Michel, The *History of Sexuality: An Introduction Volume I*. Translated by Robert Hurley. New York, NY: Vintage Books, 1990.

Friedman Jeffry A., *Global Capitalism: its Fall and Rise in the Twentieth Century.* New York, NY: W.W. Norton & Company, Inc., 2006.

Friedman, Thomas. "Foreign Affairs; Here Comes the Sun," New York Times. May 4, 2001.

Girard, René, *The René Girard Reader*, James G. Williams, ed. New York, NY: The Crossroad Publishing Company, 2003.

[41] Wickeri "Christian Mission Impossible: The Global Role of U.S. Denominations," 4, citing Friedman, "Foreign Affairs; Here Comes the Sun," New York Times, May 4, 2001.

Hartley, Lucy, "War and Peace, or Governmentality as the Ruin of Democracy," in *Foucault in an Age of Terror: Essays on the Biopolitics and the Defense of Society*. Stephen Morton and Stephen Bygrave, eds. New York, NY: Palgrave Macmillan, 2008.

Hudson, Winthrop S. *Religion in America.* New York, NY: Charles Scribner's Sons, 1981.

Jennings, Willie James. *The Christian Imagination: Theology and the Origins of Race.* New Haven, CT: Yale University Press, 2010.

Míguez, Néstor, Rieger, Jorge, and Sung, Jung Mo. *Beyond the Spirit of Empire.* London, UK: SCM Press, 2009.

Potolsky, Michael. *Mimesis.* New York, NY: Routledge, 2005.

Suzana Sawyer and Terrence Gomez. *Transnational Governmentality And Resource Extraction: Indigenous Peoples, Multinational Corporations, Multilateral Institutions and the State*. Identities, Conflict and Cohesion, Program Paper 13. Geneva, Switzerland: United Nations Research Institute for Social Development, September 2008.

Sokolowski, Robert. *Introduction to Phenomenology*. New York, NY: Cambridge University Press, 2000.

Weber, Max. The Protestant Ethic and the Spirit of Capitalism. New York: Scribner, 1948.

West, Cornel. *Democracy Matters: Winning The Fight Agianst Imperialism.* New York, NY: The Penguin Press, 2004.

Wickeri, Philip L. "Christian Mission Impossible: The Global Role of U.S. Denominations." www.TheThoughtfulChristian.com. 2006.

5 Mission and Coloniality: Christianity and the Caribbean

Gerald BOODOO

Introduction

This Chapter will give some voice to the possible ways of understanding Christian, mainly Roman Catholic, involvement in the Caribbean in past, present and future dimensions using the lens of coloniality to try to make sense of Christian constructs in the region. Let me indicate that by Caribbean I mean geographically the territory covered by the Roman Catholic Antilles Episcopal Conference that runs from Bermuda and the Bahamas in the north to Cayenne (French Guyana) in the south including Belize to the west and all of the islands to the east. The following self description is given by the conference's website:

> The English, French and Dutch territories of the Caribbean, with the exception of Haiti, constitute the geographical area entrusted to the pastoral care of the Bishops of the Antilles Episcopal Conference. The Catholic Church within these territories comprises five Provinces, consisting of five archdioceses, fourteen dioceses and two Independent Missions, i.e., twenty-one ecclesiastical units in all. Politically, within the five Provinces there are thirteen independent Nations, three Departments of France, two parts of the Kingdom of the Netherlands having complete internal autonomy, and six British colonies. In addition, one United States Dependency enjoys observer status.[1]

One must note that this geographic division is one that is continuous with colonial divisions and not geographic contiguity so that the Guianas (Dutch, British and French) are not considered part of South America because they are not "Latin" and the Spanish speaking islands of Cuba and the Dominican Republic are not included. Colonial language and structures still divide the ways in which (what is called) the Catholic Church in the Caribbean is understood.

I also consider as part of the Caribbean, in terms of mentalities, all those persons who are from the Caribbean, living in many other parts of the world, but who draw upon their Caribbean intellectual and cultural heritage as integral to their self-identification. I include myself in this group and think of all the Caribbean

---

1 http://www.aecrc.org/joomla/index.php?option=com_content&view=article&id=44&Itemid=54

associations and festivals that appear in many parts of the world. From this perspective, the space of the Caribbean as a place linked by relationships is not limited only to immediate geographical inhabitation, and perhaps the discontinuity of colonial divisions has had an unforeseen linkage (or re-linking if you like) where what is understood as Caribbean can be said to extend well beyond the simple physical limitations of its assigned geographic location.

For a region and a people that have been brought to the region by fiat and who easily leave and come based on educational, economic, social and other factors, how does one describe the "whereness" of such existing? A globalized nomadic life style? This is especially the case when current structures of inhabitation are shaped by (and still maintain) the legacies of colonial rule which in bitter-sweet fashion, link the region to global realities. I say bitter-sweet because these global realities, spurred on by greed and lust, created the geographically contained context out of the death and oppression of Amerindians, Africans, East Indians and yes even the very Europeans that came here, but which at the very same time allow Caribbean peoples to recognize their solidarity with a world that has many voices, voices also caught up in the in-between type of existence the region is accustomed to. So what "Caribbean" means is no simple phenomenological study, it is not simply or only the geographical space of the Caribbean (though it must include that) nor is it only the mentalities and ideologies that are generated by the region. As a space that was global from its occupation in the late 1400's, it is a "world space" that has influenced and is influenced by music, food, culture, intellectual traditions, and religions of the world. So to me, the "where" of what is the Caribbean is more of an epistemic space that feeds off some patterns created by our geographical space but not limited to that space. It is about epistemic location more than it is about geographical location, and the Caribbean as a space, since 1492, has always been like that. We will pay more attention to what this epistemic location could mean as we engage notions of Christian mission in the region.

Mission in the Caribbean

For the overwhelming majority in the Caribbean, Christian entry into the Caribbean is synonymous with Spanish colonization in the 1490s, followed by the French, English and Dutch colonial presence. Scholarship on the coloniality of power[2] within the modern world system since 1500 has highlighted the atten-

[2] Cf. Anibal Quijano, "Coloniality of Power, Eurocentrism, and Social Classification", in Mabel Morana, Enrique Dussel, Carlos A. Jauregui, eds., *Coloniality at Large: Latin America and the Postcolonial Debate*, Duke University Press, Durham, 2008.

dant dark side of modernity and the global designs of Christian mission during this period. The colonial difference created by modernity has reinscribed the dominant perspective of Christianity as a civilizing mission linked to Euro-American expansion. But this global expansion has also, because of the colonial difference, created the conditions for subaltern contexts and voices from those contexts. The thinking engaged in these subaltern spaces is called border thinking by Walter Mignolo[3] or forced and dislocated reflections by me[4]. How is Christian/Catholic mission to be understood given such an understanding of our modern/postmodern/postcolonial world? If global designs such as European colonial expansion are local histories projected onto other local histories, how is the Christian message to be understood? Can Christianity authentically speak to the contexts of the subaltern or is it inextricably linked to imperial global designs?

Even after the political independence of some colonies, the system of control and exploitation established by colonization still remains in effect as a system of coloniality. How the region has experienced and continues to experience Christianity still exhibits the coloniality of power and the colonial difference. By colonial difference is meant "the place and experiences of those who have been the object of inferiorization on the part of others who, in the midst of the colonial endeavor, have come to consider themselves to be superior. It is a place and experience constituted as an exteriority to modernity according to a negative logic (a logic of inferiorization)".[5]

In 1975 four missiology conferences were held in Antigua, Guyana, Jamaica and Trinidad and the Acts were published in 1977 as *Out of the Depths* edited by Idris Hamid.[6] Catholic and Protestant participants and contributors hailed from Puerto Rico, Cuba, Santo Domingo (Dominican Republic), Jamaica, Antigua, St. Lucia, Guadeloupe, Trinidad, and British Guyana.

In the introduction to the published texts Hamid lists some traits that the participants indicated represented the "old missiology": (1) Mission was tied to an

---

3 Walter D. Mignolo, *Local Histories/Global Designs: Coloniality, Subaltern Knowledges, and Border Thinking*, Princeton University Press, Princeton, New Jersey, 2000.

4 Gerald Boodoo, "De Schrijver's Wager, Theology and Dehumanization: The Meaning of Liberation in Forced Theological Contexts", in Jacques Haers, Edmundo Guzman, Lope Florente Lesigues, Daniel Franklin Pilario, eds., *Mediations in Theology: Georges De Schrijver's Wager and Liberation Theologies*, Peeters, Leuven, 2003; "Understanding Church and Theology in the Caribbean Today", in Peter C. Phan and Diana Hayes, eds., *Many Faces, One Church: Cultural Diversity and the American Catholic Experience*, Sheed & Ward, 2005.

5 Gregory A. Banazak & Luis Reyes Ceja, "The Challenge and Promise of Decolonial Thought to Biblical Interpretation", *Postscripts* 4.1 (2008) 113–127, p. 116.

6 Idris Hamid, ed., *Out of the Depths*, Rahaman Printery, San Fernando, Trinidad, 1977.

ideology that created, sustained and justified a system of wickedness and brutality; (2) it greased the colonial machinery; (3) it held an unflattering and demeaning evaluation or estimate of the peoples of the Caribbean; (4) it was afflicted by the blinding factor of power; and (5) it consistently skirted the burning social issues that weighed heavily on the lives of the colonized.

Following upon this Hamid then presents what the "new missiology" should engage. First, it should arise out of the depths of the historical and spiritual experience of the peoples of the region, recalling the religious intuitions of our people with a re-reading of our history which locates our spiritual lineage on a different historical sphere that allows us to cease being appendages to European history. Second, it rejects the prevailing definition of man as a producer or consumer, that *to have* is *to be* or *to consume* is *to be* or *to produce* is *to be*. It affirms that *we participate* therefore *we are, we share* therefore *we are, we love* and *serve* therefore *we are*. Third, it requires new structures of worship, organization, witness, theological training and dialogue. It will affirm that God has been and still is at work in other religions and that God was at work in the religious traditions of our forefathers.[7]

On my part, I would like to highlight what I consider to be the more significant prevailing points mentioned by all the participants. First, the most common and strident calls in all of the authors was the need for decolonization. Colonialism is a "historical reality that both divides and unites the Caribbean."[8] The need to decolonize the churches, the peoples of the region and the very faith that Christians hold has been and continues to be a necessity in the region. The end of the physical period of colonial occupation is not the end of coloniality, the ideologies and structures that further the colonial designs of modernity, that show themselves as the necessary accompaniment to modern expansion. The benefits derived from modernity have as their necessary counterpoint the "dark" side of modernity. There is no modern project without its losers. All of the participants point to this; and I think the notion of coloniality will help to highlight this.

Second, all of the authors speak of a re-reading of our historical context in a manner that "recalls" the religious intuitions of the people of the region. There are three sub-points here of interest. The first sub-point has to do with the curious fact that most of the people in the region are not native to the region. The descendants of Africans, East Indians, Chinese, Arabs and Europeans were either brought involuntarily or came to the region with the promise of material reward. The deci-

[7] *Ibid.*, pp. 5-9.

[8] *Ibid.*, p. 256.

mation of the Amerindian population in the islands, leaving miniscule reserves in Trinidad and the Dominican republic, and their disenfranchisement in the Guianas and Suriname have left the call to "recall" the religious intuitions of people to be more a call to remember some "homeland" that is distant geographically, cosmologically and spiritually. Recalling religious intuitions becomes a tricky business and keeps seeking some prior state that is either illusory or ever shifting. This is why, and this is the second sub-point, in the Caribbean the term inculturation has never taken hold. Instead, all of the participants speak of highlighting and cherishing *indigenous* cultures, structures, and forms of worship. Again, what this means in a region that is made out of fiat is unclear but it points to the sensibility for organic expressions and structures. Indigenization has been and is the Caribbean's call for local expression and seems, at least methodologically, to be a call to lift up the popular religious expressions of the region, recognizing in them some "original call" from the space of inhabitation of the peoples of the region. And this leads to the third sub-point, how then do we go about understanding and creating history? Given some of the external and internal interpretations of the region as being devoid of history, in the sense that there aren't any native narratives of the land (as in Africa and Asia for example), where or what is the basis for a historical reading of the region? Against an argument that the region is void of native history Guyanese writer and thinker Wilson Harris would argue that it has to be based on the native matrix, the narratives generated not only by the peoples of the region but by relationships that have taken place in its space, even and especially the involuntary associations that occur amongst peoples. Historiography becomes a way of arriving in tradition,[9] a sort of "creolization of the chasm within illuminations drawn from, or nursed from, the fabric of involuntary associations embedded in humanity".[10] In other words, traditions, and native cultures are never "pure" and one unearths the "native" in the cross cultural associations that involuntarily take place routinely. The native is not an archetype of purity.

Third, there is a recognition among the participants that a new way of thinking is required, a new way of thinking about what it means to be Christian, the calling of the Christian, the mission of the Christian in this struggle for decolonization. I think some insights from decolonial thought can be of help.

---

9 Wilson Harris, "Creoleness: The Crossroads of a Civilization?", in Andrew Bundy, ed., *The Unfinished Genesis of the Imagination: Selected Essays of Wilson Harris*, Routledge, New York, 1999, pp. 243.

10 *Ibid.*, p. 241.

Colonialism and Coloniality

There are three main points I want to make with regard to decolonial thinking. The first is that we need to understand that modernity has created a world system that for the first time in the history of the world has linked all (or virtually all) parts of the world and subsumed them into a connected system. Along with this comes the realization that not everyone and everywhere have benefited from these connections. There is a dark side to this modern system of coloniality so that you have those who benefit from the modern project, those who are "inside" modernity and wield the power of modernity and who can be too easily blinded to the millions who are negatively affected by modernity, who are "outside." This "outside" of modernity is termed the "colonial difference". As noted above "colonial difference" is "the place and experiences ... constituted as an exteriority to modernity according to a negative logic (a logic of inferiorization)."[11]

Second, there is a "coloniality of power"[12] which privileges and enshrines Euro-American thinking by constituting itself in (i) the classification and reclassification of the planet population (the concept of culture becomes crucial in this task); (ii) institutional structures which function to articulate and manage such classifications (state, university, church etc.); (iii) the definition of spaces appropriate to such goals; (iv) an epistemological perspective that articulates, legitimates and channels its production of knowledge. Walter Mignolo explains that "Eurocentrism becomes, therefore, a metaphor to describe the coloniality of power from the perspective of subalternity. From the epistemological perspective, European local knowledge and histories have been projected to global designs. . . ."[13]

Third, decolonial thought seeks to produce knowledge formed from the colonial difference. What is needed is a new way of thinking, not new ideas. As such, if one speaks from the perspective of the colonial difference, one also speaks from what Mignolo calls the "colonial wound" and therefore the "other paradigm" does privilege the knowledge from these spaces of oppression, the victims of modernity, but with the realization that even though it is produced from "outside" modernity, it still is linked to the modern project. The colonial wound is created by coloniality. So decolonial thought gives rise to an ethics and a politics of *pluriversality*

---

[11] Gregory A. Banazak & Luis Reyes Ceja, "The Challenge and Promise of Decolonial Thought to Biblical Interpretation", *Postscripts* 4.1 (2008) 113–127, p. 116.

[12] Cf. Anibal Quijano, "Coloniality of Power, Eurocentrism, and Social Classification", in Mabel Morana, Enrique Dussel, Carlos A. Jauregui, eds., *Coloniality at Large: Latin America and the Postcolonial Debate*, Duke University Press, Durham, 2008.

[13] Walter D. Mignolo, *Local Histories/Global Designs: Coloniality, Subaltern Knowledges, and Border Thinking*, Princeton University Press, Princeton, New Jersey, 2000, p. 17.

(a combination of the words "plural" and "universality"). "Standing in opposition to global and totalitarian designs, created in the name of universality (which usually means a particularity claiming to be universal), pluriversality is an attempt to make visible and viable a multiplicity of knowledges, forms of being, and visions of the world. Pluriversality is equality-in-difference, the possibility that many worlds can fit in one world. It is the future alternative to modernity/coloniality."[14] Decolonial thinkers see this as occurring across many disciplines and many facets of life, hence they assert the "transdisciplinary" and "transcultural" nature of decolonial thinking. This mixture of perspectives works to unmask the "purity" of disciplines and the so-called "universality" of modernity.

Making this distinction between colonialism/colonization and coloniality is significant. For many in the Caribbean, invoking the colonial past is seen as anachronistic. Many think "dat gone already" and easily agree that we have overcome that past. However, while I was in Jamaica in the summer of 2011, the local paper reported that 65% of Jamaicans thought they should become a British colony once more! No doubt driven by economic, cultural and global realities, but also the heavy residue of colonial aspirations. Sixty-five percent! Many of those responding have no experience or critical knowledge of the legacy of colonialism and have not been educated in the abiding effects of it. Understanding coloniality helps to change those aspirations and give greater emphasis to epistemic locations from the colonial difference which aid decolonization.

Indigenous History?

I have found Wilson Harris to be one of the finest minds in the Caribbean and the writer/thinker who has dared to imagine a philosophy of history for the region. Of all the writers in the Caribbean, Harris is concerned to create an architecture of native imagination, an outline of structures of consciousness native to the region. By native, Harris does not mean local. Native is not local/insular or pseudo universal and has application beyond its local context. This does not mean that native consciousness is not location driven, shaped and formed in the landscape of its inhabitation. But that, though exhibited in location, the native expression is not limited to or by local conscription and therefore relates beyond the shores of its genesis. What this means for re-reading the history of the region is the profound partiality of one's tradition (any tradition). Harris speaks of the "numinous

14 Gregory A. Banazak & Luis Reyes Ceja, "The Challenge and Promise of Decolonial Thought to Biblical Interpretation", *Postscripts* 4.1 (2008) 113–127, p. 118.

partiality"[15] we present in our historical and fictional expressions that allow us to "arrive in tradition".

> Indeed, in this scenario we come abreast of the self-deceptions in a purely formulaic (some would say Cartesian) education, in which a so-called dialogue with the past rests on *descriptions of, not numinous arrival in,* the complex, disturbing life of tradition.[16]

He is arguing here against the retrieval of some magical "pure" native consciousness or calcified structure which is presupposed with dominant historical descriptions. Instead, to arrive in tradition "involves an appreciation of profound tension between originality and tradition." There is a deep sense of owning and appreciating the partiality of any interpretation. How will Christian narratives, imperial narratives, colonial narratives, dominating narratives fare in such an exercise when their aims and goals are toward total description? None of these narratives lay claim to partiality nor are they interested in doing so. How would Christian mission be understood with such claims of partiality? Theological and dogmatic expressions recoil at this because of the specter of *relativism*. Perhaps we have given that term a bad rap by not embracing the partiality of our native histories.

> There can be no perfect or absolute arrival in tradition, and some measure of descriptive logic is necessary; but we need a narrative that helps us to sense the partiality of linear progression and brings home to us in genuine stages of creativity (rather than purely intellectual experimentation) the simultaneity of the past, present and the future in the unfinished genesis of the imagination.[17]

This arriving in tradition depends on our use of the arts of the imagination which seem to have been shunned in the technologically driven modern age. In our rush to invest absolutely in partial traditions (modernity, coloniality, and religious economies) we do not partake of the creative capacity to "*read* ourselves in the book of reality ... as *partial* creatures."[18] Instead of arriving in tradition, we encapsulate it with descriptors that make us essential to its existence. We become not just necessary to the tradition, we become the tradition itself! This has been the history of missiological activity in the Caribbean. A new historical reading from the native partiality of our contexts, struggling with the tension between originality and tradition that address the heart of our presuppositions must work with

[15] Wilson Harris, "Creoleness: The Crossroads of a Civilization?", in Andrew Bundy, ed., *The Unfinished Genesis of the Imagination: Selected Essays of Wilson Harris*, Routledge, New York, 1999, pp. 247.

[16] *Ibid.*, p. 243.

[17] *Ibid.*, p. 244.

[18] *Ibid.*, 247.

our imaginative capacity for re-creative genius. Such indigenous history is possible and not reliant solely on a historical description of origination. The originary consciousness, or the unfinished genesis of the imagination, can be found in the re-creative capacity for narrative in the arts. It is no mistake that a discarded oil drum has now become, as a result of the re-creative imagination of the native, the only musical instrument created in the 20th century—the steel pan. This product of the creative arts of the imagination is native to the Caribbean region but not "owned" by or local to the region. How do we re-create Christian mission with similar re-creative imaginations?

Mission as Border Epistemology

I see in what Mignolo calls border thinking or border gnoseology some way forward with this. For Mignolo

> ...transcending of the colonial difference can *only* be done from a perspective of subalternity, from decolonization, and therefore, from a new epistemological terrain where border thinking works...Border thinking can only be such from a subaltern perspective, never from a territorial (e.g. inside modernity) one. Border thinking from a territorial perspective becomes a machine of appropriation of the colonial differe/a/nces; the colonial difference as an object of study rather than as an epistemological potential. Border thinking from the perspective of subalternity is a machine for intellectual decolonization."[19]

So border thinking is not a territorial/geographic grounded space that can then become commodified but an epistemological space that generates intellectual decolonization. This border thinking is still within the imaginary of the modern world system but is repressed by the coloniality of power which controls the conceptualization of knowledge, however, it is exposed in the moments "in which the imaginary of the modern world system cracks."[20] This is similar to the recognition Harris suggests of the partiality of our traditions. If our traditions begin to be seen and understood as partial then there is the space for an "other" imaginary, an "other" epistemology.

Mignolo describes border thinking as

> a way of thinking that is not inspired in its own limitations and is not intended to dominate and to humiliate; a way of thinking that is universally marginal, fragmentary,

[19] Walter D. Mignolo, *Local Histories/Global Designs: Coloniality, Subaltern Knowledges, and Border Thinking*, Princeton University Press, Princeton, New Jersey, 2000, p. 45.

[20] *Ibid.*, p. 23.

> and unachieved; and, as such, a way of thinking that, because universally marginal and fragmentary, is not ethnocidal."[21]

Again we see parallels with Harris' thinking, the native consciousness is not a conscriptive and/or descriptive localizing totality but a partial consciousness that does not impose tradition but arrives in it. As such, it too is fragmentary and unachieved. The key configuration of border thinking is "*thinking from dichotomous concepts rather than ordering the world in dichotomies.*"[22] This is similar to Harris' creolization of the chasm created by the involuntary associations of cultures in the Caribbean. Instead of dismissing the dichotomies and the blends that result from involuntary associations we should creatively think from the spaces of these occurrences.

This note on the configuration of border thinking is significant and should be commonplace in the Caribbean. After all, if Caribbean existence has not been ordered and ruled by dichotomies whose/where is? The still common (colonial) tendency is to reconcile dichotomies or to resolve them into whole systems which then enshrine the colonial difference and continues the inside/outside structures of the coloniality of power. The still deep desire to be the "included", the "insider" in the modern world system (in the current church structure), keeps us entrenching rather than overcoming the colonial difference. Instead of using dichotomous reality as a means for decolonization we favor coloniality and the difference it inscribes because it legitimates our existence and production of knowledge according to its own logic. Our desire *to be* (and to be highly acclaimed) in this system blinds us to the potential of *not being able to be* in this modern world system. On the contrary:

> Not being able to be where one is is the promise of an epistemological potential and a cosmopolitan transnationalism that could overcome the limits and violent conditions generated by being always able to be where one belongs. I am where I think.[23]

So how does all this relate to mission, if at all? Especially since Mignolo sees in Christianity "the first global design of the modern/colonial world system"?[24] Harris however still has use for Christianity and religion in so far as he speaks of the numinous arrival of tradition. Is decolonization/border thinking amenable to Christian mission?

---

21 *Ibid.* p. 68.
22 *Ibid.* p. 85.
23 *Ibid.* p. 334.
24 *Ibid.* p. 21.

First, the decolonial notion of pluriversality in relation to religions or Harris' native consciousness can be of help. If being Catholic, for instance is not simply nor only where Catholics are, but the engagements and relationships Catholics have with all people who could also be people of diverse faiths, could we not also call the epistemic locations at the crossroads of these encounters also Catholic space? And at the same time Methodist, Anglican, Presbyterian, Hindu, and Muslim space? The dichotomous nature of such spaces (Catholic-Hindu, Catholic-Presbyterian etc.) opens the possibility of border thinking in relation to religion. Instead of trying to resolve these dichotomies into homogenous narratives, allow for what Mignolo calls "macronarratives"[25] that allow for these seemingly contradictory experiences which people experience every day the world over or "partial traditions" which allow us to be inserted without totalization or conquest. This is not strange to Christian self-understanding since we do hold another religion (Judaism) as the genesis of our own. We are constituted in our originary architecture of consciousness in dichotomous form! That there are plural universal claims add to the epistemic locations that can crack totalizing systems and decolonize the knowledge that informs our sense of mission. Such decolonial thinking, to my mind, has to be engaged without fear of losing one's faith or faith tradition. I would contend that a totalizing descriptive dogmatic reasoning does not do justice to our situated experiences as a people of God and our mission to cross the borders in voluntary or involuntary associations. Aligned with this we have to assert that the myth of a "pure" tradition has to be excised from our missiological understandings. This is one certain epistemological step towards decolonization. The premise that what we have is "full" and thereby requiring preservation and not creative adjustment must be replaced by Harris' notion that what we have is partial and re-creative. Our faith must serve and be served by the epistemological perspectives that are generated out of the colonial difference, the dichotomous experiences of our situations, the border thinking that comes from our forced and dislocated spaces.

Second, who actually gets to interpret and make decisive judgments about the reality, text, situation under consideration? The coloniality of power has to be given consideration. Again, if border thinking has any value, then the so-called "uninformed, unconsecrated" subaltern must have a voice at the table along with the voices already speaking. Authentic interpretation, canon, should not be used to silence the already silenced. Pluriversal readings and interpretations from the colonial difference need to be heard and used in the continuing shaping of our

[25] *Ibid*. p. 22.

dynamic *traditio* (not a static *tradita*) which means that no one voice can carry the weight of all. This is not about numerical or classificatory representation more than it is a recognition that no one experience or voice has a "zero point" perspective and thus we have to always be negotiating and renegotiating what is considered a "classic" or a "canon". The time of the *summa* in any production of knowledge is long over! Indeed, we need to entertain the idea that our traditions (and scriptures) only reveal their full meaning in relationship to other traditions (and scriptures). This adjusts worship, cultural hegemony and the privileging of Western productions of knowledge. I am always amazed at how Western theologians consider themselves the default perspective for authentic theology yet have little and in some cases no familiarity with theological authors and works from the so-called other universal spaces of Christianity. Theological education and curricula are still part of the problem.

Third, we have to recognize the complicity of secularity with Christianity yet recognize the need for post-secular thinking. As Nelson Maldonado-Torres suggests, secularism has been pitted as the enemy and/or negation of religion in the modern/colonial world system. Both secularists and religious thinkers have made this claim without recognizing how the secularist thesis builds off the religious reality in that it continues the dual opposition of what is considered sacred and what is profane or unacceptable. Given Christianity's role in the domination and subjugation of non-Western cultures and races there is a bias towards secular forms of redress that do not see anything but an imperial colonially implicit role for religion. But Maldonaldo Torres claims that this "secularism continues the logics of imperial Christendom" in so far as it inherits "from imperial Christianity a fundamental impetus either to convert, to control, or to radically domesticate other epistemes... The secular-religious divide has come to work in ways similar to the Christian-pagan divide. The lack of a radical critique of secularism surreptitiously serves to maintain the superiority of Western cultural epistemologies intact."[26]

By a critique of secularism is not meant the usual religious attempts at denial, denunciation, disengagement and despair over secularism, but recognition of the complicity between Christianity and secularity with regard to coloniality. We have to recognize the ways in which our scripting and acting of Catholic mission enshrine the secular dualisms that continually recreate the colonial difference and intentionally re-inscribe coloniality. From this point of view, the critique of secu-

[26] Nelson Maldonado-Torres, "Secularism and Religion in the Modern/Colonial World System: From Secular Postcoloniality to Postsecular Transmodernity", in Mabel Morana, Enrique Dussel, Carlos A. Jauregui, eds., *Coloniality at Large: Latin America and the Postcolonial Debate*, Duke University Press, Durham, 2008, p. 382.

larization is also a simultaneous critique of aspects of Catholicism in its continued colonial and imperial forms.

Conclusion

Mission still needs decolonizing. The possibility or impossibility of this may be the reason that many have stopped using the term, or at the least find it unhelpful. I think the question is not whether mission is helpful or has meaning for us today more than what epistemological locations drive mission today and how we can undertake missiology speaking from the colonial difference. If this border thinking is impossible for missiological understandings, which I dispute, then the problem is not about mission but about intractable structures and understandings that resist decolonization and still desire too strongly *to be* inside a system of coloniality that ensures their privileges.

Part II:

Impact of Vatican II on Church and Mission

6 Vatican II and the Church in Africa: An Overview of 50 Years

Laurenti MAGESA

Introduction: Pope John XXIII and Vatican II

The Second Vatican Council (1962-1965) was, without any doubt, the immediate brainchild of one individual, Pope John XXIII. The Council was born of Pope John's profound spiritual vision about God, the Church, humanity and the world. Pope John intuited that the relationship between the Church and the world should be mutually benevolent and supportive, not antagonistic and hostile. The divine kingdom was for him intimately associated with the plenitude of life in and of the world. Although the church is not *of* the world, it seemed to be his profound conviction, it is *in* the world: It is in the world that God, through the Holy Spirit, continually accomplishes the divine design of recreating and renewing everything in Christ.

Pope John described his decision to convoke the council in terms of "a spontaneous inspiration." Perhaps that was the reason why, as the analyst of the Council, John W. O'Malley, puts it, "The announcement took everybody else by surprise, including the other cardinals of the Curia." It certainly astonished the bishops and the Catholic faithful of the world. "After the definitions of papal primacy and infallibility at Vatican Council I, some theologians predicted that there would never be another council because it seemed to them that now the pope would solve all the problems."[1] Again, this perception was widespread. For the majority of Catholics in Europe and the Americas, the Councils of Trent (1545-1563) and Vatican I (1869-1870) were generally presented as councils to end all councils. The faithful in the rest of the Catholic world, and certainly in Africa, did not know much about these councils, nor cared about them. Few even had an indigenous word for "ecumenical council." For them, the pope, mediated by the local bishop, was the extent of their ecclesiology and faith. Of course, there was no such thing yet as conferences of bishops.

The reading and interpretation of the Scriptures were hitherto, therefore, restricted to the priests and hierarchy in the church. Since the upheavals of the

[1] John W. O'Malley. *What Happened at Vatican II* (Cambridge, Massachusetts: The Belknap Press of Harvard University Press, 2008) 17-18

Protestant Reformation in the 16th century, there had grown a strong suspicion in the Catholic Church against reading, let alone studying the Scriptures by the general faithful. But Martin Luther had translated the Bible into German and published it in 1534. The Bible in the vernacular had consequently become more accessible to the common people in the Protestant tradition as they could read it for themselves for spiritual inspiration and nourishment without the intervention of priests. After this initiative, more translations in other European vernaculars, namely, French, Dutch and English, soon followed, and they had the same effect. However, the Catholic Church was not to accommodate itself to this change until four centuries later. It was not before 1943, with Pope Pius XII's encyclical letter, *Divino Afflante Spiritu*, that a spirit of openness towards reading and a critical study of the Bible slowly began to emerge in Catholic Christianity.

Significance of Pope John's Encyclicals

Pope John and Vatican II, therefore, changed the inward-looking spirit that had prevailed in the Church since the Council of Trent which had set for itself the task of countering the radical effects of the Protestant Reformation upon the structure and some of the beliefs of the Church. But even before Vatican II began, Pope John seemed to have sensed the need for this change. Deeply immersed in, and guided by, a holistic and positive vision of the world and all existence, he wrote the encyclical *Mater et Magistra* in 1961, describing the role of the Church in and for the world as inherently maternal. The letter was situated against the background of the anxieties ushered in society by modernity (an intellectual movement that, in the eyes of some at the time, seemed to erode the certainties the Church had had since the late Middle Ages). With modernity, more and more individuals were coming up with theories implicitly or explicitly questioning some of the assumptions the Church thought were sacrosanct and unassailable. As a consequence, the Congregation of the Index (1571-1917), later called the Holy Office (1917-1966), had been established to prevent these "errors" from spreading. One way the Congregation did so was to periodically compile and publish an "Index of Forbidden Books." In its 1948 edition, the Index contained almost 4,000 titles. These included works in science, theology, morality, philosophy, and so on. In his spirit of openness to the world, Pope John saw no serious reason for these anxieties. As a result of Vatican II, Pope Paul VI abolished the Index and reconstituted the Holy Office into the Sacred Congregation for the Doctrine of the Faith in 1966.

In 1963, mid-way through the Council's deliberations, and barely three months before his death, Pope John issued another encyclical on peace in the world, *Pacem in Terris*. The encyclical was written in an environment of great tension: the world was being torn apart by the destabilizing conflict of the Cold War then raging between the ideological blocs of East and West. But *Pacem in Terris* had a more immediate background: the situation in October 1962 where nuclear confrontation had not only been possible but had nearly occurred with the Cuban missile crisis. In spite of this, Pope John thought it still possible and necessary for the Church to be hopeful about the future of humankind and the world. The pessimism that some harbored, that the only direction the world was headed to was a downward spiral of violence and destruction, did not constitute any part of Pope John's spirituality.

The point these two letters carried was one of positive engagement between the Church and God's creation, whatever the circumstances. This was the spirit with which they influenced in a profound, if perhaps inconspicuous, way the orientation of Vatican II's deliberations. Both were commemorative documents, belonging to and pushing forward the tradition of the social thought of the Church, initiated in modern times by Pope Leo XIII's *Rerum Novarum* (1891) and Pope Pius XI's *Quadragesimo Anno* (1931). However, Pope John's encyclicals had a different quality and flavor. They combined into one three prongs that constitute the Christian reality: deep trust in God, immense love for humanity, and unlimited openness to the goodness of world. It was not an accident that these documents addressed themselves not only to the Catholic, or even the Christian, communities. The pope deliberately intended them to speak to all people "of good will" throughout the world. In short, *Mater et Magistra* and *Pacem in Terris* were completely devoid of suspicion or fear of the world but were, on the contrary, full of trust and hope. According to the pope's own reported position: "I do not fear the habits, the politics, or the religion of any man anywhere in the world as long as he lives with an awe of God."[2] This is what his encyclicals demonstrated.

A question that must perhaps remain hypothetical, because of the fact that there is no way to answer it with certainty, is whether without Pope John's initiative with these letters and his convocation of Vatican II, Pope Paul VI would have written his encyclical masterpiece on Catholic social thought, *Populorum Progressio* (1967) on the meaning of human development. The same question applies to Pope John Paul II with reference to his encyclicals *Laborem Exercens* on human labor (1981), *Sollicitudo Rei Socialis* (1987) on human development, and *Centessimus Annus* (1991) on the contemporary political and economic situation. Further, would Pope Benedict XVI have written his *Caritas in Veritate* (2009),

2 See Ward J. Fellows, *Religions East and West* (New York: Holt, Rinehart and Winston, 1979) v.

on the idea of the economy for the common good? It seems that the style, breadth and scope that all of these later documents demonstrate are steeped in Pope John's letters and the spirit and events of Vatican II that he set in motion. It is, therefore, not far-fetched to speculate that without them, Pope John Paul II might not have undertaken his many pastoral travels throughout the world, including Africa, or that Pope Benedict XVI after him would not have visited Benin to promulgate the Apostolic Exhortation, *Africae Munus,* concerning the Second Special Assembly for Africa of the Synod of Bishops, popularly known simply as the Second African Synod. Indeed, would there have been an African Synod, or any synod, at all for that matter?

The need to have a more visible presence of the world's episcopate in the teaching and government of the Church beyond the Roman curia had been long felt worldwide since Vatican I. Pope John had been aware of this feeling in convoking the Second Vatican Council. Shortly after his election in 1963, his successor, Pope Paul VI, immediately broached the idea of the reform of the curia, at the beginning of the second session of the Council, and formally established the office of the Synod of Bishops as a permanent institution in September 1965. This was also in response to the conciliar desire for collegial oversight of the Church as well as a concrete expression of the Council's understanding of the Church as "the People of God" (*Lumen Gentium*, 9-17). There were, however, some strictures to this institution that were unsatisfactory to many. Rather than being an organ of the practice of collegiality of the bishops with the pope, as the Council had envisioned, the synods turned out to be an organ of the papacy, "an instrument of the primate to use as he wished," as Joseph Ratzinger complained.[3]

Nevertheless, since the end of the Council, the ecclesiology of the Church as People of God and the structure of collegiality included in the institution of the Synod of Bishops have been somewhat reflected in the ordinary processes of the synods. These hang on two ancient principles in the history of the Church: first, the principle of listening and, second, the principle of reception. In terms of the synods, the first principle underlines the importance of the participation of the entire Church in their preparation, in line with the ancient principle of listening to the voice of the people as inspiration from God. The second emphasizes the necessity of the positive reception of teaching on the faith, according to the equally ancient theological rule that teaching becomes "an effective guide for the

3 Ratzinger Joseph,. *Theological Highlights of Vatican II* (New York: Paulist Press Deus Books, 1966). 140.

believing community" only when it is effectively accepted by the community in question.[4]

The Council and the African Church: Two Approaches

For the 50 years since the council ended, what concerns us directly in this assessment is whether, on account of Vatican II and the events it set in motion, the Church in Africa has any reason to celebrate. Celebration is in the final analysis an occasion of rejoicing because something positive has taken place in one's life on account of the agency of a person or thing or event. We understand celebration in theological language as a moment of grace, when we recognize that God, through the Holy Spirit, has involved us in some divine creative activity in the world for the purpose of our own growth towards salvation. At the same time, through the power of the same Spirit, we acknowledge our own grace-filled participation in the particular moment of grace.

As far as Vatican II is concerned, the issue involved in determining the situation of the Church in Africa—whether or not to rejoice—may be approached in two complementary directions. From one angle, we might ask whether the African Church through its bishop representatives present at the Council contributed anything distinctive to the Council deliberations during its four sessions, from 1962 to 1965. If so what? In other words, was the sense of the faith of the African continent adequately presented? What, indeed, was that view? Given the sources available about the proceedings of the Council, this aspect of the question is relatively easy to answer. The other aspect, however, the issue about the way or ways the teaching of the Council in its sixteen documents has influenced and shaped the different dimensions of life in the African Church and continent in general during the last 50 years is much more complex. Taking into account the time period that has elapsed, as well as the size and the many and often dramatic happenings in the continent, this aspect can be approached only in a rather general and tentative way.

Both considerations, however, open the door to appreciate the relationship between the Council and the African Church from a number of focal points. The most relevant of these include the social-historical and theological interactions between the two realities. Looking at these dimensions, it becomes possible to evaluate realistically two levels of the Council-Church process: first, as we have

4 James A Coriden, "The Canonical Doctrine of Reception." http://arcc-catholic-rights.net/doctrine_of Undated. Accessed on 1/26/2012.

indicated, the African Church's role in the Council as an *event*, and, secondly, the impact and challenge that the Council as a *process* has had on the African Church in the intervening half-century or so. Although each of these levels is a distinct entry into the discussion, in the end both can only be discussed fruitfully in conjunction with each other. For if, on account of historical circumstances, the contribution of the African Church to the council-event was definitely limited, the challenge and impact of the Council on the continent during the intervening fifty years may be found to be significant, giving reason for celebration.

The Council-Event: New Directions

First, I take a look at Vatican II itself as an assembly or event. Of all the ecumenical councils of the Catholic Church, Vatican II has been described as standing in a category of its own. In terms of planning, size, and the breadth of issues covered it is unparalleled in history. The positive mood that contextualized it, inspired by that of Pope John himself, has already been alluded to. Whereas previous councils had been mostly concerned with defining dogma and condemning heresies, the general character of Vatican II is that it was a pastoral council, interested in guiding the Catholic faithful on how to live their faith in the world and among other people. Accordingly, the issues discussed were extensive, covering many human concerns and dimensions. The Council treaded novel ground in many respects. It was concerned about the church's opening doors or windows to the world, as Pope John wished, not about closing them. Thus, in addition to the rather explicitly unprecedented issues discussed about ecumenism, the missionary activity of the church and, above all, religious freedom and the Church's relationship to non-Christian religions, there was the document *Gaudium et Spes*, the Pastoral Constitution of the Church in the Modern World. The Constitution is generally regarded as the Magna Charta of the Council that set all the other council documents into the context of openness and appreciation of divine grace working in the world.

Unlike any previous Council, Vatican II's preparation was long and elaborate, taking the better part of four years and involving, for the first time ever for an ecumenical council, wide consultation. The preparatory commissions to draw up pre-council documents did extensive work. Father Joseph Ratzinger (then university professor but since 2005 Pope Benedict XVI) who was present at the council as theological expert to Cardinal Josef Frings, reports that the commissions produced 70 working plans, "enough to fill 2,000 pages." He notes that "This was more than double the quantity of texts produced by all previous councils put together".[5]

Furthermore, the number of participants was huge, covering all parts of the Catholic world. O'Malley notes that although the number of people actually present at the assemblies in St. Peter's Basilica varied throughout its four sessions (considering sicknesses, deaths, and other factors), "generally there were about 2,400 council fathers participating at any given time".[6] Compare this with 750 fathers at Vatican I and Trent's approximately 200 voting participants at its peak, and the difference between these councils and Vatican II in this respect becomes very clear.

Thirdly, if there were from the beginning attempts to control the Council by a few cardinals from the curia, they did not succeed. The conciliar bishops rejected many of the *schemas* or documents prepared by curial officials for endorsement and commissioned new ones. This was unprecedented. Another Council historian, Norman Tanner, notes that "Before the council the Roman curia had been allowed to prepare draft documents, but these quickly proved unacceptable to the council, so new decrees had to be hammered out almost from scratch".[7] Ultimately, the assembly took its own uncharted course. It can truly be said that a palpable sense of freedom of spirit pervaded the discussions. No single group of bishops was able to manipulate the agenda or the discussions on the floor. This constituted another uniqueness of Vatican II, perhaps the most important one of all. Just as internal manipulation was nipped in the bud, so to speak, there were similarly no significant power plays from external civil sources. This was quite unlike many of the previous councils where the hand of political authorities was often obvious.

The sense of freedom during the Council proceedings allowed for the introduction into the agenda and discussion aspects of current theological developments that would otherwise have not surfaced at all if liberty to speak had been muzzled. On this point Ratzinger wrote:

> Previously it had seemed that Roman officialdom was the only really formative and active authority in the Church, and that apart from the curia there was really nothing but non-authoritative outsiders. Now it became clear that, besides the official curia organs (subordinated to the pope), the body of bishops was a reality in its own right, infusing into the dialogue and the very life of the Church its own spiritual experience.[8]

5 Ratzinger, *Theological Highlights of Vatican II*. 5

6 O'Malley *What Happened at Vatican II*. 21; Ratzinger, *Theological Highlights of Vatican II*. 6

7 Norman P. Tanner, *The Councils of the Church: A Short History* (New York: The Crossroad Publishing Company, 2001). 98

8 Ratzinger, *Theological Highlights of Vatican II*. 9.

Of course, the liberty experienced at Vatican II was not sudden; it had a long history, championed by many of the theologians who attended the Council as advisers to the bishops. Ratzinger notes that this desire for freedom was something that had been percolating within the church and was now coming into the open. Many of the theologians spearheading the change in their writings had been previously censured in one way or another.

Fourthly, quite apart from the universal representation at the Council which helped to get the Council's message to more parts of the world than before during recesses when the cardinals went home, there was the role that the media of mass communication played during the entire Council process. At the beginning, the curia was rather hostile to the press and no significant details of the Council discussions emerged publicly. But slowly this changed and some aspects of the Council were broadcast by the electronic and print media to the world. This event that was Vatican II was, therefore, followed not exclusively by Catholics but by many others who cared to know. It is important to recall also that there were at the Council observers from other Church groups, Protestant and Orthodox, who must have reported their impressions to their member churches.

Role of the African Church in the Council-Event

The question that must be asked concerning the relationship of the African Church and Vatican II is this: Did the church in Africa have any significant input in the conciliar event? Do the conciliar deliberations reflect much contribution specific to the church in Africa? Is this evident in the sixteen official documents that emerged from the council? Are there sentiments there that touch directly the concerns and needs of the Church in the continent at the time? Probably the most important social-political issue in Africa at that time was the struggle for political independence. Did the bishops from Africa articulate this aspiration of the African peoples so that it is reflected in the deliberations and some of the Council documents? Looking at the theological and pastoral territory the Council-event covered, one had to answer these questions largely in the negative.

The needs and concerns of the European churches appear clearly in the documents. In fact some analysts have said that despite its universal reach that we have noted in terms of the geographical representation of the bishops, the theology and the pastoral concerns of Vatican II were fundamentally European. The council was basically a European council. "Europe, its concerns and the legacy of its history, provided the framework within which Vatican II operated," writes O'Malley. "The story of the council is almost exclusively the story of Europeans fighting over issues arising out of European history."[9] By and large, even at Vatican II, the conviction famously phrased by Hillaire Belloc that "the faith is Europe, and Europe is the faith" was still, even if unconsciously, very much alive among practically all of the Council Fathers.[10] At any rate, such was the theology of the universal Church, where the center of the Church since Trent and Vatican I was literally Rome, in particular, and Europe in general.

Statistics tell part of the story and lend credence to this assertion. There were about 300 bishops from Africa (only 10 percent) as compared to more than a thousand from Europe (36 percent). Nine hundred bishops came from the Americas (34 percent) and the remaining 20 percent from Asia and Oceania.[11] But more important than numbers were the ideas presented and influence exerted in the council floor discussions. These formed the substance of the official documents. A list of "Council Participants Frequently Mentioned" includes only one bishop from Africa, Marcel Lefebvre, archbishop of Dakar, Senegal, a member of the missionary order of the Holy Ghost Fathers, and only because of his arch-conservative positions.[12] Although bishops from Africa did not lack organization among themselves, there were factors that did not allow much original, that is genuinely African, contribution from them.

To appreciate this situation, one has to keep in mind the facts of history which are rather widely known. But in order to contextualize and highlight the situation, they deserve quick mention. At the time of the Council the African continent was only slowly emerging from a very long period of colonial rule, but structurally and economically it was still firmly tied to and dependent on Europe. It would be so for a long time even after independence. The same situation existed in the Church. The Church in Africa in the 1960s was in every way an extension of the European Church, so that the relationship between them was vertical rather than horizontal. There was the Mother Church of Europe and the Daughter Church of Africa. Europe dictated the terms of the Church's existence in Africa and Africa had little to say about it. Thus, although the population of Catholics in Africa was already sizable, other crucial factors that would have genuinely constituted the identity of the Church in the continent as a distinctive "African church" were

---

9 O'Malley, *What Happened at Vatican II* 13.

10 John L. Allen, *The Future Church: How Ten Trends Are Revolutionizing the Catholic Church* (New York: Doubleday, 2009). 14.

11 See Maureen Sullivan, *101 Questions and Answers on Vatican II* (New York/Mahwah, N.J.: Paulist Press, 2002).21.

12 For a list see O'Malley, *What Happened at Vatican II*. 321-328; see also Tanner, *The Councils of the Church: A Short History*. 111.

sorely missing. The Church in Africa lacked not only the face but also a distinctive content, which led to its presence at the Council to become basically an augment of Europe. This situation was inevitable.

Additionally, the vast majority of the Council fathers from Africa were European missionaries, trained in European philosophy and theology, and basically carrying identical attitudes about the African people and the Church in Africa that their counterparts from the global North held. They were convinced, for example, that the authenticity of the Church in Africa consisted in faithfully mirroring the theology and structures of the European Church and theology. The episcopate from Africa, once again, therefore, generally gravitated towards and reflected European positions. Specifically, these bishops generally reiterated positions taken by their counterparts from their countries of origin and their religious congregations. The organizer of the episcopate from Africa at the Council was Joseph Blomjous of Mwanza in Tanganyika, a Dutchman and member of the Missionaries of Africa (White Fathers). On account of insufficient theological and pastoral immersion into the African spiritual and cultural realities, issues of immense consequence to the African faithful were treated perfunctorily, or not at all.

One example is the issue of polygamy which, even the forward-looking Pastoral Constitution of the Church in the Modern World lumped together in one sentence with "the plague of divorce" and "so-called free love," and described it as "disfigurements" of the nobility of marriage and the family.[13] One truly wonders whether the bishops from Africa would have concurred with this formulation if they had cared to argue out the case of this issue on its own merits from the African experience. The institution of polygamy as practiced traditionally in African societies does have its shortcomings, of course, but these do not include "the plague of divorce" and "free love." On the contrary, it radically excludes them and insists on love and fidelity, some of the most important and cherished values of marriage.

Also, the *Decree on Priestly Formation* (*Optatam Totius*), though granting that formation programs should be the responsibility of individual churches, still put forward as the ideal the study of Latin (no. 13) and "speculative reason exercised under the tutelage of St. Thomas" (no. 16). Having no clear alternative in this respect, and not wanting their clergy to appear "inferior" or "second-class" if trained under a different, but more adapted system of formation, the majority of the conciliar bishops from Africa were unable to see the flexibility afforded them in this decree for the training of their clergy.

---

13 See Vatican II, *Gaudium et Spes*, # 47.

Lastly, the validity of Hinduism, Buddhism and Islam as forms of a genuine search for the divine was acknowledged by name in the *Declaration of the Relationship of the Church to Non-Christian Religions* (*Nostra Aetate* nos. 2-3). African or other indigenous religions were not, except in the rather reluctant admission that there is also a spark of the divine among peoples whose cultures are not "advanced," in distinction from "religions bound up with cultural advancement" (see no. 2):

> From ancient times down to the present, there has existed ... a certain perception of that hidden power which hovers over the course of things and over the events of human life; at times, indeed, recognition can be found of a Supreme Divinity and of a Supreme Father too. Such a perception and such a recognition instill the lives of these peoples with a profound religious sense (no. 2).

At the time, in 1965 when this document was promulgated, African Religion could not even be given the dignity of the title as a religious orientation. Again this was a fact reflecting Western perspectives on African worldviews, which were generally negative towards the latter. The reluctance of African Christians to completely abandon some of their indigenous religious practices was interpreted as lack of conversion, not as a shortcoming in the evangelization methods and processes. Judging by the situation in the Catholic Church today, this is still the case in many areas. Some documents which have come out long after the Council make one wonder whether the *Declaration on Religious Freedom* (*Dignitatis Humanae*) also contemplated the liberty of the followers of African Religion to worship God as their spirituality directs them.

Assessing the Council as a whole, Tanner is therefore correct when he writes that

> Reception of the council's decrees has ... been generally less engaged outside the western world than inside it. Christians of Latin American [sic], Asia, and Africa, central and eastern Europe, have not felt the same affinity with the council. Their interests and concerns were not addressed so directly: for example, oppression and structural injustice, for which the western world bears much responsibility, popular religion of a non-western kind, and so on. Nevertheless this distance should not be exaggerated. Even if these churches outside Europe subsequently pursued paths of their own, the new directions may well have become possible only because of the changes initiated by the council.[14]

Evidence from developments in the Church in the past 50 years in Africa demon-

[14] Tanner, *The Councils of the Church: A Short History*. 110-112.

strates that Vatican II is perhaps more justifiably celebrated for what it subsequently offered to the Church in the continent in terms of theological and practical insights and possibilities. During this time, the Church has made strides from being merely a Church in Africa (as was the case before the Council), to some degree identifying more closely and realistically with the continent. What this means is that the Council's teaching has indirectly inspired the African Church to begin the process of becoming a "local," and not just a "particular" Church.

Reasons for Cautious Celebration

Need for a Local Church

Perhaps the most important inspiration of Vatican II as far as Africa is concerned has been the need to construct an African local Church or African local churches. The Council used the term "particular churches" because many in the Council, following curial conviction, argued that in the diocesan structure we already have local churches. But this is not how the idea has been understood and developed in Africa.

The term "particular church" is seen in Africa as a juridical-structural term; it usually identifies the Church with the diocese. The term "local Church," however, is favored in Africa because it is seen as going beyond that geographical and juridical circumspection by taking in theological-pastoral implications. It emphasizes the necessity of culture and inculturation in preaching and liturgy, and accepts the reality of the faith at any level: continental, regional, diocesan, parochial, small Christian community, and even family.[15] In the understanding of local Church, the focus of evangelization is "to make the Gospel truly enter into the cultures of the people so that the church is no longer looked at and treated as a mere foreign accretion," as Bishop Francisco F. Claver from the Philippines writes. In Africa the Church could not be credible if it continued to present itself "fully clad in Western garments, speaking in a foreign tongue, and, hardest of all, seemingly disdaining to assume a native face."[16] As has been the case throughout history, a particular Church, while remaining in the union of faith with other churches, must forge an identity as a local Church, one that is necessary to bring about the horizontal

---

15 See Joseph A. Komonchak, "The Local Realization of the Church," in Giuseppe Alberigo, Jean-Pierre Jossua, and Joseph A. Komonchak, eds. *The Reception of Vatican II* (Washington, D.C.: The Catholic University of America Press, 1987), 77-90.

16 Francisco F. Claver, *The Making of a Local Church* (Maryknoll, New York: Orbis Books, 2008). 13-14.

level of relationship with other particular and local churches. Only in this way can genuine dialogue and mutual sharing for growth in maturity be possible.

There is no serious reason to doubt that the number of Catholics in Africa would have continued to increase phenomenally even without Vatican II. Although harboring often unarticulated reservations concerning the Catholic Church's approach to evangelization in several respects, African people saw in the message of the Gospel the Church carried something beautiful and readily acceptable to them. This was especially so as the Gospel was made concrete in the social services the church provided in the form of education and health care facilities. There is reason to believe, however, that without Vatican II, the Church in Africa would not have taken the initial steps towards becoming local. It can be credited to the Council that almost just a decade afterward, at the 1974 Synod on evangelization, the Church in Africa had solidified the idea of having its own identity. "Africa was concerned with becoming an autonomous church, led by native clergy and not treated as an immature ward of the old churches of Europe."[17] The call for a "moratorium" on foreign personnel and finances had been broached by the Protestant churches in the continent. Its echo, although muted in Catholic circles, was not totally absent there.[18]

Leadership

The need for a Church with a local face in Africa was recognized immediately after the Council, helped by developments in the political sphere. As we have mentioned, Vatican II coincided with the period when many African countries were gaining independence from their colonial masters and taking the first steps to becoming fully fledged nations. At the same time, however, many dioceses were under the leadership of foreign bishops, even though the number of native clergy in many of them was growing impressively. This discrepancy appeared to many an odd situation, leading at least one political leader to wonder loudly why, "if we can govern ourselves politically, we cannot do so in the Church"? The unease did not go unnoticed by the missionary leadership itself in Africa as well as, obviously, by Rome. Native ordinaries were rapidly installed in various dioceses, so that within a short time the structural face of the Church dramatically changed.

These developments flowed from ideas broached in various conciliar documents, especially *Gaudium et Spes*, the *Constitution on the Church in the Modern World*, *Lumen Gentium,* the *Constitution on the Church*, and *Dignitatis Humanae,*

---

[17] Ibid. 14.

[18] Ibid.

Declaration on Religious Freedom. The *Decree on Priestly Training, Optatam Totius,* was particularly instrumental in insisting on the promotion of priestly vocations and establishing houses of formation. From being a Church which was hardly self-ministering at the time of the Council, the African Church grew to send out men and women as missionaries to minister to the churches of the global North. One might mention as well that a number of Missionary Institutes founded in the global North have grown to depend on vocations from the global South, including Africa, for their vitality.

Small Christian Communities (SCCs)

Thanks to Vatican II, a dimension of major structural and pastoral significance in parts of the Church in Africa, which is now playing a major role in making the Church truly local, is the reality of Small Christian Communities (SCCs). As Joseph G. Healey, a well-known researcher on the ecclesiology of SCCs in Africa, writes:

> Small Christian Communities ... developed as a result of putting the ecclesiology of the Second Vatican Council (1962-65) into practice. Latin America, Africa and Asia (especially the Philippines) all pioneered the development of a SCC Model of Church or a BCC Model of Church. After considerable research and debate, many specialists feel that quite independently of one another these three areas of the Catholic Church in the Global South *simultaneously* experienced the extraordinary growth of SCCs. Thus the African experience did not come from Latin America but developed on its own ....[19]

A key moment in their historical development came in 1973 in Nairobi, Kenya, at a study conference of the regional Association of Member Episcopal Conferences of Eastern Africa (AMECEA) on "Planning for the Church in Eastern Africa in the 1980s." There the bishops resolved on "building church life and work on Basic Christian Communities in both rural and urban areas." They explained that "Church life must be based on the communities in which everyday life and work take place: those basic and manageable social groups whose members can experience real inter-personal relationships and feel a sense of communal belonging, both in living and working."[20]

---

[19] Joseph G. Healey,. "Timeline in the History and Development of Small Christian Communities in Africa Especially Eastern Africa." 2012 (http://www.smallchristiancommunities.org/africa/africa-continent/107-timeline-in-the-history-and-development-of-small-christian-communities-sccs-in-africa-especially-eastern-africa.html).

[20] Ibid.

Theological Evolution

There has also been a remarkable theological development in Africa after the Council. Already in the mid-1940s, the Belgian missionary Placide Tempels had published his pioneering, largely positive, and influential study on African systems of thought titled *La philosophie bantoue*.[21] This publication marked a daring leap of intellect and courage, given the mood of the times about Africa. In the 1950s a few African and Haitian priests, in a collection of essays published as *Des prêtres noirs s'interrogent*[22] had also expressed their dissatisfaction with European theology applied indiscriminately to African faith realities. And in Kinshasa in January 1960, Tharcisse Tshibangu and Alfred Vanneste had debated the merits and demerits of developing an African theology. These must be considered the seeds for the birth of African Theology. The consolidation of this genre of doing theology in Africa must be attributed to the spirit of openness of the Council to the world. Special credit goes again to *Gaudium et Spes*, but especially to *Dignitatis Humane* and *Nostra Aetate*.

Nostra Aetate, it is true, distinguishes between "religions bound up with cultural advancement" and supposedly others less so. That is why, as we have pointed out, African Religion is not referred to by name. However, the famous statement the declaration makes in paragraph 2 was soon understood by students of African culture to include also African Religion. If, according to the document, the Church must reject "nothing which is true and holy" in any culture, she must not do so in African Religion. On the contrary, she should look "with sincere respect upon those ways of conduct and of life, those rules and teachings which ... often reflect a ray of that Truth which enlightens all men" (*Nostra Aetate*, no. 2). From this small seed, an African theology, seriously affirming this statement in terms of African culture and religion, has flourished also in various schools of higher learning.

The Synods on Africa

As a result of a number of factors, including the numerical growth of the Church in Africa, its political instability, and the orientation of African theology, within the space of a decade and a half the office of the Synod of Bishops in Rome has

21 First published 1945; English translation 1959, See Placide Tempels, *La Philosophie Bantoue*. Paris: Présence Africaine, 1949. (*Bantu Philosophy*. Paris: Présence Africaine, 1969.)

22 See Léonard, Santedi, Meinrad Hebga, and Gérad Bissante, eds. *Des Prêtres Noirs S'interrogent; Cinquante Ans Après*. Paris: Karthala; Présence Africaine, 2006; 1956.

called two special assemblies on Africa, one in 1994 and the other in 2009. This is no small achievement for the African Church. The themes discussed in both synods were extremely relevant, having to do with evangelization, reconciliation and justice and peace. Although questions remain as to the influence of these synods on the African Church, their symbolic value cannot be underestimated.

One dissatisfaction involves the way the questions in the preparatory documents, the *Lineamenta*, were structured. If they were intended to involve all the People of God into the process, they failed to do so. Secondly, the language of the post-synodal exhortations also does not seem to render itself to ready understanding, nor does it touch the deep concerns of the general faithful. The most critical question regarding these synods, however, concerns follow-up methods. What is being done to implement their major conclusions? Since, in the main, the synods take up and advance themes the Vatican II touched upon in its historical and theological contexts in the 1960s, if the synods were truly implemented, they would advance considerably the teaching of the Council in Africa.

Prospects: Progress or Regression?

Why caution?

For any celebration, Africans usually go all the way to make the event memorable. Celebration is for them always a spiritual occasion where all the forces of existence, the visible as well as the invisible, concentrate in and cooperate with nature to move life forward in expectation of better and greater things to come. This is how it should be when the African Church is celebrating the golden jubilee of Vatican II. But looking at the concrete scene, it is both necessary and important to be realistic. One must not do a disservice to the Church by painting an unrealistic picture of theoretical expectations.

Integral Healing

The desire for the healing ministry in African spirituality is well known, but in the Catholic Church not much is being done about it. As Michael Katola put it, many African Catholic Christians “seek deliverance, healing, and exorcism from other denominations because [Catholic] priests do not realize they have redemptive powers”.[23] However, it might be an exaggeration to assert that African priests

[23] Allen, *The Future Church: How Ten Trends Are Revolutionizing the Catholic Church*. 36.

"*do not realize*" that by their ordination they are tasked with this responsibility; it is the theology so far in force in the African seminaries, a result of European rationalism, enforced rigorously in diocesan policies, that considers the intrusion of spiritual forces into human life as "irrational" and "superstition." There are numerous examples in many an African diocese where a priest or a catechist has been disciplined for attempting exorcism. The famous case is, of course, that of the then archbishop of Lusaka, Zambia, Emmanuel Milingo. Fortunately, he is one of a few who has exhaustively recorded his experience in that area.

Since the beginning of evangelization witchcraft, for example, has been dismissed as a nonsensical belief. However, for numerous Africans, whether Catholic or not, "Witchcraft is a reality," affirms Katola, and if we dismiss it, "we cannot deal with it." John L. Allen notes that a document from a possible future African pope presenting Christ as Victor over the forces of evil, over spells, and witchcraft "would arguably stand a better chance of finding an audience at the global Catholic grassroots [particularly in Africa] than virtually any other subject that Western theological elites might desire a future pope to address."[24]

The Laity in the Church

The conciliar *Decree on the Apostolate of the Laity*, *Apostolicam Actuositatem,* brought the reality of the laity and their vocation through Baptism forcefully to the center of the experience of the Church. There can be no Church without the laity. Through Baptism the laity are members of the Body of Christ, charged as much as anybody else with the ministry of bringing the Gospel and holiness, which is Christ's kingdom, to society. Especially in these fast changing times, the role of the laity is indispensable and could be realized in practice through the structure of Small Christian Communities (SCCs).

Although the development of acceptance of SCCs in many African dioceses has been a welcome ecclesiological development, it would not be correct to say that their ecclesiology has been fully thought out, or even that in every diocese they are accorded the status that some of the official documents of the Church accords to them. Can they, in their present state in many dioceses, be described as a truly "new way of being church," incorporating within them and expressing many of the characteristics of the early, apostolic communities in terms of organization, the celebration of the Eucharist, and the growth of focused ministries? There is still a long way to go to realize the Church as truly "a community of

[24] Ibid. 37.

believers" through SCCs. What the Australian bishop, John Heaps, has written captures some important elements of what as yet still needs to be done to realize the deep theological and pastoral implications of SCCs:

> To make this truly the Church, the bishop would approve these communities, accept their leaders and ordain their priests. All this would be done in consultation with the community. Leaders would emerge, candidates for ordination and the non-ordained ministries would present themselves for acceptance by the community and ordination or induction by the bishop. Some would need to undertake further studies, many of which would be part-time in the same way that many people undertake part-time studies.

Members of the communities which make up the diocese would be very much involved in the consultation process leading up to the choice of their bishop.[25]

Ecumenical and interreligious Relations

Though not much mentioned in African Catholic circles, one of the most scandalous aspects of Christianity in Africa—indeed, the Council itself recognized it as "a stumbling block to the world" (*Unitatis Redintegratio*, no, 1)—is the division and divisiveness in Christianity, which in the past often amounted to rancor. This division does not have its origin in Africa; it was introduced here as part and parcel of the Christian "faith" throughout the experience of evangelization in the continent. Africans in general fail to comprehend why, if all Christian churches preach the same Jesus Christ, there should be so much malice among them. Yet so far, ecumenical initiatives, even on the level of practical ecumenism, are few and far between. Of course, ecumenical initiatives in the West have mostly been based on doctrinal understanding, something of little interest to the average African Catholic or Christian. Exceptionally baffling, given their religious and spiritual culture of hospitality and sharing, is the exclusion that Catholic doctrine insists on with respect to Eucharistic sharing in times of joy and celebration.

The African Initiated Churches, though much more fractured than the mainline denominations as a result of the circumstances of the origin of each, seem not to be as acerbic against one another as the mainline Christian churches. They have also put dialogue between them and African Religion in practice, respecting the latter as possessing God-given values that are a useful and valid expression of faith in Christ. The Council counts "Promoting the restoration of unity among all

[25] John Heaps, *A Love That Dares To Question: A Bishop Challenges His Church* (Grand Rapids, Michigan: William B. Eerdmans Publishing Company, 1998 ... 105-106

Christians [as] one of [its] chief concerns" (*Unitatis Redintegratio,* no 1). Nevertheless, if there is one area where the Council has failed to inspire any meaningful movement in African Catholicism, it is in this area. As well, although African theology is trying to make dialogue between Christianity and African religion a reality in the Church, sadly little reflection has appeared concerning dialogue between Christianity and Islam in Africa.

Conclusion: The Hermeneutical Circle/Spiral Again and Again

According to Walter Kasper, the impact of the Council depends on nothing other than "the people who translate its words into terms of real life." Thus, "What is at issue for Catholic theology," Kasper argues, "is not the council in itself. What is in question is the interpretation and reception of the council".[26] According to Kasper, the conversation about the Council in the following years should be about this, and this alone.

The partners in this conversation in Africa are twofold: the tradition of the Church as received from the missionary Church on the one hand, and the great tradition of African Religion and spirituality on the other. This conversation is carried on by three indispensable mediators, namely, the Christian experience of the African laity, interpreted by the African theologians and examined and confirmed or disputed by the hierarchy. There will always be a healthy tension here, one that must not be eliminated but creatively fostered on all sides. This is the same tension that made Vatican II itself possible. It is a similar one that should constitute the process of Christian hermeneutics of doctrine and its development.

The African Church has already a certain experience and overall view of the Council during these past 50 years. This experience must be brought to bear, or "applied" ever anew, to particular questions that face the faith every day. This dynamic will help to give further understanding of the spirit and spirituality of the Council. "This back-and forth process of questioning from whole to part and back again, from general to particular and back again to general knowledge, is the rhythm of the hermeneutical circle or spiral." As Ormond Rush explains, this "is not a vicious circle; I don't just return to the same point in the circle. When I come back and take the helicopter view of the landscape, I understand it differently than before".[27] At every moment of the application of the spirit of the Council in the

[26] Walter Kasper, "The Continuing Challenge of the Second Vatican Council: The Hermeneutics of the Conciliar Statements," in *Theology and Church* (New York: Crossroad, 1989), 168.

[27] Ormond Rush, *Still Interpreting Vatican II* (Mahwah, New Jersey: Paulist Press2004). xi.

African local Church, it will bring with it different and greater divine gifts than before.

References

Allen, John L. *The Future Church: How Ten Trends Are Revolutionizing the Catholic Church* (New York: Doubleday, 2009).

Claver, Francisco F. *The Making of a Local Church* (Maryknoll, New York: Orbis Books, 2008).

Coriden, James A. Undated. "The Canonical Doctrine of Reception." http://arcc-catholic-rights.net/doctrine_of Accessed on 1/26/2012.

Fellows, Ward J. *Religions East and West* (New York: Holt, Rinehart and Winston, 1979).

Healey, Joseph G. "Timeline in the History and Development of Small Christian Communities in Africa Especially Eastern Africa." (http://www.smallchristiancommunities.org/africa/africa-continent/107-timeline-in-the-history-and-development-of-small-christian-communities-sccs-in-africa-especially-eastern-africa.html). 2012.

Heaps, John. *A Love That Dares To Question: A Bishop Challenges His Church* (Grand Rapids, Michigan: William B. Eerdmans Publishing Company, 1998.).

Kasper, Walter. "The Continuing Challenge of the Second Vatican Council: The Hermeneutics of the Conciliar Statements," in *Theology and Church* (New York: Crossroad, 1989), 166-176.

Komonchak, Joseph A. "The Local Realization of the Church," in Giuseppe Alberigo, Jean-Pierre Jossua, and Joseph A. Komonchak, eds. *The Reception of Vatican II* (Washington, D.C.: The Catholic University of America Press, 1987), 77-90.

O'Malley, John W. *What Happened at Vatican II* (Cambridge, Massachusetts: The Belknap Press of Harvard University Press, 2008).

Ratzinger, Joseph. *Theological Highlights of Vatican II* (New York: Paulist Press Deus Books, 1966).

Rush, Ormond. *Still Interpreting Vatican II* (Mahwah, New Jersey: Paulist Press, 2004.)

Santedi, Léonard, Meinrad Hebga, and Gérad Bissante, eds. Des Prêtres Noirs S'interrogent; Cinquante Ans Après. Paris: Karthala; Présence Africaine, 2006; 1956.

Sullivan, Maureen. *101 Questions and Answers on Vatican II* (New York/Mahwah, N.J.: Paulist Press, 2002).

Tanner, Norman P. 2001. *The Councils of the Church: A Short History* (New York: The Crossroad Publishing Company).

Tempels, Placide. *La Philosophie Bantoue*. (Paris: Présence Africaine, 1949)

7 Vatican II and the Agency of Asian Churches

Felix WILFRED

One of Karl Rahner's celebrated statements concerns the abiding significance of Vatican II. He saw in Vatican II the Church becoming for the first time truly "catholic," universal.[1] Though the statement is well-meant, I have been skeptical of its presupposition. It implies that the Church is a reality of the West, and now it has become universal by reaching out to the other parts of the world. Those from the other ends of the world by participating in the council witnessed to its universality. The view of Rahner was developed later by Walbert Bühlman who spoke of *The Coming of the Third Church.*[2] There is an unintended eurocentrism here regarding the origin and expansion of Christianity. This is true also of the more recent work of Philip Jenkins, titled *The Next Christendom. The Coming of Global Christianity.*[3]

But the facts tell us that Christian presence was an accomplished reality in several parts of Asia—India, Iran, China, etc.—even before many parts of Europe heard of the Gospel. There was a flourishing "Church of the East" which predates sixteenth century European mission expansion into Asia. There has been in India a community of Thomas Christians who have maintained their faith almost from the beginnings of Christianity; and in China Christianity was present from the seventh century onwards, attested by the Nestorian monument in Xian.[4] So, then,

---

1 Cf. K. Rahner, "Basic Theological Interpretation of the Second Vatican Council," in *Theological Investigations,* vol. 20(New York: Crossroad, 1981), 77-89.

2 Cf. Walbert Bühlman, *The Coming of the Third Church* (New York: Orbis Books, 1979).

3 Cf. Philip Jenkins, The *Next Christendom. The Coming of Global Christianity* (New York: Oxford University Press, 2002). When he speaks of "The Next Christendom" referring to the Churches in the South, including those of Asia, it would give the impression as if Christianity in Asia were a later expansion of Western Christianity. Moreover, the presentation of Christianity today as a religion of the poor in the South needs to be analyzed in depth. Perhaps here there are unintended prejudices. For example the claim that reason is something Western and modern, and hence the critical attitude towards Christianity and its rejection in Europe, while it is being increasingly accepted and is flourishing in the pre-modern societies of the South wanting in reason, and rich in emotion. I thank Dr M.P. Joseph for this insight on the work of Philip Jenkins in his paper presented at the Silver Jubilee Conference of SATHRI held at Serampore during 15-17 August, 2014.

4 See Felix Wilfred, ed., *The Oxford Handbook of Christianity in Asia* (New York: Oxford University Press, 2014); see also Samuel Hugh Moffett, *A History of Christianity in Asia, Vol. I, Beginning to 1500* (Bangalore: TPI Publications, 2006), 288.

what does it mean for Asia when Rahner says that for the first time in Vatican II, the Church has become truly "catholic," a world Church? For us Asians, the significance of Vatican II lies somewhere else, as will be clear in the following reflections.

Once Again Active Agents of Their Faith

One of the beautiful things about Vatican II was its spirit of freedom in living out one's Christian life. Thanks to it, for the first time, Asian Christians, after the colonial period, became once again active agents in the practice of their faith—something they were denied during the Western missionary expansion. There was a sense of freedom, unfettered by the past, to shape the way they worship, understand and interpret Christian faith in the Asian context and cultural universe. It brought about renewal in the Christian communities, facilitated the bridging of faith and culture, and evolving of innovative theological perspectives.

By and large, the mission historiography in Asia has been one in which the people of the continent were viewed and treated as passive recipients of a message preached to them; they were objects to be spiritually acted upon. Vatican II has reactivated Asian Christians who have a long history of their own. If the missionary epoch made Asian Christians dependent, Vatican II promoted the maturing of Asian Christians. What happened at the Asian Synod of 1998 could be viewed as the result of this maturation process set free by Vatican II. At the Synod,

> What was new is not what the Asian bishops said, but *that* they said it and *how* and *where* they said it. In front of the pope and the Roman Curia, with surprising boldness and candor, humbly but forcefully, the Asian bishops affirmed that the Church of Asia not only learn but also have something to teach the Church of Rome as well as the universal Church, precisely from their experience as Churches not simply *in* Asia but *of* Asia.[5]

Contribution of Asian Bishops at the Council

Vatican II, as is well-known, was a theological battlefield where the titans clashed on a number of doctrinal issues and questions. The conciliar documents themselves bear the imprint of the conflicts, and not in few instances, compromises were made to be able to take everybody along—something that would pave the

---

[5] Peter C. Phan, "Reception of Vatican II in Asia: Historical and Theological Analysis," in *FABC [Federation of Asian Bishops' Conferences] Papers* no. 117 (Hong Kong, 2006). 125,

way subsequently for a conflict on the interpretation of the council.[6] There is hardly anything remarkable in the contribution of Asian bishops to the doctrinal issues debated in the council. Rather, they saw the council eminently as *a pastoral event*, and became in the council itself increasingly active whenever issues of pastoral nature came up. For, the doctrinal issues were mostly done within the frame of traditional Western theology and in the context of its past debates and controversies.

Since the Asian bishops viewed the Council in its pastoral significance, the reception of it was made easy; in many areas, it corresponded to the expectations of the Asian bishops. In fact, many of the innovations brought about by the council were expressed by Asian bishops and bishops' conferences as *vota* in the ante-preparatory period and sent to Rome. In an important study on the participation of Indian bishops at Vatican II, Paul Pulikkan notes some of the *vota* or proposals sent by reform-minded Indian bishops.

> Some of the important 'reform-minded' proposals of the Indian *vota* were thus: the use of vernacular, liturgical renewal, the restoration of the permanent diaconate (also the married), ecumenical dialogue with the non-Catholic Churches, reform of the Roman Curia, adaptation and inculturation of Christianity in India ...[7]

The same could be said of the *vota* from other parts of the continent. It is easy to see then that the reception of Vatican II was a matter of joy since it vibrated with Asian pastoral aspirations, though the bishops were not able to provide articulate theological foundation to what they intuitively felt were necessary and important. But this lacuna was made good deftly in the post-conciliar period by Asian theologians who have helped the Asian Churches by developing indigenous theological reflections. Already while the council was in progress, there was a conference held in Mumbai in connection with 38th International Eucharist Congress (1964) in which Indian theologians voiced open views on the salvation of peoples of other religious traditions and the need for dialogue with them. Once again we note the active role played by the Asian Christians in the reception of the council, which was by no means anything passive.

---

6 For an analysis of the conflict in ecclesiology of Vatican II, see Antonio Acerbi, *Due ecclesiologie: ecclesiologia giuridica ed ecclesiologia di lumen gentium* (Bologna: Edizione Dehoniane, 1975).

7 Paul Pulikkan, *Indian Church at Vatican II: A Historico-Theological Study of the Indian Participation in the Second Vatican Council* (Trichur: Marymatha Publications, 2001), 568.

The Three Dialogues—Continuation of the Council

Asian bishops tried to relate and reflect on the teachings of the council in relation to the larger concerns of their respective societies and nations. The Federation of Asian Bishops' Conferences (FABC) became the catalyst and clearing house for the major ideas and orientations of Vatican II.[8] It is this body which translated the dialogical impetus of Vatican II in Asia in three major directions most relevant to the situation of Asia—dialogue with the *cultures*, with *religions* and with *the poor*.[9] The most stimulating re-interpretation of Christian faith took place in Asia not by the reading of Christian dogmas through Asian conceptual categories, as through the concrete dialogical praxis in these three major areas. The new conception of culture—far from the evolutionary one, to be found throughout the documents of the council—and the orientations of *Nostra Aetate* provided the seminal thoughts to develop the practice of dialogue with cultures and religions.

As is well-known, though there was no focused treatment on the "Church of the Poor" (Pope John XXIII), the council did speak of the poor.[10] In fact, Vatican II is but the second council in the history of the Church which spoke of the poor, the first being the Council of Jerusalem which gave the injunction to "remember the poor."[11] The spirit of Vatican II and the stimulus it gave led the Asian Churches to engage themselves in dialogue with the poor, and rightly so. For, Asia is still the home for the largest number of the poor in the world. The numerous initiatives of the FABC have again and again with insistence come back on the realities and experiences of the poor of the continent. This is true also of some of the local Churches. As Bishop Teodoro Bacani of the Philippines noted with reference to the situation in his country,

> The Church of the Poor is the Church in the Philippines' way of receiving and inculturating one of the most potent but undeveloped seeds which Vatican II sowed in the

8 At the institutional level, there have been assemblies of local Churches which helped to deepen the life and practice of Christians and the teachings of the Council and its orientation. By way of example, I may refer here to the "All India Seminar: Church in India Today" held in Bangalore, in 1969, with the participation of large number of bishops, priests, religious and laity. Similarly *The Second Plenary Council of The Philippines* in 1991 could be viewed as an important milestone in the reception of Vatican II in that country.

9 These three dialogues announced by the First General Assembly of FABC (Taipei 1974) became programmatic for the subsequent developments in the thought of FABC and in its pastoral orientations.

10 Cf. Jon Sobrino, "The Church of the Poor from John XXIII to Oscar Romero" in *Concilium* 2013/1, 99-107.

11 Cf. Aloysius Pieris, *Give Vatican II a Chance* (Gonawala-Kelaniya: Tulana Research Centre, 2010), 44.

Lord's orchard. There was enough in Vatican II to inspire Medellin and Puebla to a new way of evangelization. There was enough in Vatican II to inspire the Church in the Philippines also towards a new way of being Church.[12]

Unfazed Asians Sing Their Own Tunes

The vitality behind Vatican II is often attributed to *ressourcement*.[13] Asian Christians found exciting the return to the *pluralism* of earliest Christian tradition as it is in harmony with the Asian cultural ethos. Be it in the field of Christian worship, theological developments, interpretation of Scriptures, shaping of the life of the local communities, Asian Christians worked out, thanks to the council, ways to be themselves, without having to conform to any one single pattern. The centralizing type of universality seemed to wane giving place to the pluralism of the Pentecost (Acts 2:1-12).

It is the deep imbibing of Vatican II that prompted the Asian Churches to view with apprehension some of the Roman positions, which they felt were going contrary to the spirit of the council. Whereas Rome has been loud on explicit preaching of the Gospel, baptism and conversion, Asian bishops and the Asian Christians have been quietly insisting that the kind of mission most effective in the continent is that of silent *witnessing*. While Roman documents laid stress on preaching Jesus Christ as the only Savior, Asian Churches focused on following *the path of the historical Jesus* in his commitment to the poor, in his spirit of dialogue and in his way of life reaching out to the other. This, they felt was the way to gain a deeper understanding of the mystery of Jesus Christ. As the Japanese Bishops' Conference wrote in their response to the *Lineamenta* of the Asian synod, "Jesus Christ is the Way, the Truth and the Life, but in Asia, before stressing that Jesus Christ is the Truth, we must search much more deeply into how he is the Way and the Life."[14] Here we find reflected the absorption of the pastoral nature of Vatican II. That the Asian Churches have consistently maintained all this is itself a great sign of the continued reception of Vatican II, unfazed by the trends of restoration and integrism. Suffused with the spirit of pluralism, diversity and dialogue, Asia is, probably, too elusive to be caged within such trends, as many interventions of the bishops showed at the Asian Synod.

---

12 Theodoro C. Bacani, "Church of the Poor: The Church in the Philippines' Reception of Vatican II," *East Asian Pastoral Review* 42, 1&2 (2005), 157.

13 Cf. Gabriel Flynn – Paul D. Murray, *Ressourcement: A Movement for Renewal in Twentieth-Century Catholic Theology* (Oxford: Oxford University Press, 2012).

14 Peter C. Phan, ed., *The Asian Synod. Texts and Commentaries* (New York: Orbis Books, 2002), 30.

Contextual Interpretation and Reception

The past few decades have seen heated debates and writings on the way Vatican II is to be interpreted. Key categories in these debates are "continuity" and "discontinuity," namely, whether Vatican II is to be viewed as a council in line with the tradition of the Church, or whether it represents a caesura from the past. The question was discussed also during the extraordinary synod of 1985. To my knowledge, this question has not excited the Asian Churches or Asian Church leaders and theologians as it has done perhaps those in Europe and in Americas—at least North America. The discussion within continuity-discontinuity frame would seem to suffer from a static view of the Church without regard to God's continuous revelation. For some partners in this discussion, the identity, cohesion and continuity of the Church could be maintained only when borders and boundaries are clearly demarcated. One should clearly know who is in and who is out; what tradition is and what innovation is; what is past and what is present.[15]

More than trying to make a historico-critical analysis of the documents, its genesis, its borders and boundaries to arrive at the meaning of the council, Asians have preferred to interpret them through their life and context. They have approached the conciliar documents with the specific and unique questions and concerns of the Asian peoples, and have continued to draw inspiration for the life of faith and for Christian engagement.

Moreover, the interpretation of the council in terms of continuity or discontinuity reflects a particular hermeneutics which is being increasingly challenged today. It presupposes that the meaning of the text is identical with the meaning of the author, and hence all efforts directed to find out what exactly the council meant by this or that expression. Developments in the field of hermeneutics tell us that the meaning of any text goes beyond the meaning of the author.[16] That is true of the council and its vision.

In hermeneutically reconstructing what the council envisaged and what it outlined in its documents, it is helpful to keep in mind "the hermeneutical function of distanciation."

---

15 This is Philip Endean's motive in his critique of the apophatic and mystical theology of Rahner. Cf. Philip Endean, "Has Rahnerian Theology a Future?," in Declan Marmion – Mary E. Hines, eds., *The Cambridge Companion to Karl Rahner* (Cambridge: Cambridge University Press, 2005), 281-296.

16 Cf. Felix Wilfred, Keynote address at the "International Conference on Themes and Issues in Eastern and Western Hermeneutical Traditions" held at the Faculty of Philosophy, Jnana-Deepa Vidayapeeth, Pune, 31 Jan. & 1 Feb. 2014.

> An author of a text world (in the world behind the text) commits a vision to writing by producing a text that imagines "a world" (the world of the text). The text projects and proposes this world to an implied reader and ultimately to a reader in the "real" world, inviting the reader to imagine that proposed world in his or her own context (the world in front of the text). In the reader's application to the real world, vision can become a reality, no matter how distant in time the receiver is from the production of the text.[17]

The role of the interpreter is crucial today to understand the meaning of the text. Asian Christians as interpreters in their Asian context, continue to derive new meanings by reading the conciliar texts. These texts are for them not historically distant, but a present reality, and hence reception of the council is a continuous process. It is a creative interpretation of the council in dialogue with Asian experiences and realities of life. This is why discussion on interpretation in terms of "continuity" or "discontinuity" does not cause any excitement to me, for example, as an Asian, and I view it basically a Western discussion, and even an unproductive polemics and a deflecting theological sophistry.

Asian thinkers are aware that the council could not offer answers to all their questions and the problems they face today. They are not upset at that, since for Asian Christians Vatican II remains a point of departure of a journey, a journey which they themselves should make. More than individual texts, it is the overall spirit and orientation of the council which matters for the Asian Churches to build their future in conversation with their contexts. For example, as I noted earlier, there was little in terms of texts on the poor in Vatican II, and yet, Asian Churches and FABC have derived so much from the spirit of the council to face the reality of poverty in the life of the continent. In fact, "dialogue with the poor" was viewed by FABC as the legacy of Vatican II.

It looks to me that in modern times there has been no other Roman Catholic document more relevant for mission in Asia than *Gaudium et Spes*—even though it was not the document that dealt explicitly with mission. Why? Here is a document with which one could sensibly begin a serious discourse on mission in this continent. Its orientation vibrated with Asian concerns. For one thing, here we do not find the kind of *triumphalism* and *self-righteousness* which are the major obstacle to the witnessing of the Gospel; instead, we find a humble recognition that the Church is groping and struggling with the rest of humanity,[18] and that it has

---

[17] Ormond Rush, "Toward a Comprehensive Interpretation of the Council and Its Documents," *Theological Studies* vol. 73, no. 3 (2012), 565.

[18] Cf. Felix Wilfred, "Asian Christianity and Modernity: Forty Years after Vatican II," *East Asian Pastoral Review*, 42 (2005), 191-206.

its own weakness among its members.[19] The document opens up a large space for dialogue and for a *missio inter gentes*.

Carrying Forward a Legacy

Asian Churches not only have tried to actively realize in real life the spirit of Vatican II, but also in some crucial areas have carried forward the council one step further. I should mention at least two important areas—one is the *theology of religions*, and the other, *understanding of mission*. Though in Asia, there have been fresh thinking and initiatives to relate to peoples of other faiths right from the nineteenth century,[20] it is with Vatican II that interreligious dialogue became programmatic, and got a new impetus. Asian theologians have drawn not only from *Nostra Aetate* but also from important insights in the other documents such as *Gaudium et Spes* and *Lumen Gentium* to build a relevant theology of religions. If we read synoptically the following conciliar texts *Lumen Gentium* 16, *Gaudium et Spes* 22, *Ad Gentes* 22, *Dignitatis Humanae* 3, *Nostra Aetate* 1, they will take us to a broad vision of God's salvific plan for the entire human family across all borders, and make us realize that the responses in human freedom to the offer of God's grace take place through many channels. FABC and Asian theologians have been inspired by these texts and found in them a solid support for their work.[21] The actual practice of dialogue has helped them take forward the conciliar teachings to a new level. A reading of conciliar teachings coupled with praxis of dialogue has made Asian Churches realize that the Spirit of God is actively operative in and through the religious experience, symbols and signs of neighbors of other faiths; that we need to consider their scriptures seriously and ask whether they are also not inspired; and that other religions could be channels of God's salvific grace.

---

19 Cf. *GS* 43.

20 Since for about one hundred years before Vatican II, there have been numerous initiatives—intellectual as well as practical—for dialogue with peoples of other faiths, especially in India. I may refer here to the original views and practices of the Indian thinker Brahmabandhab Upadhyaya (1861–1907) on Hindu-Christian relations; the work of J.N. Farquhar, *The Crown of Hinduism* (1915) where he presented the theory of Christianity as the fulfilment of other religions; the ashram movement which adopted Hindu world-view and way of life to interpret Christianity.

21 Cf. FABC Plenary Assembly in Taipei (1974) Final Statement. See also "Theses on Interreligious Dialogue" by the Theological Advisory Committee of FABC. For the text, see Felix Wilfred – J. Gnanapragasam, ed., *Being Church in Asia* (Manila: Claretian Publications, 1994).

Asian theologians went on also to discuss against this background on the question of *communicatio in sacris* with peoples of other faiths.[22]

The theology of religions inspired by the council, if taken seriously, needs to be matched by *a new theology of mission*. There has taken place in the post-conciliar period a mismatch between the two. Asian Christians on their part have worked out an approach to mission that is in keeping with conciliar theology of religion and its larger implications. On the other hand, they were told from Roman central offices to follow a theology of mission that has again and again proved by history and experience as not workable in the context of Asia. For example, Asian theologians have resisted the efforts to make dialogue as a *means* of mission, as they believe that dialogue has in itself an intrinsic value, its own scope and dynamism, and cannot be turned into a means. A joint consultation of FABC-CCA in which several Catholic bishops and theologians participated stated:

> We affirm that dialogue and mission have their own integrity and freedom. They are distinct but not unrelated. Dialogue is not a tool or instrument for mission and evangelisation, but it does influence the way the Church perceives and practices mission in a pluralistic world. Mission invites us to participate in God's continuing activity through the Spirit to mend a broken creation, to overcome the fragmentation of humanity and to heal the rift between nature, humanity and God.[23]

Asian theologians felt that the spirit of the council was vindicated by the event of Assisi in October 1986 when Pope John Paul II brought together leaders of many religious traditions to be united in prayer. A further consolidation of the conciliar teaching was the statement in *Redemptoris Missio* that "the Spirit's presence and activity affect not only individuals but also society and history, peoples, cultures and religions."[24] I see in this statement an instance of the influence of Asian theology of religion on the universal Church.

At the same time, Asian theologians have critically questioned some of the post-conciliar documents which, unlike the council, exhibit negative attitude to other faiths and their spiritual practices. Even a cursory look into the documents of the Theological Advisory Commission of FABC (later renamed as Office of

---

22 Cf. D.S. Amalorpavadass, ed., *Research Seminar on Non-Biblical Scriptures* (Bangalore: NBCLC, 1974); Paul Puthenangady, ed., *Sharing Worship. Communicatio in Sacris* (Bangalore: NBCLC, 1988). See also Felix Wilfred, *Beyond Settled Foundations. The Journey of Indian Theology* (Madras: Department of Christian Studies, University of Madras, 1993).

23 FABC and Christian Conference of Asia (CCA), Joint Statement of the Consultation no. 5. See *Living and Working Together with Sisters and Brothers of Other Faiths in Asia* (An Ecumenical Consultation, Singapore, July 5–10, 1987) (Hong Kong, 1989), 104-105.

24 Cf. *Redemptoris Missio*, nos. 28 & 29.

Theological Concerns) will convince anyone about the depth and breadth of the theological creativity of Asia, taking seriously the injunction of Vatican II to open up new avenues to truth. The Commission has produced with a lot of courage documents of high theological quality on such issues as local Churches, interreligious dialogue, Church and politics, Spirit at work in Asia today, methodology of doing theology in Asia.[25] These reflections are triggered from the experiences of Asia.

The Change of Mood

Besides the above developments, I should also mention a slack in the spirit of Vatican II in the Asian Churches, especially from 1990s. There are several reasons for this. Let me name what I think are two important ones. It is a truism to say that leadership matters. Asian Churches experienced from 1990s a decline in the quality of Church leadership.[26] There was a time when the Asian Churches felt being moved forward on the path of Vatican II, through such charismatic figures as Cardinal Stephan Kim of Korea, Cardinal Fumio Hamao of Japan, Archbishop Soter Fernandez of Malaysia, Archbishop Angelo Fernandes of India—to name only a few. The engagement of these leaders meant for the Asian Churches a springtime. But then subsequently Asian Churches, unfortunately, had a set of Church-leaders quite mediocre and lacking in vision and sensitivity to the challenges of the Asian context. Asian Churches slowly started becoming "maintenance Churches" with routine activities wanting in the spirit of renewal and innovation. A second important reason was the Roman intervention since the Fifth Plenary Assembly of FABC in Bandung in 1990, out of a preoccupation that FABC is going too far and too fast. There was an effort to restrain and control the Asian Churches which stunted many new initiatives in the continent, and FABC has not recovered from it.[27] This is one part of the story.

---

[25] These documents are collected together into a volume: Vimal Tirimanna, ed., *Sprouts of Theology from the Asian Soil. Collection of TAC and OTC Documents [1987-2007]* (Bangalore: Claretian Publications, 2007).

[26] Cf. Felix Wilfred, "Rethinking Church-leadership in India in the Light of Pope Francis," in *Jeevadhara* (January 2014), pp. 48–67. The whole issue is dedicated to a critical reflection on Church-leadership.

[27] Cf. Felix Wilfred, "Fifth Plenary Assembly of FABC. An Interpretation of Its Theological Orientation," *Vidyajyoti Journal of Theological Reflection* 54 (1990), 583-592. I have shown in this article the kind of Roman intervention by Cardinal Jozef Tomko, for example, to force upon Asia at this Assembly a particular a-historical understanding of mission, whereas Asian bishops tried to underline the importance of the *context* in understanding mission in Asia as was delineated in my talk to the Assembly immediately following that of the cardinal.

On the other hand, in spite of this situation, the Church at the grassroots has been active and vibrant in the reception of the council. Individual Christians and groups have forged ahead in their engagement with the socio-political and cultural situation at the micro and macro levels. The spirit of *Gaudium et Spes* continues to inspire several movements centered on the issues of justice, human dignity and rights. There has been a deepening of Christian faith, efforts to reach out to peoples of other faiths and dialogue with them. Especially, Asian theological pursuit has been quite active in exploring many dimensions of the teachings of Vatican II.

Dark Clouds

Some of the developments in the Church under Benedict XVI have been a matter of preoccupation to Asian Christians. One of the great innovations of Vatican II was to allow the celebration of God's Word in one's own tongue. *Sacrosanctum Concilium* (the liturgical document of Vatican II) stated: "The Church has no desire, not even in liturgy, to impose a rigid monolithic structure. Rather, on the contrary, it cultivates and encourages the gifts and endowments of mind and heart possessed by various races and peoples."[28]

The worship in Christian communities in the local language and through their symbols and signs brought faith closer to life. The numerous creative initiatives in India, Indonesia, Japan and many other parts of the continent bear witness to the seriousness with which Asian Christians have put into practice the council.

But Asian Christians were aghast at the efforts under Benedict XVI to ease restrictions on the use of Tridentine mass and the encouragement to the use of Latin. Asian Christians are not able to make much sense of all this nor reconcile it with the spirit and teachings of Vatican II. Such efforts have to be read in conjunction with the attempts to dampen Asian practices of inculturation. The spirit of the Christian Pentecost is that every language is the language of God, of the Spirit. The "pastoral initiative" of Tridentine mass, apparently, to avoid rift in the Church, can be the source of new division and dissension in Christian communities. No less preoccupying have been more recent Roman efforts to water down initiatives of interreligious dialogue. This has justifiably raised alarm among Asian Christians. We hope Pope Francis will set at rest such retrograde and Eurocentric trends in the Church and encourage the Churches in Asia and in

[28] *SC* 37.

other parts of the world in their efforts to bring the Gospel closer to the people, especially to the poorest of the poor.

Conclusion

To get back to the thought of Rahner on the enduring significance of Vatican II, for Asians it is too restrictive to think of it in terms of the *ecclesia* becoming truly universal. For Asians, the abiding significance of Vatican II is not bound up with such an ecclesiological vision. *Rather, the most significant thing for Asians is the council's theological vision that the revelation and self-communication of God has truly a catholic or universal reach.* And this is a key point in the reception of the council in Asia. It crystallizes their many experiences, and especially helps them see in a new light millions of their neighbors of other faiths as part of a single God's plan of revelation and salvation. This has consequences for the life of Asian Christians in all spheres of life and mission.

Asian Christians have paid great attention to the approach and orientation Vatican II attuned to God's creation, revelation and relationship to the entire humanity. Here lies the key to the understanding of the Asian reception of the council. The council has brought new impetus to Asian Christians to view and enter into new relationship with their neighbors and concern themselves with what affects all. As the FABC-CCA consultation observed, "God's recreating activity is prior to and more comprehensive than the Church's mission, and it directs our attention beyond the Church to the Kingdom."[29]In the reception of the council, Asian Christians have been attentive to whatever in the council that orients them in the direction of the Kingdom of God.

By involving themselves in these questions and concerns, Asians have made the council their own. The accent is more on the renewal of relationships with neighbors of other faiths, and with the larger society, rather than on the Church. In the light of these relationships Asians have come to understand also the ecclesiological vision of the council. Asians carry forward the legacy of the council in a living manner by trying to renew Christian life and mission in a multi-religious and pluri-cultural continent. It is challenging, of course; but it makes Christian life exciting as well.

Being inspired by the Council for us in Asia is to overcome the temptation of creating a self-centered Church, but to become truly a Church of the people,

[29] See *Living and Working Together with Sisters and Brothers of Other Faiths in Asia*, 105. http://www.fabc.org/fabc%20papers/fabc_paper_49.pdf

dialoguing continuously with peoples of other faiths and engaging oneself with those issues and questions that concern the lives of everyone across religious borders. Here is truly the test of universality. This spirit of universality practiced at the local level will enable the Asian Church also to make its contribution for a better Asia.

8 New Wine in Old Wineskins: Liturgical Reform of Vatican II (the 50th Anniversary of *Sacrosanctum Concilium)*

Michael S. DRISCOLL

Recently I attended the anniversary of the ordination of a priest friend whose First Mass I sang forty years ago. Jokingly I offered to sing the same songs that we did back then. Of course, forty years ago we really did not have a body of liturgical music appropriate for the occasion, so we sang songs from "Up With People," Hootenany, and Broadway tunes. For this particular occasion we sang, "Prepare, Ye, The Way of the Lord," from *Godspell*[1] along with other tunes from this show. He politely acknowledged my request and suggested that this be done at the reception. Of course, I was only joking but the mere mention of what we did four decades ago makes me blush and serves as a vivid reminder of how far we have come. Twenty years later, I was speaking to a leading American bishop about liturgical music. He declared that he was glad that Michael has beached his boat, referring to "Michael, Row the Boat Ashore,[2]" but that he now could not celebrate the liturgy without carrying a canteen, since we were always "crossing the barren desert." Again he was referring to another phase of liturgical movement which moved beyond folk music to now using biblical texts. Virgil Funk, the founder of National Pastoral Musicians Association in the United States, has written about the development of liturgical music through the decades which I find very interesting and compelling. I do not want to pretend that we have now arrived, since that is not the point. As a Pilgrim People we will always be on the way. Arriving is not as important as being a pilgrim "en route." I would like to review several articles of the Constitution on the Liturgy, *Sacrosanctum Concilium,* that lie at the heart of the liturgical reforms to see what was proposed fifty years ago and where we are today.

Personally I am particularly interested in the role of sacred music in the reform of the liturgy having come into liturgical studies through the back door of music. For this reason my life's dream was to establish a program in sacred music that

1 *Godspell*: A Musical Based on the Gospel According to St. Matthew (1973).

2 *"Michael Row the Boat Ashore"* is an old American folk song that hails from the slave era, and became a popular anthem during the civil rights movement, http://folkmusic.about.com/od/folksongs/qt/MichaelRow.htm (accessed 1/17/2015)

would be as strong in liturgical studies as much as musical formation. I was able to accomplish this to some degree about a decade ago at the University of Notre Dame when I founded the Masters Program in Sacred Music. In 2013 we added a doctorate (Doctor of Musical Arts) to the program. But there is still so much to be done for the formation of pastoral musicians. And still more to be done for the on-going liturgical renewal.

As I travel around the United States speaking about the liturgy the two biggest complaints that I hear concern the music and homilies. Parishes are divided by the style of music and people are willing to travel great distances to churches that are not their parish if the music and the homily is deemed "good." The example I love to give about this concerns a parish in Chicago that found itself in bad straits. The highway passes next to the church; the area had become unpopulated and the church was dying. The pastor who took charge, declared that he would bring the parish back to life with good music and good preaching, with a huge emphasis on hospitality. He and his staff worked diligently in this regard and behold his dream was realized. In fact, it was more than realized. This church (Old St. Pat's) is so popular today that you have to arrive early and almost have to carry a shoe horn to get into the building. They now offer masses upstairs and downstairs, and often have to use large screens to broadcast the mass to those who cannot get inside the main liturgical space. This is a great success story, but there are also stories that attest to the contrary.

Looking back to *Sacrosanctum Concilium* we note that it has had a profound and far-reaching impact on the reform of the liturgy and liturgical renewal. While today we may take its principles and provisions for granted and easily quote important sections from memory, early on there was confusion about how to interpret its principles and disagreement about how to implement its provisions. Since the document is long and very comprehensive, I am tempted to look at chapter six dealing with music, but I will resist this temptation. Instead I will focus on the second chapter that speaks about the promotion of liturgical instruction and active participation with an eye retrospectively towards what the council mandated and with another eye to where we are currently.

The Promotion of Liturgical Instruction and Active Participation

Chapter II of the Constitution on the Liturgy set out the fundamental principles regarding liturgical reform and strategies on how to achieve this. I will look at articles 14-19 in some detail to see what was prescribed, what was achieved in the past fifty years and what remains to be done. As an educator I am particularly interested in what the academy has done to further liturgical renewal.

Article 14 lies at the very heart of the liturgical reforms mandated at the first session of the Second Vatican Council. The call for *full participation* is the cornerstone of the liturgical reforms and has been called the "refrain" of the Constitution on the Liturgy appearing sixteen times throughout the document (see CSL 12, 14, 19, 26, 27, 30, 41, 50, 55, 113, 114, 121, 124). The sentence "*This full and active participation by all the people is the aim to be considered before all else*" has caused much ink to flow in recent decades as authors have debated the meaning of the Latin expression *actuosa participatio.* Nevertheless, the expression *participatio actuosa* is classic. Pius X called for active participation in his *motu proprio "Tra le sollecitudini"* (1903).[3] Again in his apostolic constitution, *Divini cultus,* he wrote in 1928 that the restoration of Gregorian chant for the use of the people would provide the means whereby they "may participate in divine worship more actively." However, emphasis was also laid upon an appreciation of the beauty of the liturgy that is capable of stirring the heart of the worshipper, who thereby enters into the realm of the sacred mysteries. Pius XII in his encyclicals *Mystici Corporis* (1943) and *Mediator Dei* (1947) also used the term, but insisted that true participation was not merely external. *De musica sacra,* an instruction issued in 1958 by the Sacred Congregation of Rites, distinguished between the various levels of participation, indicating thereby that the possibility of profound interior participation was linked to high standards of execution.

What then is meant by full and active participation? What did the Council Fathers intend by using the expression *plena et actuosa participatio?* Mark Searle in his posthumously published work *Called to Participate*[4] delineates three levels of participation: participation in ritual behavior, participation in the liturgy of the Church, and participation in the life of God. In this manner, he avoids the false dichotomy between outward and inward participation. Both inward and outward participation are sought in the reforms and they complement one another. Therefore, participation should not be limited to the outer forms, but these should help the faithful enter the deeper interior dimension of praying "in spirit and in truth" (John 4:24).

[3] "The faithful assemble to draw that spirit from its primary and indispensable source, that is, from active participation in the sacred mysteries and in the public and solemn prayer of the Church." Pius X, *Motu Proprio "Tra le sollecitudini"* on Sacred Music, November 22, 1903, par. 5.

[4] Mark Searle, *Called to Participate: Theologial, Ritual, and Social Perspectives* (Collegeville: Liturgical Press, 2005).

The theological reason for the liturgical demands of participation flows directly from the waters of baptism: "*Such participation by the Christian people as 'a chosen race, a royal priesthood, a holy nation, a redeemed people' (1 Pet. 2:9; cf. 2:4-5), is their right and duty by reason of their baptism.*"[5] The council sought to lead the baptized not simply to a more active engagement in the exterior ritual action of the liturgy but to bring about a fuller participation in the paschal mystery of Christ celebrated in the Eucharist as the source and summit of the Christian life. Two (or perhaps three[6]) qualifiers are found in the various citations from the constitution modifying participation, namely fully conscious and active. In order to insure that the participation of all the baptized faithful is "fully conscious," that is, knowing, responsive, informed and fully understanding the meaning of the rites and gestures of each celebration, the constitution recognized the necessity for liturgical formation. Thus the five articles that follow (#15-19) deal specifically with the need for liturgical education and formation. In order to insure that the participation of all the baptized faithful is "active," all the rites beginning with the Eucharist were reformed in order that the baptized faithful "take part by means of acclamations, responses, psalmody, antiphons, and songs, as well as by actions, gestures, and bodily attitudes. And at the proper times all should observe a reverent silence."[7] But the mention of the importance of baptism had consequences on the subsequent sessions of the council and on the Dogmatic Constitution on the Church (*Lumen Gentium*). Massimo Faggioli[8] has written extensively on how the ideas of the constitution on the liturgy bore fruit in the overall ecclesiology that emerged from the council. Twenty years after Vatican II, a synod of bishops met in Rome to discuss the role of the laity. Out of this came the Post-Synodal Apostolic Exhortation of John Paul II *Christifideles Laici*, in which the Pope declared that "In the wake of the Second Vatican Council, at the beginning of my pastoral ministry, my aim was to emphasize forcefully the priestly, prophetic and kingly dignity of the entire People of God…"[9] A new appreciation of baptism

---

5 *Constitution on the Sacred Liturgy* (hereafter *CSL*) 14.

6 See footnote 1

7 *CSL* 30.

8 Massimo Faggioli, *True Reform: Liturgy and Ecclesiology in* Sacrosanctum Concilium (Collegeville: Pueblo, 2012). John Baldovin notes, "A profound theology of the church based on baptism and the common priesthood of the faithful undergirds the whole document [CSL], one that the historian Massimo Faggioli has argued was not adequately embodied in the other constitutions and decrees of the council." See "An Active Presence," *America* 208.18(May 27, 2013), 11-14.

9 John Paul II, *Christifideles Laici*: *On the Vocation and the Mission of the Lay Faithful in the Church and in the World* (Post-Synodal Apostolic Exhortation) (Libreria Editrice Vaticana,

was shaped at Vatican II which continues to shape the Church and her ecclesiology. The Holy Father continues:

> Life according to the Spirit, whose fruit is holiness (cf. *Rom* 6:22;*Gal* 5:22), stirs up every baptized person and requires each to *follow and imitate Jesus Christ,* in embracing the Beatitudes, in listening and meditating on the Word of God, in conscious and active participation in the liturgical and sacramental life of the Church, in personal prayer, in family or in community, in the hunger and thirst for justice, in the practice of the commandment of love in all circumstances of life and service to the brethren, especially the least, the poor and the suffering.[10]

The link between participation in the liturgy and the sacraments logically leads to engagement with the world and social justice. This theme was in the forefront of the liturgical movement well before the Council and the connection between liturgy and social justice, between Eucharist and ethics, continues to be made.

On the fiftieth anniversary of the promulgation of the Constitution on the Liturgy, after five decades of experience of the reformed liturgy, it is timely to consider again what the council meant by *participatio actuosa*. After the Bishops' Synod of 2006 dealing with the Eucharist, Pope Benedict XVI reflected upon this in his Post-Synodal Papal Exhortation *Sacramentum Caritatis*:

> It should be made clear that the word "participation" does not refer to mere external activity during the celebration. In fact, the active participation called for by the Council must be understood in more substantial terms, on the basis of a greater awareness of the mystery being celebrated and its relationship to daily life.[11]

But he goes on to say:

> In their consideration of the *actuosa participatio* of the faithful in the liturgy, the Synod Fathers also discussed the personal conditions required for fruitful participation on the part of individuals. One of these is certainly the spirit of constant conversion which must mark the lives of all the faithful.[12]

Active participation in the Eucharistic liturgy, therefore, requires that one enters deeply into the mystery requiring an examination of the inner disposition. Purifying one's mind and heart makes genuine participation possible. So Benedict

---

1998), no. 14. The term "participation" appears 76 times in various contexts. It is clear that this is the continuation of the trajectory established in the very first session of Vatican II.

10 *Ibid.*, par 16. Emphasis mine.

11 Benedict XVI, *Sacramentum Caritatis* (Post-Synodal Apostolic Exhortation) (Libreria Editrice Vaticana, 2007), no. 52.

12 *Ibid.*, no. 55.

concludes: "The faithful need to be reminded that there can be no *actuosa participatio* in the sacred mysteries without an accompanying effort to participate actively in the life of the Church as a whole, including a missionary commitment to bring Christ's love into the life of society."[13]

A word must be said about *the use of vernacular languages*. The constitution on the liturgy was very clear that "particular law remaining in force, the use of the Latin language is to be preserved in the Latin rites."[14] But then in the next sentence it goes on to say, "But since the use of the mother tongue, whether in the Mass, the administration of the sacraments, or other parts of the liturgy, frequently may be of great advantage to the people, the limits of its employment may be extended." It seems that this provision had missionary countries in mind where use of Latin would be an impediment to evangelization. The shift from Latin to vernacular languages was one of the most hotly debated topics at the council.[15] There were some bishops present at the council who contended that Latin, even if it was not understood by most, was what gave Catholics their identity. The conciliar debate over language in the liturgy, however, pointed to a much deeper tension that would affect the entire liturgical schema proposed to the bishops in council. It should not surprise us that debates over liturgical languages ensued and continue today, fifty years after the council, as evidenced by the translation of the 2000 Missal that came into use in November 2011. Father Anscar Chupungco, former professor of liturgy at the Pontifical Liturgical Institute at San Anselmo in Rome, emphasized that *the vernacular plays an absolute role in assuring the active participation* of the faithful in the liturgy. That absolute role demands that liturgical texts be easily understood in order to enable active and prayerful participation. It is little wonder that following the council the movement to translate the liturgical texts into the vernacular languages took shape so quickly.

---

13 *Ibid.*

14 *CSL* 36.1. 101. 1. "In accordance with the centuries-old tradition of the Latin rite, the Latin language is to be retained by clerics in the divine office. But in individual cases the ordinary has the power of granting the use of a vernacular translation to those clerics for whom the use of Latin constitutes a grave obstacle to their praying the office properly. The vernacular version, however, must be one that is drawn up according to the provision of Art. 36."

15 For a more thorough treatment of use of the vernacular and the history of the vernacular movement, see Keith Pecklers, *Dynamic Equivalence: The Living Language of Christian Worship* (Collegeville: Pueblo, 2003). For an appraisal of vernacular usage from an ecumenical perspective, see Maxwell Johnson, "The Loss of a Common Language: The End of Ecumenical-Liturgical Convergence?" *Studia Liturgica* 37 (2007), 55-72.

From the Liturgical Movement to the Emergence of Liturgical Studies

It is clear that the reforms mandated by Vatican II did not fall from the sky, like Dorothy's house falling from Kansas into the land of Oz. The foundations for the liturgical reforms of Vatican II were laid by the Liturgical Movement. Historians mark the beginning of the liturgical movement in France when Dom Prosper Guéranger (1805-1875) in 1833, along with several priests of the diocese of Le Mans, moved to the Abbey of St. Pierre at Solesmes on the banks of the Sarthe river in order to restore it so that they might live the Rule of St. Benedict and celebrate the Divine Office according to the original and most authentic form. As an essential part of the restoration, these priests undertook a comprehensive study of the liturgy in order to restore the French church to a purer liturgical form that Guéranger believed was found in the Roman rite. Restoration of Gregorian chant was the keystone to this project. At about the same time the Oxford movement was beginning in England under the leadership of E. B. Pusey. The Liturgical Movement spans roughly 150 years, from Guéranger's initial work in the 1830s to Vatican II and the subsequent reforms of each sacrament up to the 1980s. The movement which embraces a range of practices and thinkers, in both Europe and North America, had three phases: monastic, parish and academic, and official.[16]

Who can say precisely when and where a movement of this kind begins? There are those who have marked the time when the meaning of the liturgical movement became clear to them. And there are others to whom it seems to have come as a progressive and continuous experience from childhood. Many scholars mark the beginning of the modern liturgical movement to the year 1909, localizing it to the Benedictine Abbey of Mont César in Belgium. There a monk named Lambert Beauduin, recognized both as a liturgical reformer and an ecumenist, brought his interests in liturgy together with his zeal for social justice. Drawn to the *Société des Aumôniers du Travail*, he was ordained to the diocesan clergy but felt drawn to the monastic life. In 1906 he left for the life of a Benedictine monk at Mont César where he prepared to teach dogmatic theology (ecclesiology). It was here that he dreamed about a renewed liturgy both in parishes and monasteries that would renew the Church. In 1909 he attended the general chapter of the Benedictines in Beuron that led him to the Congress of Catholic Works in Malines, which he declared as the official beginning for his work in liturgical reform and

[16] For more detailed information on the liturgical movement see J. D. Chrichton, *Lights In the Darkness: Forerunners of the Liturgical Movement* (Collegeville: Liturgical Press, 1996); Keith Pecklers, *The Unread Vision* (Collegeville, MN: Liturgical Press, 1998).

ecumenism. But it was during his years at Rome (1921-1925) while preparing his lectures on ecclesiology, that Beauduin became acutely aware of the problem of Christian Unity through his contacts with Anglicanism and with the Christian East. He taught university level courses both at San Anselmo in Rome and the *Institut Supérieur de Liturgie* in Paris.

Article 15 of the Constitution on the Sacred Liturgy, therefore, represents an impetus already underway in three centers of learning in Europe: Trier, Paris and Rome. The first center developed in Germany in 1946, with the establishment of a chair of liturgy in the theology faculty of the University of Trier. In 1947 the Liturgical Institute of Trier was founded and in 1948 the Herwegen Institute for the Promotion of Liturgical Studies at Maria Laach soon came into being. A decade later in 1956 a French center was created with the establishment of the *Institut Supérieur de Liturgie* in Paris. Dom Bernard Botte[17] tells of the institute's early years and his apprehension at the news of a similar institute that was to be established in Rome at the Benedictine Athenaeum of Sant'Anselmo in the early 1960s. A few years later, in 1966, a doctoral program in liturgy began at the University of Notre Dame, built on the foundations of the M.A. summer program begun by Michael Mathis C.S.C. in 1947. Initially it was these schools that produced the professors of liturgy to teach in universities, colleges and seminaries. Other schools in turn followed suit by adding doctoral programs in liturgical studies, most notably the Graduate Theological Union in Berkeley founded in 1962 representing Catholic, Protestant, Unitarian Universalist, Greek Orthodox, Jewish, Muslim, and Buddhist faith traditions and the Catholic University of America in Washington DC which began its graduate program in liturgy in 1970.[18]

There are several Catholic institutions offering graduate degrees other than the Ph.D. in liturgy, which provides an alternate route for those preparing to teach liturgical studies in seminaries and colleges. For example there is the pontifical de-

[17] Bernard Botte, *From Silence to Participation: An Insider's View of Liturgical Renewal* (Washington, DC: Pastoral Press, 1988), 104-06.

[18] As a social history of the liturgical movement in the United States, Keith Pecklers S.J. in his *The Unread Vision* (op. cit.) introduces readers to the movement's pioneers and promoters and to the issues that emerged from the movement in the U.S. in the years 1926-1955. *The Unread Vision* explores the foundational years of the movement and its major themes and discusses how the movement, its goals and principles, was received by the broader community of American Catholics. Chapters include "The European Roots: 1833-1925," "The Beginnings of a Movement: Toward Full and Active Participation in the Liturgy," "The Liturgical Movement and Social Justice," "The Liturgical Movement and Education," and "The Liturgical Movement and the Arts." Biographies on leading figures of the liturgical movement, as well as histories of related organizations, are also included.

gree in theology (STD) with a specialization in liturgy and sacramental theology. This degree is required for pontifical faculties who grant pontifical degrees and is very appropriate for seminary teachers. There is also the Doctorate in Ministry degree (D.Min.) that could have a strong liturgical component.[19]

From the beginning the study of liturgy has been very ecumenical.[20] Within the United States Ph.D. programs with some form of liturgical concentration exist at Duke University, Emory University in the Chandler School, Drew University (although this degree has been withdrawn recently), and Garrett-Evangelical Theological Seminary (Evanston, IL), just to mention a few.

Suffice it to say that liturgical studies, as its own discipline, is a relatively new field. The intentional training of professors of liturgy for seminaries is of recent origin. Prior to this time, seminarians were taught how to "say Mass" and perform the sacraments in courses of canon law where a rubrical approach dominated the discussion, whereby following the liturgical rules was enough to insure the sacramental effect.[21] There was more of an interest in the "how" rather than the "why." With the creation of schools with doctorates specializing in liturgical studies, this new field was born. Initially the principal methodology was historical. To this was added a more theological dimension. Finally the human sciences were incorporated with the advent of ritual studies, a method that had been pioneered in theatrical circles under the form of semiotics and later applied to ritual performance.

On the fiftieth anniversary of the *Constitution on the Sacred Liturgy*, the Catholic Academy of Liturgy (CAL) at its annual meeting in Albuquerque looked at articles 15 and 16 reflecting on the future of liturgical studies and the mission of CAL in light of the last half century of experience of liturgical reform and teaching. A survey was prepared and administered electronically to all the members of CAL. Although the survey is still in progress, preliminary results show

---

19 For example, the Chicago Theological Union offers a Doctor in Ministry (D.Min.) degree with a certificate in liturgical studies.

20 Speaking from my experience I can report that as of 2013 among the eighty-five people who have received doctorates in liturgy at the University of Notre Dame, about half represent Protestant and Orthodox Christian traditions. See Maxwell Johnson, "Liturgy and Ecumenism: Gifts, Challenges, and Hopes for a Renewed Vision," *Worship* 80, 1 (January 2006), 2-29.

21 Frederick McManus, the well-known American canonist, comments: "Our concern is with the existing liturgical law, in particular as this has moved in recent years from its post-Tridentine inflexibility to the norms of a renewed liturgy, one that has now been profoundly reformed and in the process made more flexible and open to creativity." "Liturgical Law," Handbook for Liturgical Studies, vol 1, Anscar Chupungco, ed, (Collegeville, MN: Liturgical Press, 1997), 399.

much hopefulness in the group. The largest cohort of respondents are in their 60s, and well over half the respondents see themselves continuing in their present profession for 10 years or less. Most respondents (about 75%) see their current position continuing after they retire. A minority, but a fairly sizable one, would *not* counsel young people to go into graduate studies in liturgy. But the vast majority of respondents, more than 9 out of 10, *would* pursue graduate studies in liturgy if they themselves had it to do over. There was optimism that the quality of liturgical music will improve in most places, that preaching training will improve, that laity will increasingly claim their baptismal dignity and insist on active liturgical participation, that institutional support for academic liturgy will remain strong. But there was concern expressed about training in presiding skills, about whether preaching will improve, about diocesan support for good liturgy, about future rates of Mass attendance, about bishops wanting liturgical experts in their diocese, about bishops' commitment to multicultural issues (questions that concerned Asians, African-Americans, and Native Americans).

Liturgical Studies and Liturgical Formation in Seminaries and Religions Houses of Studies

The broad background of this article demonstrates the tremendous development that took place in the study of liturgy over the past century reflecting both scholarly research and widespread pastoral experience. This article then deals with two distinct questions: (a) the formal teaching of the science of liturgy in seminaries, religious houses of study, and theological faculties; and (b) the relation and integration of other ecclesiastical disciplines and the study of liturgy. Since Vatican II there has been a movement towards the study of liturgy as a field of its own and not simply as a subset of Canon Law. Kathleen Cahalan notes:

> There were no dramatic changes in the official theology and practice of the sacraments between the Council of Trent and Vatican II. Sacramental practice was defined according to the moral and legal obligations that were summarized in the third part of moral theology manuals, according to the rubrics of canon law.[22]

Bernard Häring used to recount that as a young seminarian he was taught that a priest could sin countless times just by saying Mass if the rubrics (the ritual directions printed in red ink) were not followed to the letter. The preparation of

[22] Kathleen Cahalan, *Formed in the Image of Christ: The Sacramental-Moral Theology of Bernard Häring, C.Ss.R.* (Collegeville: Michael Glazier Press, 2004), 49.

professors must be in accordance with the whole intent and purpose of the *Constitution*, certainly more than an education in the history of liturgical law. The intent of the *Constitution* was to promote the pastoral purpose of the liturgy; nevertheless professors of liturgy would need the same scientific background as other seminary professors in the other disciplines therefore necessitating specialized institutes for higher liturgical training.

Following the Council the mandate for liturgical formation had to be interpreted and implemented by each episcopal conference and religious order. In the United States the American bishops drafted and approved the Program of Priestly Formation (PPF) now in its fifth edition.[23] Liturgical practice and studies were interwoven among the four pillars of formation: human, spiritual, intellectual, and pastoral. The program provided a way of life permeated by the three-fold charge given priests at ordination to teach, to sanctify, and to govern. College-level seminarians were encouraged to begin the study of theology, with undergraduate courses that focus on the fundamental beliefs and practices of the Catholic faith. College-level theology courses should study the themes contained in the *Catechism of the Catholic Church,* including courses on Catholic doctrine, liturgy and sacraments, Catholic morality, Christian prayer, and Sacred Scripture.

At the post-baccalaureate level, the theology studied in preparation for priestly ministry in major seminaries, in a particular way, had to find integration and focus in the liturgy as the celebration of the Mystery of Christ. To enter the major seminary a minimum of 12 semester credit hours or their equivalent are required in appropriate courses of undergraduate theology. These courses should study the themes of the Catechism (doctrine, liturgy and sacraments, morality, prayer) as well as Sacred Scripture. In liturgy, the core included studies in the theological, historical, spiritual, pastoral, and juridical aspects of liturgy.[24] Courses in theology, history, and liturgy, where appropriate, include the role and contribution of the Eastern Churches.[25]

Liturgical formation goes beyond the classroom. Liturgical formation is regarded as a part of a life of steady prayer first and foremost centered in the sacraments, especially in the Eucharist, the Liturgy of the Hours, and the liturgical

[23] *Program of Priestly Formation, Fifth Edition* (Washington, D.C.: United States Conference of Catholic Bishops, 2006) (hereafter *PPF*). This document builds upon the foundation of previous editions. The principal and new direction of the fifth edition stems from its reliance on the Post-Synodal Apostolic Exhortation *Pastores dabo vobis* (I *Will Give You Shepherds: On the Formation of Priests in the Circumstances of the Present Day,* 1992) to organize and integrate the program of priestly formation.

[24] *PPF* 213.

[25] *PPF* 223.

cycles, but also in prayer that is personal and devotional. Therefore, either the director of spiritual formation or the director of liturgy provides for the liturgical life and prayer of the seminary community, making provision for the daily celebration of the Eucharist, the Liturgy of the Hours, and opportunities for celebration of the Sacrament of Penance. Liturgical formation includes retreats and days of recollection, making sure they are well planned and carefully executed. Thus good liturgy is taught best by experiencing good liturgies.[26]

An oft quoted passage about the role of good liturgy is found in the American bishops document *Sing to the Lord*: "Faith grows when it is well expressed in celebration. Good celebrations can foster and nourish faith. Poor celebrations may weaken it."[27] This is particularly true in seminary education. Well prepared and celebrated liturgies go a long way in the formation of the seminarian both liturgically and spiritually. Over the past half century, attention has been given to the mystagogical nature of liturgy.[28] The mystagogical method is very experiential. One learns best through experience. But following the experience, there is need for some reflection and sharing. Much like a three-legged stool, if any of these dimensions are missed, the stool falls over.

Reference is also made to the role given to popular devotions. Instances of popular devotions commended by the Apostolic See may be found in the encyclical *Mediator Dei* (nos. 172-85). The Council clearly provided norms by which existing devotions (such as evening observances, holy hours, novenas, etc.) should be reappraised: (1) harmony with the liturgical seasons (an easily violated rule); (2) conformity to the liturgy itself and certainly not oppositions to its celebrations; (3) derivation from the liturgy, that is, at least a broad observance of the liturgical pattern of common worship, its hierarchical, communal, pastoral, didactic shape; (4) encouragement by the devotional practice of popular participation in liturgy itself, for example, frequent reception of the Holy Eucharist.

The relationship of devotions or popular piety to the official liturgy is more complicated than it first seems.[29] Rather than pitting devotions against the liturgy in binary opposition, it is necessary to plot the gesture of popular piety on a spectrum ranging from liturgical to anti-liturgical with two intermediary points of

---

26 *PPF* 331

27 *Sing to the Lord: Music in Divine Worship* (Washington, D.C.: United States Conference of Catholic Bishops, 2008), par. 5.

28 See Kathleen Hughes, *Saying Amen: A Mystagogy of Sacrament* (Chicago, Liturgical Training Publications, 1999).

29 For a more detailed account, see Leonard Boyle, "Popular Piety in the Middle Ages: What is Popular?" *Florilegium* 4(1982) 184-93.

para-liturgical and quasi-liturgical. For example there are certain gestures, which originated as an expression of popular piety that were later incorporated into the liturgy. The distribution of ashes on Ash Wednesday, for example, is such a case.[30] A modern example of how a popular practice is gradually making its way into the liturgy is the lighting of the candles of the Advent wreath during the opening rites of Mass. Although this is not officially sanctioned, it is gradually becoming a part of the liturgy. There are many examples of quasi-liturgical devotional forms of prayer. Morning and evening prayer is often patterned after the Liturgy of the Hours but is not a strict liturgical form *per se*. In this case, it is adapted from and patterned after the Liturgy of the Hours and would constitute what might be called a quasi-liturgical form of prayer. The third category is para-liturgical forms of devotional prayer. Many prayers and practices that correspond in some way to the liturgical year, respecting the various feasts and seasons, but which are not derived from the official liturgy might fall under this category. The example of the lighting of the advent wreath in the home would constitute but one example of this kind of devotional form of prayer. Finally there are devotional forms of prayer that can be classified as anti-liturgical. I hesitate to give an example here but one that readily comes to mind is the Novena for Divine Mercy. When Sister Faustina had her visions in the 1930s, the liturgies of Holy Week had not yet been reformed. About 20 years after her life, however, Pius XII mandated the reform of Holy Week with the result that the penitential novena, which begins during the Paschal Triduum comes into direct conflict with the Church's liturgical practice of the feast of all feasts—Easter. It seems inconceivable that the Paschal Triduum would be overshadowed with a penitential practice. So that which began as a fine expression of popular piety eventually came into direct conflict with the Church's liturgical year. Now that this feast has been incorporated into the general liturgical calendar, it presents its own set of challenges in harmonizing the feast with the Easter Triduum celebrated a week earlier. Finally, there are other forms of devotional prayer, which seem to have no rapport with the official liturgy but are not harmful to the liturgy. The *Constitution on the Liturgy* provides a helpful principle in judging the value of devotions if they flow from the liturgy and bring the faithful back to the liturgy. Using the aforementioned criteria might be a further way to evaluate the rapport between devotions and liturgy.

30 Of course, the distinction between liturgical and devotional seems anachronistic for the Middle Ages, since certain elements began as a popular expression and only later were made official. There are many examples of this but certainly the private dispositional prayers that a priest would say before, during and after Mass are an example. At the second Vatican Council, many of these private prayers were eliminated but some still remain like the "Confiteor" prayer.

Regarding the study of liturgical law, until the Council, Canon Law made provision for the study of liturgy as a subsection of law. Until then, this was felt to refer to the courses in the manner of celebration, that is, the study of liturgical legislation and more especially the rubrics. The challenge was to move liturgical studies into the broader understanding of the "spirit of the liturgy" rather than reducing good liturgy to a matter of blindly and slavishly following rules.

Pastoral Care and Liturgical Life of Priests

The retooling of priests already ordained before 1962 was a great challenge in the years following the council. But the challenge was expanded to include the liturgical formation of religious women and men as well as the laity. At a diocesan level offices of worship were established, in-service programs were developed, and workshops were conducted in order to educate priests who had been trained in the manualist tradition in vogue before the Council. This kind of formation is not done in graduate programs but on the diocesan level. More clergy would go to these events than to summer programs. It is fair to say that the implementation of this was fairly spotty with a focus on externals (the "new" rubrics). Also, since this kind of liturgical formation requires development of skills, this means that practical training as opposed to just listening to lectures or reading was imperative. In a similar way, surgeons learn in clinical situations. There was some aversion to this approach, however, since it might put priests in a situation where they might make a mistake and be embarrassed.

At regional and national levels, liturgical weeks were organized, probably the most important one sponsored by the Liturgical Conference. The Liturgical Conference began in 1940, as an annual "liturgical week" under the leadership of the abbots of the Benedictine communities in the United States. In 1943 it was constituted under an independent board of directors. From 1940-1968, the national liturgical weeks brought together priests, religious, and lay people from all over the United States, often attracting several thousand participants. In the years immediately following the promulgation of the Constitution on the Sacred Liturgy, the liturgical weeks brought together close to 20,000 people.

In the United States much credit in the on-going liturgical formation of the clergy is due to the Federation of Diocesan Liturgical Commissions (FDLC). As a national organization composed primarily of members of diocesan liturgical commissions and offices of worship, the FDLC serves as an official collaborating agent between the local churches and the USCCB Bishops' Committee on Divine Worship (BCDW). Diocesan liturgical personnel, appointed by their bishops, have responsibility for the promotion of the liturgical life of their dioceses. The stated goal of this federation is to promote the liturgy as the heart of Christian life—especially in the parish community. But as a pastoral and professional organization, the FDLC is committed to assist the Catholic Church in the United States, its hierarchy, the local churches, and the individual bishops in their responsibilities of providing positive leadership in liturgical celebration, education, and development.

In recent decades other societies and associations have come into existence that help in the task of ongoing liturgical formation. Some thrive and grow while others have come and gone. Many could be named, but for the sake of space let me point to one that has special merit: the National Association of Pastoral Musicians, founded in 1976, gathers pastoral musicians together with the clergy. The genius of this association was the notion of the dual membership—pastoral musicians and pastors both received the magazine and both groups are welcome and encouraged to attend the national and regional conventions. Special sessions for clergy are offered allowing for the ongoing education of the clergy, while sessions aiming at pastoral musicians assist them in their liturgical and musical formation.

For some but not all, the ongoing formation of priests, religious women and men and lay ecclesial ministers lie in the domain of summer programs. These programs are numerous and have been successful in educating thousands of people who have worked diligently for liturgical reform within religious communities, parishes and diocesan offices of worship. Some of the summer programs emphasize liturgy and music, while others may have several foci. Summer programs in liturgy have attracted many priests and religious which later were extended to lay ecclesial ministers. Several summer programs in liturgy distinguished themselves nationally and internationally and attracted thousands of students over the years. The summers-only format initially catered to priests and religious women and men who could take time away from their apostolic activity to study. Later it suited well lay faithful with full-time professional and/or family responsibilities allowing students to implement in their own ministerial settings what they learn as the program unfolds, and then to bring their experience to bear on further study. Three of the oldest summer programs were at the University of Notre Dame (IN), Collegeville (MN), and Rensselaer (IN). Father Michael Mathis, C.S.C. founded the liturgical studies program at the University of Notre Dame in 1947. Out of his summer programs in liturgical studies grew the Notre Dame Center for Liturgy (previously the Center for Pastoral Liturgy), established in 1970, and the annual pastoral liturgy conferences, sponsored by the Center since 1971. In 1947, he petitioned university authorities to allow him to hold a summer session in liturgy. It was for undergraduates only, and consisted of three courses: History of the Sacred Liturgy in the Latin Rite, Theory and Practice of Gregorian Chant, and a miscellany entitled Important Features of the Liturgy. By 1948, he was given permission to launch a graduate school of liturgy. Thus, he scoured Europe and the United States for the very best of the liturgical scholars. The summer faculty rosters he assembled read like a "Who's Who" of the liturgical movement.

Another great center for liturgical studies was at the monastic school of St. John in Collegeville, MN, and the monk whose name is recognized as the driving force behind the beginnings of liturgical studies there was Fr. Virgil Michel, OSB. There is perhaps no other single individual to whom more credit is due for the inception and promotion of the liturgical movement in America. For the movement in this country, in its organized form, may truly be dated from the foundation of the liturgical review, *Orate Fratres*, near the end of the year 1929. During the time of Virgil Michel the name of the journal was changed in 1951 to *Worship*, already an indication of the growing desire for the vernacular. Those who knew Virgil Michel well were in admiration of the broad range of his activity, and of its intensity, and of its sureness.

Finally, St. Joseph College in Rensselaer (IN) has sponsored a summer-only program of Church Music and Liturgy for many years. It provides opportunities for study in liturgy and church music. Grounded solidly in liturgical tradition, the program maintains a pastoral focus on liturgical celebration in local communities. The program prepares students to promote quality liturgy in small rural communities as well as in large, urban and suburban churches. Liturgy calls for full, conscious, and active participation in every kind of worshiping assembly—in every region and ethnic community.

Normally the Master of Arts in Liturgical Studies theologizes from the liturgies themselves, introducing students to the historical, theological, and pastoral dimensions of the church's liturgical traditions, the nature of the ritual process, and the relationship between culture and liturgy. Academically specialized, this kind of study presumes a solid background in theology and scripture and prepares students for service in liturgical formation, liturgical ministries, liturgical leadership, or further academic study. The following are some of the other programs that offer masters degrees and have played a key role, in the ongoing formation of clergy and pastoral liturgists: Santa Clara (CA), Yale Divinity School and Yale Institute of Sacred Music (CT), St. Michael College (VT). By and large these programs emphasize the necessity of integrating academic work with practice. Study of the liturgy is always situated in the context of a praying, worshipping community. The most recent program specializing in liturgical studies is the Liturgical

Institute of the University of Saint Mary of the Lake at Mundelein (IL). Since 2000, The Liturgical Institute focuses on training, research and publication in the fields of sacramental theology and liturgy. The Institute offers a professional master of arts in liturgy, an academic master of arts (liturgical studies), and a licentiate in sacred theology.

Liturgical Instruction of the Faithful

Later in the Constitution on the Liturgy, art. 41, mention is made of the Bishop as the chief liturgist of a diocese.[31] Thus, he has the responsibility to provide for liturgical instruction of the faithful. But because it is impossible for the bishop always and everywhere to preside over the whole diocese, he depends upon priests and deacons working in parishes. The experience for the past half century is that this responsibility is shared with all the faithful, particularly lay ecclesial ministers, many of whom have received special training and formation in liturgy.[32] In many places, the experience of the Sunday Celebration in the Absence of a Priest (SCAP) has become quite common. Thus, the liturgical life of the parish and its relationship to the bishop must be fostered among the faithful and clergy and efforts made to encourage a sense of community within the parish, above all in the common celebration of the Sunday Mass or the Sunday Communion Service.

In addition to the formational work done in dioceses, there was also the creation of national and diocesan liturgical centers to assist in this process. Various centers for liturgy have emerged over the years to assist in the formation of liturgical ministers. Three are of special note: Notre Dame, Georgetown and Collegeville. Out of the summer programs in liturgical studies begun in 1947 grew the Notre Dame Center for Liturgy (previously the Center for Pastoral Liturgy), established in 1970, and the annual pastoral liturgy conferences, sponsored by the Center since 1971. The Georgetown Center for Liturgy, founded in 1981 by George-

[31] "The bishop is to be considered as the high priest of his flock, from whom the life in Christ of his faithful is in some way derived and dependent. Therefore all should hold in great esteem the liturgical life of the diocese centered around the bishop, especially in his cathedral church; they must be convinced that the pre-eminent manifestation of the Church consists in the full active participation of all God's holy people in these liturgical celebrations, especially in the same eucharist, in a single prayer, at one altar, at which there presides the bishop surrounded by his college of priests and by his ministers" (CSL 41).

[32] Parallel to the Program of Priestly Formation (mentioned above), the American bishops have authored and published a program for the formation of lay ecclesial ministers. See *Co-Workers in the Vineyard of the Lord: A Resource for Guiding the Development of Lay Ecclesial Ministry* (Washington, D.C.: United States Conference of Catholic Bishops, 2005).

town University and Holy Trinity Catholic Church, is an education, research, and consultation center dedicated to transforming American Catholic parishes through the Liturgical renewal initiated by the Second Vatican Council. Finally the Godfrey Diekmann, OSB Center for Patristics and Liturgical Studies, created in 1997, seeks to deepen contemporary understanding of early Christian theologians of the first through seventh centuries, and to promote the liturgical renewal called for by the Second Vatican Council.

Finally a brief word must be said about the number and kind of liturgical publications that has assisted in the on-going liturgical formation and education.[33]

[33] In alphabetical order, the following is an incomplete but representative list of journals and magazines:

Antiphon: a Journal for Liturgical Renewal: A new journal founded in 1996 and published by the Society of Catholic Liturgy. Appearing three times per year, its focus is the renewal of the liturgy in the spirit of Vatican II with an emphasis on a wide range of topics including sacramental theology, art, architecture, and sacred music. This journal has quickly become an important resource for all who are interested in Catholic liturgy.

Catechumenate: a Journal of Christian Initiation: A resource of the Archdiocese of Chicago published six times per year by the LTP, this journal focuses on practical topics and questions concerning the RCIA.

Ecclesia Orans: A serious scholarly liturgical journal found in 1984 and published by the Pontifical Liturgical Institute headquartered at the Anselmo in Rome. International in scope, this journal publishes articles in the major European languages pertaining to the liturgical life of the Church. Recently the book review section has been expanded.

E & A: Environment and Art Letter: A bimonthly newsletter from LTP focused on art, architecture, and the environment of worship. Each issue contains 1 or 2 major articles with numerous short brief items about renovations, design, artists, craftspeople, etc. Focus is on the practical and is heavily illustrated with photos. Publication has ceased.

Ephemerides Liturgicae: A major international journal founded in 1887 and published in Rome. Includes articles in the major European languages on all aspects of liturgy.

Faith and Form: The professional journal of the Interfaith Forum on Religion, Art and Architecture which appears 3 times per year. Focus is on art, architecture and related subjects. The annual awards issue features new buildings, renovations, project designs, and artworks that have received awards.

GIA Quarterly: Publication of the liturgical publisher GIA, with a focus on music and practical aspects of liturgical planning. Each issue contains 4-5 major articles with additional short notices and columns.

Liturgical Ministry: A quarterly pastoral journal now published by the Liturgical Press. The editor states that the publication attempts to awaken pastoral ministers to academic concerns and sensitize academics to pastoral issues. Many issues are thematic with topics including: GIRM, the liturgical calendar, holiness, and saints and relics. A good resource for all engaged in pastoral ministry. Publication has ceased.

Liturgy – Liturgical Conference: A quarterly publication of the Liturgical Conference, an interdenominational group headquartered in Washington, D.C. Articles are focused on practical matters of liturgy and worship with many issues centered on the liturgical season.

Some are decidedly academic while others tend to be more popular. Still there are others which straddle the divide. Some are specialized tending towards the

---

Liturgy – Cistercians of the Strict Observance: Published very irregularly, this publication from Our Lady of Gethsemani Abbey is the work of a single monk, Father Chrysogonus Waddell. A scholarly journal focused primarily on monastic liturgy and related historical topics often publishes writings of Thomas Merton. Publication has ceased with the death of Fr. Waddell.

Ministry & Liturgy: Formerly entitled, *Modern Liturgy*, this glossy, illustrated publication appears 11 times per year and is directed towards all who are engaged in pastoral ministry. Includes practical articles on music, art, environment, and individual rites.

National Bulletin on Liturgy – Canadian Conference of Catholic Bishops : Quarterly publication of the National Liturgy Office of the Canadian Conference of Catholic Bishops. Articles are written for all engaged and involved in liturgical planning: priests, deacons, religious, musicians, teachers, liturgy committee members, and readers. Its goal is to provide sound theological information and pastoral insight on liturgical questions, issues and practices. Publication has ceased.

Newsletter: Bishops Committee on the Liturgy: A publication of the United States Conference of Catholic Bishops that provides documentation on liturgical matters from the Vatican, Roman congregations, and the USCCB. A basic resource for all liturgical ministers.

Notitiae: Official publication of the Sacred Congregation for Divine Worship and the Discipline of the Sacraments. Contains texts of papal pronouncements and decrees, interpretations of liturgical law and information on current issues in worship and liturgy. Most documents and articles are published in Latin or Italian and on occasion are published in English, French and German.

Pastoral Music: Bimonthly publication of the National Association of Pastoral Musicians. Focus is on serving the life and mission of the Church through fostering the art of musical liturgy in Catholic worshiping communities in the United States.

Questions Liturgiques – Studies in Liturgy: Quarterly journal founded in 1910 and published by the Liturgical Institute at the Catholic University of Louvain. A scholarly journal publishing articles in French and English on all aspects of liturgy from the early Church and patristic period through the current day.

Rite: A bimonthly publication of LTP and the Archdiocese of Chicago featuring 1 or 2 major articles per issue that are focused on practical aspects of liturgical ministry, music, art, environment or culture. Formerly entitled *Liturgy 90.*

Sacred Music: Published by the Church Music Association of America, this is the oldest continuously published music journal in the United States. Formerly entitled *Caecilia* and *Catholic Choirmaster*, its aim is to assist church musicians to maintain the highest artistic standards and preserve the treasury of sacred music especially Gregorian chant and encourage composers to write new music for the active participation of the people.

Studia Liturgica: An international ecumenical review for liturgical research and renewal published by Societas Liturgia. A semi-annual publication devoted to Christian liturgy, history and theology from the patristsic era through the 20th century.

Worship: The foremost Catholic liturgical journal published in the United States. Founded in 1926 at St. John's Abbey, Collegeville Minnesota as *Orate Fratres* it publishes both scholarly and practical articles on all aspects of liturgy and worship. A basic resource for all liturgical ministers.

liturgical arts and architecture, while others focus on sacred and liturgical music. A special word should be said about *Worship*. This journal has been in existence since 1926. Formerly known as *Orate Fratres*, it is published by the monks of Collegeville, Minnesota. The first issue appeared on the First Sunday of Advent, 1926. In 1951, twenty-five years after the founding of the journal, its name was changed to *Worship*, an indication of the growing interest in the use of the vernacular in liturgical celebrations.

In terms of other kinds of publications, certainly The Liturgical Press has dominated the scene, particularly with the acquisition of Pueblo Books and Michael Glazier Press. Finally Liturgical Training Publications bridges the gap of academic and popular publications with a wide variety of products like books, pamphlets, clip art, videos, CDs, magazines, and the like. Founded by the Archdiocese of Chicago, the mission statement summarizes best its *raison d'être*: To promote the liturgical formation "of the faithful and also their active participation in the liturgy both internally and externally, taking into account their age and condition, their way of life, and their stage of religious development" (*CSL* 19) so all the faithful may "become thoroughly imbued with the spirit and power of the liturgy."(*CSL* 17)

In summary then, I think we can admit that much progress has been made in the renewal of the liturgy. But liturgical renewal is like ecclesial renewal. The maxim *ecclesia semper reformanda* holds equally true for the liturgy. Some people have mistaken the reform of the liturgical books for liturgical renewal and have judged that it is over. This simply is not the case. If the liturgy of the Church is to keep abreast of changing cultures and times, then liturgical renewal is constant. The *Dogmatic Constitution on the Church* (*Lumen Gentium*) speaks about this well when it uses the metaphor of a Pilgrim Church. Being on the way is as important as arriving. Indeed progress has been made over the past fifty years, but much remains to be done to achieve the fundamental goal of "full, conscious and active participation" in the liturgical life of the Church.

Bibliography

John Baldovin, *Reforming the Liturgy: A Response to the Critics* (Collegeville: Pueblo, 2008).

Joshua Brommer, *et al.*, *A Pastoral Commentary on* Sacrosanctum Concilium: *The Constitution on the Sacred Liturgy of the Second Vatican Council* (Chicago: Liturgical Training Publications, 2013).

Annibale Bugnini, *The Reform of the Liturgy – 1948-1975* (Collegeville: Liturgical Press, 1990).

Ives Congar, *At the Heart of Christian Worship: Liturgical Essays of Yves Congar*, Paul Philibert, tr. and ed. (Collegeville: Pueblo, 2010).

Remi de Roo, *Chronicles of a Vatican II Bishop* (Toronto: Novalis, 2012).

Massimo Faggioli, *Vatican II: The Battle for Meaning* (New York and Mahwah: Paulist Press, 2012).

—, *True Reform: Liturgy and Ecclesiology in* Sacrosanctum Concilium (Collegeville: Pueblo, 2012).

Rita Ferrone, *Rediscovering Vatican II: Liturgy* (New York and Mahwah: Paulist Press, 2007).

Richard Gaillardetz and Catherine Clifford, *Keys to the Council: Unlocking the Teaching of Vatican II* (Collegeville: Liturgical Press, 2012).

Piero Marini, *A Challenging Reform: Realizing the Vision of the Liturgical Renewal* (Collegeville: Liturgical Press, 2007).

John O'Malley, *What Happened at Vatican II* (Cambridge, MA: Harvard University Press, 2008).

Carmel Pilcher and Elizabeth Harrington, eds, *Vatican Council II: Reforming Liturgy* (Adelaide: ATF Theology, 2013).

Michael Prendergast and M.D. Ridge, eds, *Voices from the Council* (Portland, OR: Pastoral Press, 2004).

9 Celebrating 50 Years of John XXIII *Pacem in terris*: Its Relevance Today and Tomorrow[1]

Kenneth R. HIMES, OFM

In October of 1962 much of the world was focused on a tense confrontation between the United States and the Union of Soviet Socialist Republics. The thirteen-day confrontation was among the most tense incidents in the more than four decades long Cold War between the Americans and the Soviets. It was also a moment when the threat of nuclear war seemed most real to a young boy in Brooklyn, NY, who along with eighth grade classmates practiced drills of hiding under our school desks in the event of nuclear attack.

Even then it was not clear to me what protection our desks would provide given that I sat near a wall of windows each about ten feet high. I was unconvinced that my desk would save me from nuclear radiation, but I did take some consolation when my teacher explained that the Communists would almost certainly aim their missiles at Manhattan rather than my Brooklyn neighborhood. Once again the East River provided a sense of safety from what might befall those Manhattanites.

Six months later on April 11, 1963 John XXIII issued an encyclical, a new word for me, entitled *Pacem in terris*, Peace on Earth. Although we were told then that the pope wanted to respond to what had come to be called the Cuban missile crisis, the papal letter was more accurately described by an Italian journalist as "the utopia of Pope John XXIII."[2] That is, it was an encyclical less concerned with commentary on current events and more of an effort to explain the papal viewpoint on what peace might mean in the modern age and how it might come about.

In this essay I am not going to rehearse the content of John's letter in a summary manner. Instead I wish to do three things: (1) I'd like to begin with a brief word about the tone and impact of the document; (2) highlight several important topics—human rights, global common good, and peacebuilding—that are raised

---

1 Portions of this essay also appear in Kenneth Himes, OFM, "Papal Thinking About Peace Since *Pacem in Terris*: the World Day of Peace Messages, 1967-2013" *Journal of Catholic Social Thought* 11/1 (2014): 9-32.

2 Giancarlo Zizola, *The Utopia of John XXIII*, trans. Helen Barolini (Garden City, NY: Doubleday, 1985).

by the encyclical and illustrate the legacy of those topics for the work of his papal successors; and (3) suggest a future agenda for moving the legacy of *Pacem in terris* forward.

Tone and impact of *Pacem in Terris*

The first thing a reader of *Pacem in terris* might have noticed is that it is addressed to all people of good will. The original audience for papal encyclicals was all the Catholic bishops. Encyclicals were simply circular letters sent to the worldwide episcopate and the texts of Catholic social teaching prior to *Pacem in terris* were addressed to that audience. Beginning with Pope John's letter, and ever since, papal social encyclicals are now addressed to all people, whether Catholic or not, religious believer or unbeliever.

This universal audience is appropriate not only because of the topic of the letter, the universal concern for peace. The broad audience also reflects the papal conviction that what is being taught is rooted in the natural law, a philosophical method that claims not to be reliant upon the specific revelation of Christian faith but rooted in the exercise of right reason examining human experience.

This natural law approach with its outlook that human reason can apprehend truths acceptable to all people is a staple of Catholic social teaching. One of the most commonly cited convictions throughout the tradition is that the purpose of the state is to secure and promote the common good of society. By definition this means that Catholic social teaching claims there is something that is shared by all in even the most pluralistic human communities. John and other popes believe all people of good will can reach a shared sense of what is good for society and that Christians have a duty to work with other people in order to secure those shared goods.

There is both an epistemological and moral optimism in the Catholic tradition and nowhere are those qualities more evident than in *Pacem in terris*. For John the natural law found within the heart of the human person guides a moral order that includes the relations between individuals with one another, between individuals and the state, between states with other states, and relations within the global community. The norms governing these relations can be known, according to John, and the resulting social order can be attained if people demonstrate the requisite good will. It is rather remarkable that the pope could issue such a positive vision and maintain such a hopeful stance towards the achievement of peace just a few months after the world had been at the doorstep of nuclear war.

But good pope John was nothing if not optimistic about the possibilities of human transformation.

Like any utopian vision the encyclical was open to criticism from those who held a more skeptical view of the possibilities of a peaceful world order, or at least the relative ease with which John envisioned it coming about. Reinhold Niebuhr, the influential proponent of Christian realism in theological ethics, thought that John's hope in an institution like the United Nations as an instrument of world order was misguided.[3] And even the prominent Jesuit John Courtney Murray thought that it was unclear "how this hope is concretely to be realized."[4]

Pacem in terris was well received by many in the peace movement, however, and John's letter did encourage a generation of Catholic activists who became involved in the anti-war movement during the decade of the sixties. The impact of the encyclical led, I believe, to the willingness of the bishops at Vatican II to reconsider the church's teaching on nonviolence. John did not explicitly deny the theory of just war but his silence about the right of national self-defense coupled with his opposition to nuclear war created a mood of questioning on the topic of warfare. It was that context which found expression in the statement of the council that we need "an evaluation of war with an entirely new attitude."[5]

Exactly what that new attitude entails was left unstated, but it is plausible to understand it as the establishment of a moral presumption against war. Starting with John XXIII and continuing through the papacies of Paul VI, John Paul II, and Benedict XVI a teaching has developed "that a presumption against war lies at the very center of Catholic thinking on war and peace."[6] Whereas some earlier theories of just war gave the presumption to justice, and war was understood as being morally acceptable as a means to establish justice, the present formulation of the church's teaching with a presumption against war as a means to justice, reflects the "new attitude" called for at Vatican II.

An important corollary of this new attitude of a presumption against war was the approval given to pacifism as an alternative to just war theory. In 1956 Pope Pius XII had written that when legitimate political authority "in a moment of extreme danger" decides that a war of self-defense is necessary "a Catholic citizen cannot invoke his own conscience in order to refuse to serve and fulfill those duties

---

3 Reinhold Niebuhr, "*Pacem in Terris*: Two Views," *Christianity and Crisis* 28/8 (1963): 82.

4 John Courtney Murray, "Things Old and New in Pacem in Terris," in *Bridging the Sacred and the Secular*, ed. Leon Hooper (Washington, DC: Woodstock Theological Center/Georgetown University Press, 1994), 215-52 at 251.

5 Vatican II, *Gaudium et spes* (Pastoral Constitution on the Church in the Modern World), n. 80.

6 Robert McElroy, "Why We Must Withdraw From Iraq," *America* (April 30, 2007):

the law imposes."[7] Just nine years later, however, in 1965, the bishops at Vatican II declared, "We cannot fail to praise those who renounce the use of violence in the vindication of their rights ... And it seems right that laws make humane provisions for the case of those who for reasons of conscience refuse to bear arms, provided that they accept some other form of service to the human community."[8] That clear reversal of previous teaching developed in the span of less than a decade, a very brief time in church life. The influence of *Pacem in terris* as a sort of final testament of John XXIII had helped shift the way that Catholics thought about war.

Important Topics raised by *Pacem in terries*

In this section of my essay I would like to highlight three important themes of *Pacem in terris*. Those themes are human rights, the common good, and peace.

Human Rights

One astute commentator on the encyclical has observed that while the topic of *Pacem in terris* is peace, "the backbone of the document is its teaching on human rights."[9] That is, the encyclical offers a "distinctively Catholic approach to peacemaking," one that focuses on "the realization of human rights as the substance of peaceful world order."[10]

In paragraphs 8-27 Pope John provides the most comprehensive list of those rights that the church endorses in the modern era. John XXIII had been the Vatican nuncio in Paris during the period when the UN Declaration on Human Rights was being shaped. Any number of studies written about that period have noted that Angelo Roncalli was quietly encouraging the work on the Declaration, even as his boss, Pius XII, was expressing reservations about the lack of theoretical foundations being given for the UN statement.[11] For those who knew that background

---

7 Pius XII, "Christmas Radio Message" (December 23, 1956).

8 Vatican II, *Gaudium et spes*, (Pastoral Constitution on the Church in the Modern World, 1965), nos. 78-79.

9 Drew Christiansen, "Commentary on *Pacem in terris* (Peace on Earth)" in *Modern Catholic Social Teaching: Commentaries and Interpretations*, ed. Kenneth Himes, OFM (Washington, DC: Georgetown University Press, 2004), 217-243 at 223.

10 Ibid.

11 See Mary Ann Glendon, *A World Made New: Eleanor Roosevelt and the Universal Declaration of Human Rights* (New York: Random House, 2001), 13.

of Roncalli it was not a surprise that as John XXIII he provided a list of rights in *Pacem in terris* that closely mirrors those enumerated in the UN Declaration.

The reason John, and the Catholic social tradition in general, accepted an inclusive approach to human rights is that such rights are understood to be expressions of those conditions necessary for human beings to experience their dignity. Unlike the western liberal approach that sees personal liberty as the basis of rights, or the socialist tradition that considers equality as the foundation for rights, Catholic teaching adopts human dignity as the origin of all rights. The person requires a set of goods, freedoms, and relationships in order to flourish and attain full development. Seeing the dignity of the person as the source for human rights allows the church to embrace a more comprehensive roster of rights that challenges both liberal and socialist ideologies.

Years later, the papacy of John Paul II was an era not only of increased appeal to human rights in Catholic social teaching, but significantly increased and dramatic papal action on the topic. Through his extensive travels John Paul II knew the pluralism of societal models first hand. The daunting diversity of political, economic, social, and cultural institutions was undeniable, yet the pope was not hesitant in acting upon his role as universal pastor of the church. The challenge for John Paul, however, was how to formulate social teaching in a manner that permitted him to speak to widely disparate situations, for example Poland, the Philippines, Uganda, Brazil, and the United States. The primary way became the discourse of human rights.

John Paul used his teaching on human rights as a vehicle to assess, positively and negatively, the many different nations he visited in his travels. There might be significant differences between a gathering in Chicago or Manila but in both settings the pope could appeal to basic human rights to affirm or challenge his listeners. In effect, the human rights teaching of the papacy developed as an ethical framework that set limits, while permitting pluralism, in the way that a society organized itself.

Human rights can be understood as establishing a picture frame surrounding a canvas. Every society has the freedom to paint upon the canvas in a way that is most suitable given the history, culture, values, resources, and beliefs of the society. In fashioning a political system or economic system there is no single right way to do it, any more than there is only one way to paint a picture. However, whatever economic and political institutions and arrangements are fashioned, they cannot violate human rights. The painting cannot extend beyond the canvas and ignore the picture frame. There is legitimate pluralism within limits, and for matters of social life those limits are set by the framework of human rights.

In the face of twentieth century horrors such as World War II, the Shoah, the Gulag, and totalitarian regimes, the pope saw that the key for genuine politics was to establish it upon the firm foundation of an authentic humanism. For John Paul the agenda was to explicate how a Christian humanism might shape a better politics. In such a humanism, human rights plays a large part for they specify the social conditions that make human dignity possible.

In 1979 at the United Nations John Paul referred to human rights as a "humanistic criterion" for assessing all social systems.[12] Speaking before the United Nations he put the matter directly: "It is a question of the highest importance that in internal social life, as well as in international life, *all human beings* in every nation and country *should be able to enjoy effectively their full rights under any political regime or system*."[13] As the distinguished political scientist Samuel Huntington has observed, Roman Catholicism since Vatican II and particularly during the pontificate of John Paul II, became one of the dominant forces for advancing democracy and human rights in the world.[14] Such is the legacy of *Pacem in terris*.

Common Good

The second topic in *Pacem in terris* that I would like to highlight is that of the common good.

A major development in Pope John's letter is his employment of the idea of a universal or global common good. Aware of the phenomenon of interdependence the pope realizes that limiting the common good to the domestic society of the nation is no longer adequate. After all, "the social progress, order, security, and peace of each country are necessarily connected with the social progress, order, security, and peace of all other countries."[15] This growing transnational network that connects the fate of one nation with another leads the pope to a conclusion: "Given these conditions, it is obvious that individual countries cannot rightly seek their own interests and develop themselves in isolation from the rest . . ."[16]

The difficulty, however, is that even if national leaders were aware of the interdependent nature of international life, the existing policies and structures of the international community were unable to adequately address the challenges.

---

[12] John Paul II, "Speech to the 34th General Assembly of the United Nations" (October 2, 1979), n.17. Available at http://www.vatican.va/holy_father/john_paul_ii/speeches/1979/october/documents/hf_jp-ii_spe_19791002_general-assembly-onu_en.html

[13] Ibid. n.9, emphasis in original.

[14] Samuel Huntington, *The Third Wave* (Norman: University of Oklahoma Press, 1991), 76.

[15] *Pacem in terris*, n. 130.

[16] Ibid. n. 131.

The purpose of political authority is to protect and promote the common good. Existing state authorities have the resources and powers that allow them to fulfill those duties linked to their domestic or national common good. However, it does not appear to be true that it is a similar situation with the universal or global common good. As John said in *Pacem in terris*, "Today the universal common good poses problems of worldwide dimensions, which cannot be adequately tackled or solved except by the efforts of public authority endowed with a wideness of powers, structure and means of the same proportions: that is, of public authority which is in a position to operate in an effective manner on a worldwide basis. The moral order itself, therefore, demands that such a form of public authority be established."[17]

Key to the papal reasoning here is the last line of the quote: the moral order requires creation of a new kind of political authority. John's reasoning is traditional and direct. The purpose of all public authority is to protect and promote the common good within its jurisdiction. Ordinarily a town, city, county, state, or nation has the requisite power and ability to be reasonably effective in discharging its duty toward the common good. If it were chronically incapable of meeting that duty then a new structure of governance would be necessary to replace the failing institution. So if a state government cannot address issues of physical security the federal government steps into the void. When the structure of the nation-state is no longer able to satisfy the duty of protecting and promoting the universal common good a new structure is needed. The structural flaw in international politics is that there is no competent structure to do for the global common good what the national government does for the domestic common good.

When John introduced the idea of a universal or global common good in the encyclical *Pacem in terr*is, he was translating the traditional language from its local and national contexts to a new setting. He noted the existence of global problems that transcend the ability of any one nation to remedy them and the lack of any adequate transnational authority to address such problems. The pope did not call for a world-state but for creative means whereby existing public authorities might address global concerns in a fair and non-coercive way. John did not develop a fully adequate analysis of the global common good, but his insight prodded social theorists to consider those shared goods and bads that must be addressed at a transnational level. His language pointed out a necessary way of thinking as interdependence became a reality in the latter half of the 20th century.

Catholic social teaching sees globalization as a set of practices and institutions

[17] Ibid. n. 137.

that can and should be made subject to oversight by moral agents. In order for that to happen, however, there must be mechanisms for governance and regulation that take into account the new architecture of international relations. The old building blocks of nation-states have not disappeared but they now operate within a different context. States retain power yet they must wield that power in collaboration with other nations and non-state actors.

Globalization has taken some oversight power away from nations and placed economic actors in a more de-politicized global space. Just as with any other social space, however, there is a need for regulation, to codify rights and responsibilities. Honest, reasonable regulation is not an enemy of globalization but a necessity if there is to be avoidance of a backlash against the abuses of free-market capitalism. As Aquinas and other earlier thinkers knew, wherever there is society there needs to be governance.

Attention to the multiple levels of global society and the diversity of actors to be engaged in the life of that society suggests the need for greater interest in what Catholic social teaching calls subsidiarity. This traditional theme calls for keeping the capacities to assess, decide and act at the most local level possible while still being effective in securing the common good.

What is needed is a new framework within which forms of global authority may be conceived. This age of globalization requires the creation of institutions and practices for managing a different emerging world order. The challenge is to find an approach so that globalization may be regulated and directed. In his 2003 World Day of Peace message, John Paul II wrote:

> Is this not the time for all to work together for a new constitutional organization of the human family, truly capable of ensuring peace and harmony between peoples, as well as their integral development? But let there be no misunderstanding. This does not mean writing the constitution of a global super-State. Rather, it means continuing and deepening processes already in place to meet the almost universal demand for participatory ways of exercising political authority, even international political authority, and for transparency and accountability at every level of public life.[18]

John Paul returned to the theme in another speech later that same year. After listing several negative aspects of the present state of globalization, he called for guidelines that "will place globalization firmly at the service of authentic human development—the development of every person and of the whole person—in full respect of the rights and dignity of all." The pope continued by making clear

[18] John Paul II, "*Pacem in terris*: a Permanent Commitment," World Day of Peace Message (January 1, 2003), n.6.

that he did not see globalization in itself as the problem. "Rather, difficulties arise from the lack of effective mechanisms for giving it proper direction. Globalization needs to be inserted into the larger context of a political and economic programme that seeks the authentic progress of all mankind."[19] He then suggested to his audience that the time was ripe for a new international order.

Benedict XVI has also observed that due to "the unrelenting growth of global interdependence, there is a strongly felt need, even in the midst of a global recession, for a reform of the United Nations Organization, and likewise of the economic institutions and international finance." He went on to note that, "to manage the global economy; to revive economies hit by the crisis; to avoid any deterioration of the present crisis and the greater imbalances that would result; to bring about integral and timely disarmament, food security and peace; to guarantee the protection of the environment and to regulate migration: for all this, there is urgent need of a true political authority."[20]

The papal call for a new approach to global governance has been repeated by others, for it is widely acknowledged "change in our social and economic realities has outpaced change in the political institutions and processes that once firmly embedded them."[21] It is important to remember, however, that these calls for new forms of governance and political authority are not equivalent to support for one world government.

Several examples of new methods of regulation and agency reflect "globalization from below."[22] These include citizens' organizations and transnational networks combating climate change, promoting human rights, or supporting microfinancing. Grassroots activism on behalf of women's rights, public health services, and fair trade has forged links through globalized communications and travel.

While subsidiarity is needed, a renewed approach to that principle does not simply refer to vertical levels of authority interacting with each other, but horizontal interactions also with an array of organizations, institutions, and community groups, as well as governmental regimes.[23] Globalization's "democratic deficit" must be countered by ensuring that existing institutions are reformed and

---

19 John Paul II, "Address to the Pontifical Academy for Social Sciences" (May 2, 2003).

20 Benedict XVI, *Caritas in veritate* (Love in Truth, 2005), n.67.

21 John Coleman, "Making the Connections: Globalization and Catholic Social Thought," in *Globalization and Catholic Social Thought*, ed. John Coleman and William Ryan (Maryknoll, NY: Orbis Books, 2005), 9–27 at 14.

22 Lisa Sowle Cahill, "Globalization and the Common Good," in *Globalization and Catholic Social Thought*, 42-54 at 49–50.

23 Ibid. 50.

new ones designed with participation, transparency, and accountability in mind.[24] Organizations like the World Bank and International Monetary Fund "need to go through a radical change that would ensure the equal participation of both the rich and poor nations."[25] What is needed is global governance that provides the poor with access to power and voice in the regulation of globalization.

Questions such as, who rules?, in whose name?, by what means?, and for what goals?, are vital for the future of governance. It is clear that there are multiple stakeholders in globalization's governance, and each should be able to find some means of having input. The church will provide a genuine service if it can contribute to the formulation of an ethical framework that includes the legitimacy and usefulness of new models for subsidiarity, such as global policy regimes and networks, just as past reflections on subsidiarity contributed to our thinking about the nature, purpose, and role of the state in earlier eras.

Peace

Evident throughout John's encyclical, *Pacem in terris,* is the belief that peace is more than the absence of war. Peace is not what remains after war stops; rather it is a positive concept, something that requires positive action toward construction and maintenance of a certain type of social order. Key to understanding that social order is the notion of justice. That is why a significant development in the contemporary treatment of peace in Catholic teaching and practice is the evolution of the idea of justice.

When the bishops at Vatican II proclaimed that peace "is rightly and appropriately called 'an enterprise of justice' (Isa. 32,7)," it was with a particular view of justice in mind. It was biblical justice. This biblical idea is rooted, as is so much of Hebrew thought, in the experience of covenant. The fundamental reality for the pious Jew was that Yahweh had freely entered into a relationship with the Jewish people, marked by God's faithful and devoted love (*Hesed*). In those times when that fidelity and devotion was reciprocated by the Israelites the experience of covenant was that the Jewish people lived in a set of right relationships—with God, one another, and creation. Justice was the term used to characterize this state of being in right relationship.

---

[24] David Hollenbach, *The Common Good and Christian Ethics*, (New York: Cambridge University Press, 2002), 225.

[25] Vimal Tirimanna, "Globalization Needs to Count Human Persons," in *Catholic Theological Ethics in the World Church*, ed., James F. Keenan (New York: Continuum, 2007), 242-252 at 249–50.

Biblical justice is of a different nature than the way most Americans think of justice. Unlike the American idea of justice as impartial or "blind," the biblical concept of justice portrays Yahweh as being partial, with a clear bias in favor of the Jewish people in general and with the poor and marginal being a particular object of divine favor. This explains the prophet's regular citation of the treatment of the widow, orphan and alien as a test of the community. This biblical triad represents those people most at risk in a patriarchal and tribal society. In such a society, women and children without a spouse or father and aliens without kinship relations are understood as people on the margins of the community. So the test of a community's justice is whether those who might be easily neglected are instead brought into right relationship with others.

In modern Catholic teaching, this biblical perspective of justice informs the way that the church understands social justice. Community is at the heart of the Catholic vision of justice; establishing communities where people are able to live in right relationship with one another as well as with God and the rest of creation is the goal. Creating communal institutions and policies that reach out to and protect the marginal in modern societies is a key test of justice. When Catholic social teaching discusses a preferential option for the poor it is simply trying to retrieve the biblical idea of a special love and concern for those people who represent the contemporary version of widows, orphans and aliens in our societies.

When the bishops at Vatican II declared: "Peace results from that harmony built into human society by its divine Founder, and actualized by persons as they thirst after ever greater justice,"[26] they presumed an appreciation of the wider Christian tradition. One sees in this text not only the communitarian perspective of justice found in the Bible, but also the Augustinian theme of peace as an order of tranquility that eventuates from harmonious relationships.

It is with the above background that one can properly interpret Paul VI's famous statement in *Populorum Progressio* that "Development is the New Name for Peace."[27] When Paul VI surveyed the state of the globe in the late sixties, he concluded that the great social question of the time was the growing gap between rich and poor, both within states and between them. The gap is economic but also political as many experience a degree of powerlessness that prevents them from bringing about beneficial change.

For Paul VI the needed remedy was to assist the poor to undergo integral development, an approach that was not limited to the economic realm but would

---

26 *Gaudium et spes*, no. 78.

27 Paul VI, *Populorum progressio* (On the Development of Peoples, 1967), no. 76.

include all dimensions of human well being. An important aspect of such a holistic view of development is that the poor and marginal must be active agents of their advancement. What is needed is not a paternalistic charity that maintains the poor as passive objects of concern, but empowerment that enables them to participate in their development.

Justice as participation has become an important emphasis of Catholic social teaching. It suggests both the goal of justice as full participation in the life of a community, and the means to that goal, the empowerment of the poor as active agents. So development as the new name for peace must be understood as a certain kind of development process, one that is both just and participatory.

An additional item that can be added to this evolving understanding of peace as just and participatory development came nearly twenty-five years after John XXIII wrote his encyclical. In 1987 John Paul II, reflecting on the teaching of John XXIII and Paul VI's expansion of it, issued a follow-up encyclical on development stating that solidarity is "the path to peace and at the same time to development,"[28] adding a further nuance to the Catholic teaching on development as the name for peace. Solidarity provides an energy that fosters a desire to work toward a truly just and participatory development. From this work of solidarity in the pursuit of development will emerge genuine peace: "The goal of peace, so desired by everyone, will certainly be achieved through the putting into effect of social and international justice, but also through the practice of virtues which favor togetherness, and which teach us to live in unity."[29]

To summarize these comments on the evolution of Catholic thinking on peace, it is the outcome of a committed engagement (solidarity) to the project of social progress for individuals and societies (just and participatory development). The modern papacy has promoted this understanding by linking development as the new term for peace and solidarity as the crucial step in working for a just development. Solidarity is the path to development, and peace is the end result of working for a development that is integral, just and participatory.

Moving the Legacy of *Pacem in Terris* Forward

My third and final brief comment concerns the future, and an important item on the agenda for those who wish to carry the work of *Pacem in terris* forward. It is with the background above that one can see why the Catholic tradition has

[28] John Paul II, *Sollicitudo rei socialis* (On Social Concern, 1987), no. 39.

[29] Ibid.

become more and more interested in what is called peacebuilding. The just war tradition has focused on war-avoidance or war-limitation and the pacifist tradition on opposition to war. Peacebuilding takes a different tack and focuses attention on conditions for creating peace. It presumes, in agreement with the Catholic tradition, that peace is something positive not simply the absence of violence. As such, strategies to establish peace and advance its maturation can be devised and promoted.

The multiple levels of development demand that peacebuilding be understood broadly. Indeed, while some in the policy community identify several distinct tasks, the Catholic tradition stresses the way that the different tasks are related modes of working for peace and not separate stages that are hermetically sealed off from each other.

First, there is the realm of what can be called prevention, that is, identifying situations that might produce conflict and then through diplomacy removing the sources of violence before it erupts. A second concern entails peacemaking, efforts to resolve issues that have already led to conflict. Yet another task is peacekeeping, working to preserve fragile ceasefires or interim solutions in order to create space for implementing agreed upon measures to achieve a lasting change in tense relations. And, finally, there is building peace by means of renewing institutions and infrastructure destroyed by war, encouraging actions of mutual benefit to opposing groups, and addressing the larger cause of conflict found in economic, social, and political injustice.

Even as the emphasis on the proactive strategies for peacebuilding grows within Catholic thought on war and peace, there is a willingness to consider that the just war tradition continues to have relevance. In particular, there has been a recognition that armed force may be necessary to remove certain obstacles to peace, even if military force cannot be the sole cause of securing peace. The clearest illustration of the ongoing support for just war thinking within the church's teaching is the support expressed for what is called humanitarian intervention. The utility of military force to repel naked aggression against innocents, or to depose oppressive regimes engaged in extreme human rights violations such as genocide, continues to find support in Catholic social teaching.

Another aspect of the just war tradition is the convergence between peacebuilding and what has come to be called the *jus post bellum* category in just war theory. Traditionally, just war theory has been divided into two categories of concerns. The *jus ad bellum* addressed the question of when it was appropriate to go to war, under what conditions. *Jus in bello* took up questions of how to fight war, what strategies and tactics were morally defensible and what did not count as fighting fair. During the past fifteen years or so, a new set of concerns has arisen, how to end a war and what moral duties are incumbent upon combatants after a war is over.

This last set of concerns falls under a new heading, *jus post bellum*. Some interpretations of the rights and duties after war only address a narrow range of issues like war crimes or war reparations. But a more expansive view of *post bellum* obligations takes up issues of rebuilding and restoring infrastructure that is not only physical, for example, bridges and power grids, but also political and social, such as forms of government, legal systems, educational institutions. The presumption is that any attempt to return to the status quo prior to the war is neither possible—war is too destructive—nor wise, after all the status quo is what led to the conflict at the outset. Instead what is needed is an effort to create a better situation than had existed prior to the war. This is especially the case in humanitarian intervention where the avowed motive for the war was not to punish an aggressor nation but to assist an oppressed people in attaining a more humane life.

Seen in this way, developments in the just war tradition would appear to be moving in the same direction as the interest in peacebuilding with its aim of bringing about social transformation for the sake of avoiding conflict or restoring societies after conflict. However, thorny questions also accompany these developments. What changes and what level of assistance are moral duties for victors in war? In cases of civil war or intra-state conflicts, can the pursuit of justice in the face of war crimes exacerbate post-conflict tensions to the point that peacebuilding is less likely? What are the duties of an occupying force? What degree of ongoing intervention in the internal life of a people is justified by peacebuilding? Can outsiders demand political change that is not endorsed by large segments of the population? These questions suggest that, as helpful as the category may be, *jus post bellum* also creates a new set of issues about which thoughtful and fair-minded citizens can disagree.

For a tradition to be a living tradition it must have a "growing end." While rooted in the past it must engage the circumstances of the present. A living tradition permits not only the wisdom of the past to inform our response to the present, but for the present to elicit development in the tradition itself as it encounters new settings and new questions.

Clearly, an evolutionary process has been underway in Catholic thinking about peace that has led to seeing connections with the promotion of human rights and contributing to the global common good. Building upon the ancient wisdom of the Scriptures and the patristic writers, there has been further reflection on the nature of justice as it leads to peace. Justice, characterized by participation and solidarity, is what helps to bring about authentic development; and development is the new name for peace. A renewed appreciation for pacifism and nonviolence as strategies for advancing true peace is also notable. Within the just war tradition itself, the establishment of a presumption against war as part of Catholic teaching is an additional indication of ongoing change. Finally, the new concern for peacebuilding, which hearkens back to the traditional claim that peace is positive and not simply the absence of violence, gives additional evidence that Catholic teaching continues to evolve on the topics of peace and war since *Pacem in terris* in 1963.

Informed by all these new insights, dedicated disciples and faithful citizens can join in the spirit of good Pope John to address the difficult challenges that stand before us as American Catholics. By doing so, we will take seriously the words of our Lord, "Blessed are the Peacemakers, for they will be called Children of God" (Matt. 5,9).

Part III:

Mission and Dialogue – Among and With the Nations

10 The Where, Why, and Wherefore of Christian Mission Today – A Perspective from Asia

Peter C. PHAN

Two sociological facts are striking about Christian mission in Asia: it is one of the earliest missionary endeavors of the nascent church, if Saint Thomas's mission to India is a historical occurrence, and it is the least successful if the number of conversions is the criterion for judging the missionary enterprise. In this context, the questions of Where, Why, and Wherefore of Christian mission, especially in Asia, become more challenging and urgent than ever. I begin with a brief overview of the current socio-political, cultural, and religious context of Asia insofar as it impacts Christian mission. I next consider some key issues confronting the church's *missio ad gentes*. I end with suggestions on missionary activity in Asia today.

The Where of Christian Mission in Asia

Geographically, 'Asia' is the earth's largest landmass, stretching from the cluster of the former Soviet satellite states, whose names end with "*stan*" [land], in the west to Japan in the east, and from Mongolia in the north to Timor-Leste in the south and the Pacific Islands in the southeast. The map of Asia covers what is commonly called West (Central) Asia, South Asia, East Asia, and Southeast Asia but leaves out the Middle East. Asia is also the most populated continent, with slightly over half of the current world population of seven billion, China and India alone having a total of two and half billion. Today, roughly 60 out of 100 humans are Asians.

The question of "where" of Christian mission in Asia does not of course refer simply to geography. Rather, to use the famous adage "See, Judge, Act," it is necessary to "see" clearly the manifold realities of the Asian context in which Christian mission is to be carried out ("where"), before we can "judge" truthfully about the nature of Christian mission ("why"), and then "act" effectively to fulfill the mission of the church ("wherefore').

Mega-Migration, Mega-Urbanization, and Mega-Mediatization

In his presentation to the SEDOS Seminar in May 2011 entitled "The Asian Mission Landscape of the 21st Century," Pio Estepa, SVD, gives a comprehensive and informative social-scientific analysis of the Asian context.[1] He helpfully delineates three current megatrends in Asia, namely "mega-migration," "mega-urbanization," and "mega-mediatization." First, concerning mega-migration, in the decades following World War II, the main destinations of Asian migrations were the United States, Australia and New Zealand; after the 1970s they headed to the oil-rich countries of the Middle East. Within Asia, the countries that attract migrant workers were the so-called "tiger nations" (Hong Kong, Taiwan, Singapore, South Korea, Malaysia, and Thailand). These migrations were either voluntary, composed of contract workers and professionals, or forced, as the result of human trafficking and political upheavals. Second, with regard to mega-urbanization, Estepa notes that by 2030 more than half of Asians will be city-dwellers ("cityzens") in five megalopolises (i.e., Tokyo, Jakarta, Mumbai, Delhi, and Metro-Manila), each with a population exceeding 20 million (China will soon add more cities to the list). While mega-urbanization has reduced the poverty rate, especially in China and India (thanks to outsourcing and offshoring from the West), its high cost is environmental destruction. Lastly, regarding mega-mediatization, thanks to the ubiquity of electronic media, a new kind of Asians has emerged—the post-literate, media-savvy, high-tech "e-GenerAsians"—who constitute the majority of the Asian population. The main characteristics of this mediatized youth are the adoption of the "consumer culture" and the ability to communicate instantly with and understand the youth of other countries despite geographical distance and linguistic barriers.

While Estepa's description of these three megatrends in contemporary Asia is of great import for our reflections on the task of Christian mission among Asians, it must be supplemented by the familiar and still valid analysis given by the Federation of Asian Bishops' Conferences (FABC), according to which Asia is characterized by economic poverty, cultural diversity, and religious pluralism.[2]

---

1 Pio Estepa, SVD's presentation is available on the SEDOS website.

2 For the FABC's documents, see the four volumes titled *For All the Peoples of Asia* (1992, 1997, 2002, and 2007, the first edited by Gaudencio Rosales and G. G. Arévalo, and the last three by Franz-Josef Eilers) and published by Claretian Publications, Quezon City, Philippines. See also Peter C. Phan, ed., *The Asian Synod: Texts and Commentaries* (Maryknoll, NY: Orbis Books, 2002).

Economic Poverty and Cultural Diversity

As has been noted by Estepa, enormous progress has been made in the last four decades in raising the living standards in Asia. For instance, in the late 1970s, when economic liberalization was introduced in China, an estimated 30.7% of the Chinese population lived below the absolute poverty line; now only 2.8% do. Similarly, in the early 1990s, 39% of the Indian population lived under the absolute poverty line; now the number has dropped to 25%. While the benefits of globalization and its neo-capitalist economy are undeniable, they have not been evenly spread, and the divide between the rich and the poor in Asia, as has often been pointed out by economists and the FABC, has grown wider. Poverty remains widespread, especially in rural areas, with scarcity of jobs and lack of adequate health care and educational opportunities. This economic misery is systemic, causing, as noted above, widespread migration and urbanization, accompanied by ecological destruction, violation of human rights, and deleterious effects on family life. Among the social ills that are undermining Asian societies are unjust exploitation of unskilled labor, prolonged separation of family members, mail-order marriage, prostitution, sex tourism, and human trafficking, especially of children. In some countries, the caste system, military dictatorship, political oppression, ineffective government, and financial corruption exacerbate economic deprivation.

In addition to economic poverty, the richness and diversity of Asian cultures, a much-celebrated source of human development and societal cohesion, is being severely threatened by globalization and its consumer culture. The siren of the Western lifestyle, with endless accumulation of wealth and unbridled enjoyment of pleasures, with the constant creation of new desires and wants through advertisement, with glamorous celebrities held up as idols, is for the Asian youth a well-nigh irresistible call. To equip their citizens for successful competition in the global market, many countries in Asia are putting the acquisition of technical skills ahead of the ethical and spiritual formation of the whole person which was the hallmark of traditional education. English has become the "lingua franca," an absolute necessity for international communication, commerce, and diplomacy, to the detriment of local languages. Furthermore, family, tribal and national traditions and rituals are fast disappearing as quaint relics of a bygone age.

Socialist-Communist Regimes

Economic poverty and cultural impoverishment are perhaps nowhere more evident in Asia than in countries with a socialist-communist system, mainly China, Vietnam and North Korea. Long shut off from the West and its market economy, these countries experienced major upheavals when they began relaxing their grip on absolute political, economic, and religious control. As is well known, the relation between the Vatican and the Chinese government, as well as between the "Official" or "Patriotic" Church" and the "Unofficial" or "Underground" Church in China, and the modus vivendi of Christianity in Vietnam and North Korea present enormous challenges to how Christian mission is to be carried out. While both China and Vietnam are increasingly adopting the free market economy, their communist governments still regard Christianity, and especially the Catholic Church with its Vatican City State, as a threat, if not an enemy, to their survival.[3]

Lastly, there is a stubborn fact that despite centuries of Christian mission, Christianity in Asia still remains a very small minority. Except in the Philippines, Timor-Leste, South Korea and Vietnam, Christians make up only a tiny percentage of the population, especially in the three most populous countries, namely, China, India, and Indonesia. (Asian Catholics make up about 3.33% of the Asian population.) Though there are breathless reports about a vast number of conversions, especially in the Evangelical/Pentecostal Churches in China, mass conversions of Asians to Christianity are, barring an act of divine intervention, extremely unlikely.[4] Even if there were to be a massive evangelization in the future, the great majority of Asians will not convert to Christianity but will retain their own faiths. The main reason for this state of affairs, as Aloysius Pieris has pointed out, is that Asians already have their well-established religions.[5] This prognosis must not of course discourage mission work nor dampen missionary zeal. But it is important to take note of it so that missionaries will not entertain unrealistic expectations

---

3 For accounts of Christianity in China, see Edmond Tang & Jean-Paul Wiest, eds., *The Catholic Church in Modern China* (Maryknoll, NY: Orbis Books, 1993); Stephen Uhalley Jr. and Xiaoxin Wu, eds., *China and Christianity: Burdened Past, Hopeful Future* (Armonk, NY: M.E. Sharpe, 2001); Beatrice Leung & William T. Liu, *The Chinese Catholic Church in Conflict: 1949-2001* (Boca Raton, FL: Universal Publishers, 2004); Jean-Pierre Charbonnier, *Christians in China: A.D. 600-2000*, trans. M. N. L. Couve de Murville (San Francisco: Ignatius Press, 2007); and Philip L. Wickeri, *Reconstructing Christianity in China: K. H. Ting and the Chinese Church* (Maryknoll, NY: Orbis Books, 2007).

4 On Evangelical/Pentecostals in Asia, see Allan Anderson and Edmond Tang, eds., *Asian and Pentecostal: The Charismatic Face of Christianity in Asia* (Oxford: Regnum, 2005) and Wonsuk and Julie C. Ma, eds., *Asian Church & God's Mission* (West Caldwell, NJ: MWM, 2003).

5 See Aloysius Pieris, *An Asian Theology of Liberation* (Maryknoll, NY: Orbis Books, 1988).

and the lack of conversion and baptism will not be taken as evidence of the failure of Christian mission.[6]

The Why of Mission: *Missio Ad Gentes* in Asia

Christian mission, in the widest sense of the term, consists in bearing witness to the reign of God that has been inaugurated and realized, though not yet completed, by Jesus of Nazareth. This mission of the Trinitarian God (*missio Dei*), originating in the Father, realized by the Son, and brought to fulfillment by the Holy Spirit, is now taking place in the church in various forms, from announcement of the Good News to preaching, catechesis, theology, worship, pastoral care, and work for justice and peace.[7] Here I limit our consideration to the evangelization of non-Christians, and more specifically, to non-Christian Asians or the Asian *gentes*.[8]

Three Modalities of Evangelization: *Missio ad gentes, inter gentes, cum gentibus*

Christian mission to non-Christians used to be called, and still is in the documents of the papal magisterium, *missio ad gentes*.[9] Note the theological force of the

6 On the relation between mission and conversion, see Peter C. Phan, *In Our Own Tongues: Perspectives from Asia on Mission and Inculturation* (Maryknoll, NY: Orbis, 2004), 45-61.

7 Among the plethora of contemporary works on mission the following deserve mention: David Bosch, *Transforming Mission: Paradigm Shifts in Theology of Mission* (Maryknoll, NY: Orbis, 1991); J. Andrew Kirk, *What Is Mission? Theological Explorations* (Minneapolis: Fortress Press, 2000); Stephen B. Bevans and Roger P. Schroeder, *Constants in Context: A Theology of Mission for Today* (Maryknoll, NY: Orbis, 2004); Stephen Bevans and Roger Schroeder, eds. *Mission for the Twenty-first Century* (Chicago: CCGM Publications, 2001); Roger Schroeder, *What Is the Mission of the Church? A Guide for Catholics* (Maryknoll, NY: Orbis, 2008); Wilbert R. Shenk, *Changing Frontiers of Mission* (Maryknoll, NY: Orbis, 1999); Andrew Walls and Cathy Ross, eds., *Mission in the 21st Century: Exploring the Five Marks of Global Mission* (Maryknoll, NY: Orbis, 2008); Robert J. Schreiter, ed., *Mission in the Third Millennium* (Maryknoll, NY: Orbis, 2001); Francis Anekwe Oboji, *Concepts of Mission: The Evolution of Contemporary Missiology* (Maryknoll, NY: Orbis, 2006); Dana Robert, *Christian Mission: How Christianity Became a World Religion* Oxford: Wiley-Blackwell, 2009; Charles E. Van Engen, Darrell Whiteman and J. Dudley Woodberry, eds., *Paradigm Shifts in Christian Witness: Insights from Anthropology, Communications, and Spiritual Power* (Maryknoll, NY: Orbis, 2008); and Robert L. Gallagher and Paul Hertig, eds., *Landmark Essays in Mission and World Christianity* (Maryknoll, NY: Orbis, 2009).

8 For a survey of contemporary Asian Christianity, see Peter C. Phan, ed., *Christianities in Asia* (Oxford: Wiley-Blackwell, 2010).

9 See, for instance, Pope John Paul II's encyclical on mission *Redemptoris Missio* (1990). The

preposition *ad*. The *gentes*, that is, those who have not yet accepted the good news and are still to be incorporated into the church through baptism, were once termed 'pagans' or 'heathens,' and were regarded as the object or target of evangelization and conversion.

Though proselytism, that is, conversion of the *gentes* by physical force, psychological pressure, or material enticements, is frowned upon, the *gentes* are still thought to be those *to* whom the gospel is "proclaimed" and "preached." In *missio ad gentes*, the missionaries preach, the *gentes* listen; the missionaries teach, the *gentes* learn; the missionaries bestow the means of sanctification, the *gentes* receive them; the missionaries lead, the *gentes* follow; the missionaries command, the *gentes* obey.[10] In other words, the *gentes* are the beneficiaries of the threefold ministry—prophetic, priestly, and kingly—of the missionaries.

In contrast to *ad*, the preposition *inter* abolishes this one-way direction from the missionaries to the *gentes* in which the former enjoy superiority and dominance over the latter in all aspects of life, and radically reframes their relationships. It establishes fundamental interdependence and equal relationship between the two groups, Christian evangelizers and the Asian *gentes*. Mission is not something done by one group, i.e., Christian missionaries, *to* and *for* another, i.e., Asian non-Christians, but rather something carried by *both* groups to and for each other. Thus, instead of *missio ad gentes*, contemporary missiology speaks of *missio inter gentes*. Furthermore, mission in Asia is a collaborative work carried out by Christians and non-Christians *together* for a common cause so that *missio inter gentes Asiae* must also be *missio cum gentibus Asiae*.

Contemporary Challenges to Christian Mission in Asia

The social, cultural, and political megatrends discussed above bring about new challenges to Christian mission in Asia. As far as mega-migration, mega-urbanization, and mega-mediatization are concerned, according to Estepa, they create "divides," first, the *migrational* divide pitting nationals against migrants; second, the *industrial* divide separating rural communities from urban societies; and, third, the *informational* divide splitting the illiterates from the educated. Estepa argues that "*missio inter gentes* consists not in moving from the 'old' side of

pope laments the waning of *missio ad gentes* and devotes a whole chapter of his encyclical to it (Chapter IV: "The Vast Horizons of the Mission *Ad Gentes*").

10 I am not asserting that this is how all missionaries who adopt the *mssio ad gentes* model actually behave; in fact, many don't. I am only claiming that the *missio ad gentes* model of mission conceives, at least implicitly, the relation between the missionary and the *gentes* in this way.

a divide to venture into the newer other. Rather, it consists in building ecclesial 'bridges' between (*inter*) all the major divides." Furthermore, Estepa discerns in all the three divides both challenging and opportune trends for Christian mission. In light of these divides, Estepa proposes new fields for missionary endeavors in terms of *koinonia*, *diakonia*, and *kerygma*, and I will come back to them.

As far as economic poverty, cultural diversity, and religious pluralism are concerned, the FABC calls for integral human development (liberation), inculturation, and interreligious dialogue. These three activities are not to be understood as three separate and unrelated fields of Christian mission; rather, one cannot be effectively carried out without the other two. The common thread binding them together is the dialogical mode. Dialogue does not replace mission but is its fundamental and most effective modality.

In this complex and multifaceted situation of the *gentes Asiae*, what must be the why—tasks and objectives—of Christian mission in Asia? Of course, the answer depends largely on how certain key New Testament texts regarding the so-called missionary mandate are selected and interpreted, such as Matthew 28:19-10, Mark 16:15-18, Luke 24:47-48. Another possible approach is to examine both the teaching and the practice of the paradigmatic missionary, namely, the apostle Paul, as described in his letters and the Book of Acts.[11] While acknowledging the fruitfulness of these two ways, I propose a third, that is, examining the *missionary practice* of Jesus himself, and not only his words, during his public ministry as a whole. It is in the light of Jesus' practice of his mission that the above-cited biblical texts as well as Paul's teaching and practice can be correctly understood. Subsequently we will ask how Jesus' missionary practice can be a model for mission *inter gentes* and *cum gentibus Asiae.*

Peoples of Asia as *gentes*?

The first observation to be made with regard to the *missio ad gentes* in Asia is that paradoxically, in a true theological sense, Asians are not the *gentes* in the old meaning of this term, that is, 'pagans' or 'heathens.' The term *gens/gentes* has a long and complex history. It has its roots in the Hebrew *goy/goyim*, which was used to designate the 'nations,' that is, those peoples who, in Israel's view, have not been chosen to be in covenant with Yahweh, the non-Jews, the uncircumcised,

[11] There is no point in citing works on mission in the New Testament here since there are literally legions of them. For a massive, two-volume study, totaling to 3000 pages (quite a few of them with very small print!), see Eckhard J. Schnanel, *Early Christian Mission* vol. 1 *Jesus and the Twelve* and vol. 2 *Paul and the Early Church* (Downers Grove, IL: InterVarsity Press, 2004).

the impure. The Hebrew *goy/goyim* was translated with the Greek *ethne* (with the adjective *ethnikos*, meaning 'belonging to the nations'); in turn, *ethne/ethnikos* was translated with the Latin *gentes/gentiles.* Finally, the Latin *gentes/gentiles* is often rendered in English as 'pagan' or 'heathen.' 'Pagan' comes from the Latin *paganus*, literally, 'villager,' often in the pejorative sense of 'uncultured, 'as opposed to sophisticated 'city-dweller' or 'urban.'

From the third century, *paganus* was equated with 'non-Christian,' since the majority of Christians were city-dwellers. Soon, it acquired the connotation of idolatry and superstition and was applied to Hellenistic and Roman religions, which were regarded as rife with doctrinal errors, moral depravities, and idolatrous worship. After the discovery of the Americas and Asia, the term designates the indigenous religions of these continents, and their inhabitants are called the *gentes* (or *pagani*) and are considered as the primary target of Christian missions, the *missio ad gentes.*

In the aftermath of Vatican II, the Catholic Church's perception of the *gentes* and their religions has undergone a radical change. *Nostra Aetate* statement regarding non-Christian religions illustrates this theological shift well: "The Catholic Church rejects nothing of what is true and holy in these religions. It has a high regard for the manner of life and conduct, the precepts and doctrines which, although differing in many ways form its own teaching, nevertheless often reflect a ray of that truth which enlightens all men and women" (no. 2).[12] Compared with the older concept of *gentes*, Vatican II's description of the *gentes* and of the relation between them and the church represents as it were a Copernican revolution, and this sea change must be taken into account when we refer to Asians as *gentes* in either *missio ad gentes* or *missio inter gentes.* Clearly, we can no longer view Asians as people living in spiritual darkness and sin who cannot be saved except through conversion to Christianity, nor can we condemn their religions as human inventions corrupted by superstitions and vices. Needless to say, as will be argued shortly, this transformation entails a different understanding of the very Christian mission among the *gentes Asiae*.

[12] English translation is taken from Austin Flannery, ed., *Vatican II: Constitutions Decrees Declarations* (Northport, NY: Costello, 2007). For a comprehensive overview of Catholic theology of religion, see Karl J. Becker and Ilana Morali, eds., *Catholic Engagement with World Religions: A Comprehensive Study* (Maryknoll, NY: Orbis Books, 2010).

Missio inter gentes as Bridge-Building

Before exploring the tasks and objectives of Christian mission *inter gentes Asiae* in the light of Jesus' missionary practice, I would like to return briefly to Estepa's proposal that the building of bridges to join the two sides of the three divides together constitutes the primary task of Christian mission in Asia today. Without a doubt, the concept of bridge-building forms part of a "challenging" and "opportune" contemporary missiological trend. These bridges afford the opportunity for urban dwellers, nationals, and the educated to cross over into the communities of rural people, migrants, and the illiterates and vice versa. This crossing must be a mutual movement, a two-way traffic, so as to enable all the groups to communicate with each other and to live and work together for the common good, with equal rights and dignity. The ultimate goal of this crossing-over and mutual encounter is removal of all factors contributing to mutual hatred and reconciliation of the various groups living on the opposite sides of the three divides, in both society and church.[13] The hoped-for result is new human and ecclesial communities marked by justice, forgiveness, peace, and love. Needless to say, missionaries have an important role to play in promoting this bridge-building process and reconciliation.

Of course, bridge-building and reconciliation do not require forgetting, much less ignoring, past and current injustices committed by those having the power and means to control the crossing of the industrial, migrational, and informational divides and, in order to maintain their hegemony, bar others from coming over into their domains. On the contrary, genuine and long-lasting reconciliation is impossible without remembering the past truthfully, by both victimizers and victims, the former to acknowledge their guilt, and the latter to regain their human dignity in spite of their dehumanizing sufferings. Only from this truthful memory can both victims and victimizers work together to build a new society with legal and political structures promoting justice, equality, and reconciliation. Furthermore, this task of bridge-building does not in any way invalidate the "option for the poor" that was the hallmark of Jesus' ministry and has been repeatedly advocated by the FABC.

In addition to understanding *missio inter gentes* as bridge-building *between* the two sides of the three divides, I suggest that we take the preposition *inter* in

[13] On reconciliation as part of mission, see the numerous works of Robert Schreiter. See also Peter C. Phan, "Peace Building and Reconciliation: Interreligious Dialogue and Catholic Spirituality." *Peacebuilding: Catholic Theology, Ethics, and Praxis*, ed. Robert J. Schreiter, R. Scott Appleby and Gerard Powers (Maryknoll, N.Y.: Orbis Books, 2010), 332-365.

the phrase *missio inter gentes* to mean *among* or *in the midst of*, so that *missio inter gentes* means *reciprocal* mission between the missionaries and the *gentes Asiae*. In other words, mission is not a one-way activity, done by the missionaries to the *gentes*, but rather a two-way activity done by the *gentes* to the missionaries and by the missionaries to the *gentes*. It is therefore a *mutual* mission: Both the missionaries and the *gentes* "do mission" (as agents) and "are missioned" (as recipients). Furthermore, in addition to reciprocity between missionaries and the *gentes*, mission in Asia is performed *together*, so that *missio inter gentes* is also *missio cum gentibus,* which implies that there is a common cause to which both the missionaries and the *gentes* are committed and for which they labor together. I now explore these two aspects of *missio inter gentes* and *cum gentibus Asiae* in some detail.

Missio inter gentes as Mutual "Evangelization"

It is a widely common experience of mission in Asia (and of course also elsewhere) that in evangelizing the *gentes*, missionaries themselves are evangelized by them, and indeed, that the effectiveness of their mission work depends on the extent to which they are open to being evangelized by the *gentes*. By this I do not refer to the banal fact that there are *gentes* who are much wiser and holier, even by Christian standards, than the missionaries themselves, or that there are certain official actions by the church as an institution that the *gentes* deem immoral and therefore find no compelling reasons to join the church. I refer rather to the fact that in not a few areas of Christian life there are teachings and practices of the religions and cultures of the *gentes* that missionaries would do well to learn and practice in order to be a better Christian and missionary. Examples abound in areas such as sacred books, ethics, prayer, spirituality, and monasticism. This fact was recognized by luminaries such as Matteo Ricci in China, Roberto de Nobili in India, Alexandre de Rhodes in Vietnam, and countless other, lesser-known but no less effective, missionaries, both women and men, in the distant past as well as in the present.[14]

Recognizing and celebrating the goodness and holiness of people outside one's religious tradition and culture—the *goyim* or *gentes*—is not an invention of progressive missionaries. It was practiced by Jesus himself. Jesus praises the Samaritan leper who alone among the ten lepers whom he has cured comes back

[14] In this context it is vitally important, even a matter of sheer justice and historical accuracy, to recognize the role of lay women and women religious in mission. On this, see the pioneering works of Dana Robert.

to thank him (Lk 17:17-18). He also holds up a Samaritan as the model of love of neighbor (Lk10:33-35). Jesus is said to have been astonished or amazed by "such great faith" of the Roman centurion (Mat 8:10). That Jesus was—and did not pretend to be—"astonished" (*ethaumasen*) implies that the existence of such faith in a *goy* was something he did not expect or know. Thus, in a real sense, the Roman centurion's faith-filled behavior revealed to Jesus how universal God's saving grace is. Even more tellingly, the "great faith" (Mat 15:28) and perseverance of the Canaanite woman, in spite of Jesus' curt, even insulting, refusal to grant her request for her daughter's healing, and her humble retort that even "the dogs [a Jewish term of abuse for the *goyim*, which Jesus himself used] eat the crumbs that fall under their masters' table" (Mat 15:27) succeeded in changing Jesus' understanding that he was sent only to the lost sheep of Israel. Here, it is Jesus' ethnocentric understanding of his ministry that was changed and enlarged by a Gentile, and a woman to boot!

In their work, in light of Jesus' own practice, missionaries in Asia must be willing and able to open their minds and hearts to be changed intellectually and transformed spiritually by the "reverse mission" of the *gentes Asiae* to them. Admittedly, they are severely hampered in this by the fact that the traditional descriptions of mission as "teaching," "proclamation," "evangelization," and "conversion" that form part of the theology of *missio ad gentes* do not dispose missionaries to adopting a posture of listening and humility.[15] Indeed, if one comes to a foreign place with the conviction that one or one's church already possesses exclusively all the truths in all their fullness; that one's primary task is to "proclaim" these truths, as if standing at a pulpit or behind a lectern, with a megaphone in hand, and "teach" them like an all-knowing professor; and that the objective of one's mission is to "convert" the *gentes*, would it come as a surprise that the *gentes* are seen as nothing but targets of one's mission (as implied by the preposition *ad*) and that success in mission is measured by the number of baptisms, as victory in a war is demonstrated by the number of casualties and cities destroyed or occupied? Would it be strange that the *gentes Asiae* will look upon Christian mission as a neo-colonialist attempt to conquer and destroy their religions? How can we plausibly defend ourselves against this charge if in fact the goal of our mission is to convert the followers of other religions to Christianity?

In contrast, suppose, as a thought experiment, we no longer use terms that imply superior knowledge and moral excellence such as "evangelize," "convert,"

[15] On the relationship among proclamation and mission, see Peter C. Phan, *In Our Own Tongues*, 32-44.

"teach," and "proclaim" to describe the objectives and tasks of Christian mission, so prevalent in magisterial documents and used by theological watchdogs as a litmus test for orthodoxy? What would missionaries do and how would they act if they come to Asia not as proclaimers and teachers and converters and evangelizers but as guests—and uninvited, and even unwanted, guests at that—who totally depend for their physical and spiritual survival on the kindness and generosity of the *gentes* as hosts? What if we bring our Christian faith not as something to be proclaimed and taught in order to evangelize and convert the Asian *gentes* but as a humble gift, as a token of our gratitude for their hospitality, which our hosts have the perfect right to accept or refuse, use or not use? What if, as becoming of grateful guests, we do not insist that they abandon their beliefs and adopt ours, reject their moral norms and follow ours, condemn their rituals and practice ours, disown their religions and be baptized into ours? Suppose, with a sincere and humble heart, we let ourselves be "taught," "proclaimed," "evangelized," and "converted" by our hosts' beliefs, moral values, modes of worship, and religious affiliations because in fact there are things that are of great, or even greater, truth and value in these than in ours.[16]

Perhaps, someday, after we have known and trusted each other as friends, we can play host in our turn and invite the *gentes* as honored guests into our spiritual home, which we call 'church.' Then we can proudly display its splendor and *gemütlichkeit*, its welcoming atmosphere and warm hospitality. Then we can talk about our beliefs and practices; tell them our family history, from the ancient Hebrews to Jesus to us as Jesus' disciples, with our warts and all; and invite them to create with us a larger family made up of theirs and ours. But then we must reckon with the likelihood that as guests, they too will bring us their own gifts of faith, which may very well be of great use to us, or which we even may find that we are in need of very badly. In this way, our mission is no longer *ad gentes* but *inter gentes*. The "evangelizers" become "evangelized" and the "evangelized" become "evangelizers," in mutual respect and appreciation, in open honesty and genuine friendship, correcting one another when necessary, and always reaching out to greater truth and goodness.

[16] On the concept of the missionary as guest, see the insightful writings of Anthony J. Gittins. For example. *Gifts and Strangers: Meeting the Challenge of Inculturation.* New York: Paulist Press, 1989.

Missio cum gentibus: the "Reign of God" as our Shared Goal and Destiny

The above reflections on *missio inter gentes Asiae* may appear to some to deny the possibility and necessity of mission. In fact, however, what is denied is only that conversion, baptism and incorporation into the church should be conceived as the goal and fulfillment of mission. In other words, what is denied is not the possibility and necessity of mission as such. Rather it is denied that mission should be undertaken simply as *missio ad gentes,* and not primarily as *missio inter gentes.* What mission should intend to do is not simply making the *gentes* into members of our presently existing church, which with all its current beliefs, practices and institutions, is still too small and narrow in structural design, too limited and provincial (i.e., Western and Roman) in theological outlook, too imperfect and even sinful in institutional leadership, to offer the *gentes* a livable home.

Before we invite our guests into our home, even for a short visit, let alone for a permanent stay, we must, as good hosts, clean and spruce it up, even remodel and rebuild it, to meet their special needs and to make them feel welcome and comfortable. So too must we do with the church, and with the help with the *gentes.* It is also a common practice for the host to ask the guests in advance what kinds of food and drink they cannot eat and which they favor. So also must we do when we invite the *gentes* to come to (or into) the church, our spiritual home: Are there anything they find objectionable or harmful, anything to be modified and improved? In this way, our church will truly become the house of God for all peoples. Only in this way, I submit, the very goals of *missio ad gentes*, which are alleged to be denied by the above considerations, will be achieved, and even more effectively, by *missio inter gentes.* Of course, it is not guaranteed that the *number* of conversions will become thereby bigger, but no doubt the quality, that is, the depth and genuineness of faith will grow, and not least, the church itself will become more conformable to what God intends it to be.

Implicit in this theology of mission is the notion that mission is a collaborative enterprise in which both Christian missionaries and the *gentes Asiae* are engaged and which they help each other carry out. It may be objected that it is naive to expect the *gentes Asiae* to contribute to Christian mission. The point is well taken only if mission is conceived as *missio ad gentes*. Obviously the Asian *gentes* can hardly be expected to help missionaries expand the church. Nor should they be blamed for their suspicion and rejection of Christian mission that is geared toward what they perceive as a destruction of their religions by converting them to Christianity, notwithstanding the Catholic Church's official rhetoric about respecting the "elements of truth and grace" that may be found in their religions. (The Catholic Church would no doubt do as much if, let's say, Buddhists or Mormons or Protestants try to "steal its sheep," even though they may acknowledge "elements of truth and grace" in Catholicism.)

The situation would be completely different if mission is undertaken as *missio inter gentes*, since in this case the ultimate goal of mission and the final destiny of humanity are not the expansion of the church but the realization of the kingdom of God (*basileia tou theou*), however this reality is understood and named in various religious traditions.[17] To make the kingdom (or reign or rule) of God (or heaven)—and not the church—the ultimate goal of mission is not theological innovation. On the contrary, it represents fidelity to Jesus since there is no doubt that Jesus himself made the reign of God the center of his life and ministry. It is this total commitment to the reign of God that allowed Jesus to recognize that a man who drove out demons in his name, even though he was not one of his disciples ("not one of us," said John), was not against him but for him and should not be stopped from doing it, since driving out demons was part of working for the kingdom of God (Mk 9:38-40). Interestingly, there is no record that the exorcizing man ever knew Jesus personally, or that Jesus ever attempted to make him his disciple or required him to be one. It is thus possible (and indeed a fact) that a person can do something in the name of Jesus without knowing him or being his follower.

There is another reason why in Asia *missio inter gentes* must also be *missio cum gentibus.* I mentioned above both the tiny percentage of Christians among the Asian population and the unlikelihood of mass conversion of the Asian *gentes* to Christianity. This means that from a practical point of view Christians in Asia will never be able to effectively work for God's reign of justice, peace and reconciliation without the collaboration of the *gentes*. They simply cannot 'go it alone.' This is especially true in socialist-communist countries and in countries with Muslim majority, where Christianity lacks necessary resources and encounters severe restrictions to its mission. Thus, while the *gentes* cannot and must not be expected to work for the expansion of the church, they can be encouraged to work with Christians for the reign of God—however this reality is named, since Buddhists, for instance, do not even mention God— by promoting justice and peace, reconciliation and love. Indeed, in many places of Asia, they have in fact done so. Once again, it is to be noted that in *missio inter gentes* and *cum gentibus*, the goals of Christian mission can be amply fulfilled, without the *gentes* being converted, bap-

[17] On the symbol of the kingdom of God in mission, see Peter C. Phan, *Christianity with an Asian Face* (Maryknoll, NY: Orbis Books, 2003), 75-97.

tized, and incorporated into the church. Of course, there is no opposition between church and the reign of God. In fact, the former is a sign and instrument, or sacrament, or symbol of the latter. But it would be idolatrous to identify the church with the reign of God. It is the difference between the two that enables the *gentes Asiae* to work for the kingdom of God and yet not belonging to the church, *reapse* [in fact] or *in voto* [in desire].

The Wherefore of Christian Mission: Doing Things "In the Name of Jesus"

Christian mission presupposes seeing accurately and judging truthfully. However, these are only conditions for acting effectively in mission. Mission itself must be acting, doing concrete things, and not just preaching and proclaiming and teaching, even though these do constitute mission provided that they are done in the way of *missio inter gentes et cum gentibus* as proposed above. But mission must involve much more than *verbal* activities and deeds by words, important though they may be. No doubt the Western churches heavily favor the use of words and speeches and books, and, not to fall behind the time, Websites and Facebook and Twitter. Witness the tsunami of documents and pronouncements of all kinds emanating from the Roman magisterium, not to mention papal autobiographies and theological tracts, inundating churches that hardly have the time and ability to read and understand them, written as they often are in a theological idiom well-nigh incomprehensible to the average people. Sadly, some think that in issuing these documents the magisterium is fulfilling its 'prophetic' or teaching mission.

Mission as action involves of course much more than producing this deluge of words. Mission demands, at least in Asia, as much if not more, non-verbal actions. Silence, profound and contemplative, that follows speaking, still remains the most effective communication among believers. In addition, mission includes actions for liberation and development, human rights, social justice, peace and reconciliation, education, and health care, just to mention a few areas in which missionaries in Asia, both Catholic and Protestant, have labored long and well, sometimes at the risk of their own lives.

The question inevitably arises as to how to distinguish these activities as part of Christian mission from those of social activists and NGOs of various kinds. Underlying this question is the anxiety, especially among church authorities, that missionaries have become mere secular social activists and have lost what is called the "vertical" dimension of Christian mission. In response, let it be noted first of all that from a sociological point of view, there are no differences between the activities of missionaries and those of social activists in these areas. The former are not nobler, holier, or more effective than the latter simply because they are done by the church, nor should they be played against each other. Instead of competition for resources and influence, there should be collaboration between church agencies and secular groups.

Secondly, these social activities must not be viewed simply as—to use a common expression of the recent past— "pre-evangelization" (to be done by the laity, mostly), that is, a prelude to or means for "real" evangelization through preaching, sacramental celebrations, and pastoral leadership (the reserved province of the ordained). Rather, they are a constitutive and integral part of mission in which the *gentes* can fully participate.

Thirdly, the difference between church mission and social activism is not between the alleged "verticality" of the former and the "horizontality" of the latter, nor between the former's concern for salvation of the soul and the latter's concern for the welfare of the body. In fact, the one cannot be obtained in its fullness without the other. Rather the distinctiveness of Christian mission lies in the fact that it is performed "in the name of Jesus." This, as we have seen above, does not mean: with an explicit knowledge of Jesus or membership in his circle of disciples. Much less does it mean: with the official authorization or "mandatum" by the church hierarchy, or with the powers associated with the sacrament of orders, or with the spiritual sacrifices of religious vows. Rather, mission done "in the name of Jesus" means mission carried out in the way Jesus did and for the cause for which he lived and was killed, that is, the reign of God. Thus, the distinction between mission and social activism does not lie in *what* is being done and in the alleged spiritual superiority of the former over the latter, but in *how* mission is done (i.e., in Jesus' way of self-emptying and powerlessness) and *why* it is done (i.e., for the sake of the reign of God).

In summary, to carry out their mission, Christians must *see* accurately, *judge* truthfully, and *act* effectively. Mission in Asia requires that we know who the *gentes Asiae* are in their contemporary socio-political and religious contexts; that we do mission among them (*inter gentes*) and with them (*cum gentibus*); and that we work together for the reign of God. Because the goal and destiny of mission is the kingdom of God, mission is not ours nor the church's. It is rather the mission of the Trinitarian God (*missio Dei*), which the Father initiates, the Son performs, and the Spirit fulfills, for the sake of reconciling all things in God and a sharing in God's eternal life. All humanity—including the *goyim/ethne/gentes/pagans*—is called to participate in this mission, and the church is but a sacrament of the *missio Dei*, and we the unworthy servants.[18]

[18] The substance of these reflections on Christian mission in Asia was presented in my address during the May 2011 SEDOS Seminar entitled "Mission *Inter Gentes Asiae*: Contemporary Theologies and Practices of Mission in Asia," available on the SEDOS website.

11 Christian Communities in the Middle East and Islam: A Shift in the Understanding of Mission among Eastern Catholic Churches

Michel Elias ANDRAOS

> Traders, missionaries, Western citizens living in the [Ottoman] Empire, and soon Eastern Christians too, all found themselves placed under the protection of the French kings. Gradually a tradition of French protection of Eastern Christians was formed. . . . In the middle of the eighteenth century France was recognized by the Holy See and by the European powers as the protector of Christians affiliated to Rome. (Joseph Maïla)

Introduction

Christian communities in the Middle East continue to exist in many geographical locations uninterrupted since the beginning of Christianity. Without being at least mindful of this long and complex history and presence, one cannot talk about Christianity in the Middle East. The local Christian communities in the region are very mindful of this reality.

In the modern period, that is during the last five centuries, since the domination of the region by the Ottoman Empire, particular social and political developments began to take place that continue to have an impact on the present day Middle East, and that would be important to understand in order to make sense of the reality today. Two of these developments are particularly relevant to my topic. The first is the new relations and power dynamics between European Christian powers and the Christian communities in the Near East, which significantly affected the worldview of Eastern Christians, particularly in relation to Islam. The second development is the making of the Middle Eastern Christian communities into *millets,* or sects, that is autonomous groups with distinct political and ethnic identities and representations based on belonging not just to a religion, but also to a particular denomination. Originally designed for managing religious diversity in the Ottoman Empire, the *millets* became a problem in the modern nation states. These processes of social formation, identified later as sectarianism by scholars and historians, survived the Ottoman period and were reinforced by Western European colonial powers after the end of the World War I and the defeat of the

Empire.[1] In the opinion of many scholars, what is today commonly referred to as "Christian minorities," or rather minoritized Christians in the Middle East, is a direct outcome of the politics of sectarianism, which began during the late Ottoman period and became institutionalized with the new artificially created nation-states in the region in the aftermath of World War I. After that war, notes historian Kamal Salibi, both the French and the British cheated the Arabs and failed to keep their promises. They artificially partitioned the region in service of their own colonial interests. None of the newly created five countries (Syria, Lebanon, Palestine, Jordan and Iraq) had a coherent or uncontested national project. In Salibi's words, "all five of these countries were artificial creations established and given their initial organization by foreign imperial powers." This, maintains the author, was a new geographical and historical reconfiguration of the region.[2] According to historian Ussama Makdisi, sectarianism, like the new nation-states, is also a colonial construction and is not the product of the newly created nations and nationalisms; rather, it is the other way around. Makdisi argues

> Although it is constructed as the dark deviant underside of the nationalist narrative, sectarianism is a nationalist creation that dates back no further than the beginnings of the modern era when European powers and local elites forged a politics of religion amid the emerging nation-state system.[3]

The formation of group identities and self-understanding of communities along "religious" lines existed in the Middle East since immemorial times, but that took on a new function in the modern nation states. The development of sectarian identities as we know them today is a modern and colonial construction in response to a modern problem, as historian Ussama Makdisi would argue.

My final introductory remark is about the term *Near* or *Middle East*, which is used in multiple ways to convey different meanings and representations. The word "East" in Middle or Near East immediately locates the region at a periphery in relation to a center: East of what? The invention of the Middle East as we know it today, similar to the inventions of other regions and continents is a relatively

---

1 On the particular notion of sectarianism among the Christian communities in the Middle East see Bruce Masters, *Christians and Jews in the Ottoman Arab World: The Roots of Sectarianism* (Cambridge University Press, 2004); Ussama Makdisi, *The Culture of Sectarianism: Community, History, and Violence in Nineteenth-Century Ottoman Lebanon*, 1st ed. (University of California Press, 2000); Laura Robson, *Colonialism and Christianity in Mandate Palestine* (Austin: University of Texas Press, 2011).

2 Salibi, *A House of Many Mansions*, 29–31.

3 Makdisi, "Reconstructing the Nation-State: The Modernity of Sectarianism in Lebanon," *Middle East Report* (September 1996): 26.

recent construction; it dates back to the modern European colonial era. There are many conflicting inventions in the region, some old and some new, but getting into these histories is beyond the scope of this paper.[4] I will limit my essay to the Christian communities in what is generally known as the Levant (the countries on the eastern part of the Mediterranean), or the Near East, but I will continue to use the term "Middle East" simply because it is the most commonly used name of the region, despite the fact that it is problematic.

This essay has four parts. The first part briefly points to some key historical moments that influenced the self-understanding of Middle Eastern Christian communities and the formation of sectarian identities. This section of the study serves as a background for understanding the recent shift in the official teaching of some Middle Eastern churches in relation to rethinking their identity and mission in the region, which is the focus of part two. Part three presents an overview of some recent discussions on the elaboration of a contextual Arabic theology that is relevant to the new challenges of the churches and their mission. Part four offers a summary of the debates that are relevant to the main theme before and during the recent Special Assembly of the Synod of Bishops for the Middle East (October 2010). The study concludes by offering some remarks on current trends and the future of the mission of the churches in the Middle East.

Minoritization of the Middle Eastern Christian Communities

The relationship between European powers and Middle Eastern communities is very old and goes back to the period of the Roman Empire. In the modern period I referred to above, that is since the early sixteenth century, agreements, known as "Capitulations," were made between the Ottoman Empire and Western powers to grant certain privileges to their citizens and protect their interests and institutions in what is known today as the Middle or Near East. These Capitulations, notes historian and social scientist Joseph Maïla,

---

4 I am thinking here in particular of the works of Enrique Dussel and Walter Mignolo on the invention of Latin America that inspired part of my thinking about the invention of Middle East. See Enrique Dussel, *The Invention of the Americas: Eclipse of "the Other" and the Myth of Modernity*, trans. Michael D. Barber (Continuum, 1995); Walter D. Mignolo, *The Idea of Latin America*, 1st ed. (Wiley-Blackwell, 2006); The works of Benedict Anderson, *Imagined Communities: Reflections on the Origin and Spread of Nationalism* (Verso, 2006), and Shlomo Sand, *The Invention of the Jewish People* (Verso, 2010) are also helpful for understanding how within particular communities mythology about ancient history, ethnicity, religion and nationalism were used for inventing new political identities.

> began to be influenced by strong supremacist tendencies, which took them out of their specific technical, and legal context, and gave them a stronger political connotation. Traders, missionaries, Western citizens living in the Empire, and soon Eastern Christians too, all found themselves placed under the protection of the French kings. Gradually a tradition of French protection of Eastern Christians was formed.... In the middle of the eighteenth century France was recognized by the Holy See and by the European powers as the protector of Christians affiliated to Rome.[5]

Understanding how the subsequent colonial encounters with Western Christianity over many centuries have influenced the formation of the worldview and self-understanding of Middle Eastern Christian communities, particularly in relation to Islam, is crucial for understanding the Christian theology of Islam and the present Muslim-Christian relations in the Middle East. Makdisi, known for his pioneer work on American missionaries in the Middle East,[6] argues, among others, that essentializing the difference with Islam and the Muslim communities, as we know it today, is a product of nineteenth and early twentieth-century French and British colonial politics in the region. European powers, notes Makdisi, "singled out the Christian communities of the Ottoman Empire for special protection from the Muslim population."[7] He writes,

> European insistence on essential differences between Christianity and Islam provided one of the key legitimating factors to their intervention in the Middle East. [Belgian Jesuit] Henri Lammens' vision was a poignant example of French colonial ideology that used invented cultural and historical narratives of the Lebanese "nation" to justify the imposition of the mandate system in the Middle East ...[8]

Salibi has also argued that Lammens and his negative views on Islam strongly influenced both French politics and the Christian elites who studied under him at the Jesuit University in Beirut, where he taught oriental studies.[9] In the opinion of many analysts, the European colonial influence in the nineteenth and early twentieth centuries had a strong impact on shaping the culture of the Christian commu-

---

5 Joseph Maïla, "The Arab Christians: From the Eastern Question to the Recent Political Situation of the Minorities," in *Christian Communities in the Arab Middle East: The Challenge of the Future*, ed. Andrea Pacini (Oxford: Clarendon Press, 1998), 34–35.

6 Ussama Makdisi, *Artillery of Heaven: American Missionaries and the Failed Conversion of the Middle East* (Cornell University Press, 2009).

7 Ussama Makdisi, "Reconstructing the Nation-State: The Modernity of Sectarianism in Lebanon," *Middle East Report* (September 1996): 24.

8 Ibid., 25.

9 Kamal Salibi, *A House of Many Mansions: The History of Lebanon Reconsidered* (University of California Press, 1990), 130–150.

nities of the Middle East, particularly those associated with the Roman Catholic Church, in two main ways: (1) negative view of Islam, and (2) dependency on the West for protection as "threatened" Christian minorities. Joseph Maïla rightly points out that

> The constant concern shown by the European consuls for the Christian minorities, attested in numerous diplomatic documents, as well as the number of times they intervened on their behalf at the Sublime Porte, turned them into political patrons of Europe, and made them extremely dependent psychologically on the West. From minorities within the [Ottoman] Empire, Christians became children of the West.[10]

The heavy interference by European powers—and later the U.S., including churches, missionaries and educational institutions—played a significant role in the nineteenth and twentieth centuries in building particular relationships of patronage with the elites of the Middle Eastern Christian communities, which, as pointed above, contributed to the construction of both the attitude of superiority and the "minority in need of protection" identity.[11] The cultural dynamics that contributed to creating an attitude of superiority vis-à-vis Islam and Arab culture, have also, paradoxically, simultaneously created a sense of isolation and fear in these communities.

The historical developments briefly described above have also influenced the thinking of many Eastern Catholic bishops during the early decades of the twentieth century. At the time of the partition of the Middle East after World War I, the Maronite Patriarch, Elias Houayek, who led the delegation that represented the Christian and Muslim communities of what later became Lebanon and Syria at the Peace Conference in Versailles in 1919, emphasized the Phoenician origin of the Christians of the region with an intention to separate them from the Arab and Muslim communities.[12] Historian Asher Kaufman notes that at the Peace Conference the Maronite Patriarch "ethnically tied the Maronites to the French through the ancient Phoenicians by attributing the origins of the Crusaders to the ancient Phoeni-

---

10 Maïla, "The Arab Christians: From the Eastern Question to the Recent Political Situation of the Minorities," 40.

11 Obviously, not all Western missionaries thought the same, and many were promoters of the study of Islam and Arab civilization and culture. Many also had a much more positive attitude to Islam and Arab culture than some Middle Eastern Christians. Their names are too many to mention here.

12 See the chapter "Phoenicia Resurrected," in Salibi, *A House of Many Mansions*, 167–181; Makdisi, "Reconstructing the Nation-State: The Modernity of Sectarianism in Lebanon," 24; and Asher Kaufman, "Phoenicianism: The Formation of an Identity in Lebanon in 1920," *Middle Eastern Studies* 37, no. 1 (January 2001): 185.

cians, which, according to him, had established colonies on the French coast from which the Crusaders departed to the Levant."[13] Phoenicianism and similar other ideologies from that period are still alive among some Christian groups in the Middle East today. Inventing a mythology about their ancient origin in service of a constructed ethno-religious identity played an important role in the formation of minority identity among different groups in the Middle East region.

A Shift in the Pastoral Teaching and Attitude of the Eastern Catholic Churches since the 1990s[14]

The heads of the seven Oriental churches in communion with the Roman Catholic Church (Coptic, Melkite, Syriac, Maronite, Chaldean, Armenian and Latin) met together in August of 1991 for the first time as a group to discuss the pastoral situation of their communities in the Middle East. They later formed together the Council of Catholic Patriarchs of the East.[15] The pastoral letter they issued at the end of their first meeting reflected a significant development in the collaboration between the Catholic churches in the region. In the introduction to the letter, the Patriarchs noted that they were meeting at a crucial moment in the history of the region. The moment they referred to is the creation of the "new world order" and its impact on the Middle East in the aftermath of the first Gulf war. In that particular historic moment, the Patriarchs wanted to emphasize the importance of the relation between Christians and Muslims as indigenous peoples of the region. The letter articulated a new understanding of the presence of the Christian churches in the Middle East and the relation with Islam, which was one of the Patriarchs' main concerns. "We Christians and Muslims of the Middle East," notes the letter,

> drink from one cultural heritage that we share and to which we each contributed in our unique own way. ... God, exalted be his wisdom, willed us to be together in this part

13 Kaufman, "Phoenicianism," 185.

14 Other less developed versions of this section of the essay were previously published in the following articles: "Christian Churches in the Middle East and Islam: 'Standing Together before God and History'," *New Theology Review* 23, no. 3 (August 2010): 50-61; "Christian Communities and Islam in the Middle East: A Shift in the Self-Definition of Eastern Catholic Churches," *The Ecumenist* 48, no. 3 (Summer 2011): 1-4.

15 The meeting took place in Lebanon from August 19-24, 1991 and was hosted by the Maronite Patriarch. The main purpose of the meeting was to discuss the newly approved Canon Law of the Oriental Churches, but the pastoral situation of the Christian churches in the region became an important part of the agenda.

> of the world. We fully accept his will and hope that it will help us open our hearts to include everyone, regardless of their different belonging.[16]

Two other pastoral letters, issued in 1992 and 1994 respectively, focused in particular on the relations between Christians and Muslims and the mission of the churches in the Middle East. These three pastoral letters, in my opinion, inaugurated a new era in the official teaching to the Catholic communities of the Middle East about their relation to Islam and the Muslim communities. This new teaching and attitude toward the Muslim communities and Islam has been consistent in the pastoral letters of the Eastern Catholic bishops since the early 1990s.

Describing living together with Muslims as "God's will for both communities to be together" is a new language that was never so clearly used before by such an official Catholic forum in the Middle East. In this new teaching, we notice a shift from a previous understanding of coexistence with Islam as a "cross" that needs to be accepted to a new understanding of living together as the will of God and a call to mutual acceptance and shared responsibility for the common good of all.[17] Similar teaching was repeated in the second pastoral letter, "The Christian Presence in the Middle East: Witness and Ministry," issued on Easter 1992. In this document, the Catholic Patriarchs affirm that the mission of their churches is not to convert Muslims to Christianity, but rather to collaborate for the wellbeing of all as communities of faith who share a long history and many centuries of life together. Christians believe, reiterates the pastoral, that it is God's will for Muslims and Christians to live together in that part of the world.[18] The shared cultural identity of both religions is emphasized again in paragraph 48:

> The Christians of the East are part and parcel of the Muslim cultural identity as the

---

[16] The pastoral letters of the Council of Catholic Patriarchs of the Middle East are published by the General Secretariat of the Council, Bkerké, Lebanon. Most letters are available online in Arabic and French at www.opuslibani.org.lb/cpco/img006.htm. All translations to English are mine, unless indicated otherwise.

[17] There is a parallel teaching in the Qur'an: "O Mankind! We created you from a single (pair) of a male and a female, and made you into nations and tribes, that you may know each other (not that ye may despise each other). Verily the most honoured of you in the sight of Allah is (he who is) the most righteous of you. And Allah has full knowledge and is well-acquainted." 'Abdullah Yusuf 'Ali, *The Meaning of The Holy Qur'an*, 10th ed. (Amana Publications, 1989), v. 49:13. The pastoral letter of the patriarchs does not make reference to this Qur'anic verse; this is only an observation by the author.

[18] Many Muslim leaders share a similar official position towards Christians. See Imam M.M. Shamsuddin, *Muslim Christian Dialogue: Toward a Project of Shared Struggle (in Arabic)* (Beirut, Lebanon, 2004). Imam Shamsuddin was the highest Shi'a religious authority in Lebanon until his untimely death in 2001. This is just one of many examples.

> Muslims in the East are an inseparable part of the Eastern Christian cultural identity. In this sense, *we are both responsible for each other before God and history*. (My emphasis)

The third letter, "Together before God for the Wellbeing of the Human Person and Society: Living Together as Muslims and Christians in the Arab World," issued two years later on Christmas of 1994, affirms the same historical analysis and vision for a shared future and includes some concrete pastoral recommendations for collaboration in areas of common concern in social and public life. The core message of the letters, that the Patriarchs repeatedly affirm, is that the Christian churches in the Middle East are not communities coming from outside with a mission to the Muslim world, rather they are an integral part of the region's history and cultures, and they share the responsibility for building its future and work for the common good of all.

According to the Patriarchs, these letters are presented as pastoral documents for theological reflection in the context of the new challenges facing the Arab world. The challenges mentioned in the documents include the tension between tradition and modernity, political instability, social and economic development and poverty, religion and society, freedom of religion and conscience, issues of justice, peace and human rights. In addition, the Catholic Patriarchs highlight the urgent political problem of the Palestinian situation, which they say has an international dimension and has deeply troubled the region "while the Palestinian people continue to be victims of injustice, humiliation and suffering." The Patriarchs also mention concern for the situation in Iraq and other conflicts in the region. These problems are shared concerns among all the peoples of the Middle East; they are not only concerns for Christians, affirm the pastorals. None of the major issues of concern mentioned in these letters has been resolved since the writing of the documents, more than two decades ago. On the contrary, there have been more wars, occupations, refugees, internal displacement and migration, poverty, and less hope for peace. The popular uprisings in the Arab world that began in January 2011 open new possibilities of hope for change, but it is too soon to predict the concrete outcome of these movements. The current international intervention in the region, in the opinion of many analysts, is yet another *déjà vu* colonial episode.

The new pastoral approach expressed in these pastoral letters, which are the fruit of a long experience of the churches of the Middle East, is in my opinion a breakthrough similar to what happened in *Nostra Aetate*, the Second Vatican Council declaration on the relation of the Roman Catholic Church to other religions. It took the Catholic bishops of the Middle East another 25 years after the Vatican Council to write their own *Nostra Aetate.* However, in these pastoral letters, the Patriarchs pushed the boundaries of the theological vision of *Nostra Aetate* by articulating a mutuality with Islam based on a new interpretation of their pastoral experience and the context of their local churches, and on an emerging theology that was not imaginable a few decades earlier. I will say more on this theology in the following section.

One of the influential voices in pushing these boundaries has been Gregorius III Laham, the Melkite Patriarch. In the Middle East, he notes, "This Church of the Arabs, that is of the Arab world, culture and society, is a Church of Islam; it is in constant interaction with Muslims, suffers and rejoices with them, builds hope and grows with them, and loves and serves together with them."[19] The concept of a "church of Islam," or a "church with Islam," is not totally new to the Melkite Patriarch. In his pastoral letters and public interviews, since he was elected Patriarch in 2000, he often used the term "church of Islam" as a way of talking about the vocation of the Eastern Arabic churches among the Muslim communities in the Middle East. For Patriarch Laham, the church of Islam, as I understand it, simply means a church fully incarnated in the Arabic, Islamic culture that is able to articulate its witness in a way understandable to rather than in confrontation with Muslims.

There is no denial on the part of these Christian leaders that there are incidents of confrontation and persecution in certain parts of the region, but they affirm that the overall situation is not one of Christian minorities persecuted for their faith struggling to defend their presence.

An Emerging Arab Christian Theology

Many Middle Eastern theologians today acknowledge that there is no clear articulation of an Arabic Christian contemporary theology. There is no local theology yet, they argue, that is rooted in the experience of their communities; a local theology that gives expression to the lived faith of these communities in a language, not only understandable in their cultural context, but that also articulates a response,

[19] The quotation is from a lecture delivered by Patriarch Laham at the University of Cambridge, October 12-15, 2008, at a conference in commemoration of the first anniversary of the publication of *A Common Word Between Us and You*, the letter by 138 Islamic scholars, clerics and intellectuals addressed to Pope Benedict XVI after his Regensburg lecture. Patriarch Laham, along with other Melkite bishops, has been publically engaging *A Common Word* in the Arab world and beyond. See www.acommonword.com.

from a Christian faith perspective, to the challenging religious and social issues facing all the peoples of the Middle East today. This theology is yet to be developed, according to these theologians.[20] Discussing the absence of such a theology has been a topic of many conferences and meetings over the past decades.[21] I will examine below one instance of such meetings and summarize the debate on this topic to give just one example of this emerging theological endeavor.

A group of mostly Middle Eastern theologians and church leaders, Catholic and Orthodox, including also some Muslim scholars, met in 2002 to reflect on how to construct a contemporary Arabic Christian theology. They discussed the obstacles that have so far prevented the emergence of a theological discourse that reflects the experience of the Christian communities in the Middle East today. They also explored the potential contribution of such a discourse to Christian-Muslim relations in the present context of the region.[22] In the words of one key participant, the main aim of the conference was to discuss

> how to articulate the continuity of our Christian faith in a way that is appropriate to our Arabic culture? ... Our reality is that we live in an Arabic, Islamic environment ... The theological discourse must be addressed to this Arabic and Islamic culture, and be immersed in it. It also means that this discourse should have as a starting point, on the one hand, dialogue with the Qur'anic Islamic thought, and on the other, the Arab heritage and civilization.[23]

Theologian Mouchir Aoun, a main speaker at the conference and prolific writer on this topic, argues that "The essence of an Arabic, Christian theological discourse that aims to meet Arab Christians in their struggle has to be a local and contemporary discourse, that has as its main characteristics belonging to its place and time, and engaging the multiple ways of active witness to faith."[24] By active witness the author means a response by the Christian churches and communities to the concrete social and political struggles of daily life, which are not limited to Christians

---

20 The work of Jean Corbon on this topic in the 1970s was widely discussed and continues to be a point of reference today. But it had a more limited scope than the proposal discussed here. See Jean Corbon, *L'Église des Arabes* (Paris: Cerf, 1977).

21 See for example *Pour une théologie contemporaine du moyen-orient: actes du Ier Symposium interdisciplinaire, Institut Saint-Paul de philosophie et de théologie, Harissa, 15-18 octobre 1987.* (Beyrouth, Liban: Editions Saint Paul, 1988).

22 *Toward A Christian, Arabic, Contemporary Theology* (Seminary of the Maronite Patriarchate, Lebanon, 2002). Papers of a conference held in Ghazir, Lebanon, April 11-13, 2002. In Arabic.

23 Samir Khalil Samir, "The Understanding of God: An Historical and Contemporary Comparative Overview," in *Toward A Christian, Arabic, Contemporary Theology*, 11.

24 Mouchir Aoun, "Theoretical Conditions for Constructing an Eastern, Arabic, Christian, Contextual, Contemporary Discourse," in *Toward A Christian, Arabic, Contemporary Theology*, 86.

alone. These struggles are equally shared by all the people of the region. A faith response in service of social change and liberation is equally expected from other faith communities, Christian as well as Muslim, he adds.[25] According to Aoun, a contemporary, contextual Arab Christian theology would need to take three main challenges into consideration: Islam, the context of the Middle East, and liberation. The author argues that such a theology, for a variety of historical reasons, has not been elaborated yet. There is also no synthesis yet, he adds, of the main stages of development of Arabic theology from its beginnings through the middle ages up to the modern and contemporary periods that would help Middle Eastern Christians trace the continuity of this theology across the ages, if there is such a continuity.[26] This work, which has just started in a very modest way, according to Aoun, is essential for the emerging Arabic Christian theology.[27] Contemporary Christian theology in Arabic, especially among the theologians in the Catholic communities, is still mostly a work of translation and imitation of Western theology in its methods and content, remarks Aoun.[28]

It would be important to note here at least one exception to Aoun's argument. Among Palestinian Christian theologians, thanks to the Palestinian liberation theology movement that began in the 1980s, there are several theological works that reflect on the struggle for liberation by the Palestinian people under Israeli occupa-

---

25 Aoun, "Theoretical Conditions for Constructing an Eastern, Arabic, Christian, Contextual, Contemporary Discourse," 96–97.

26 *Arab Christian Religious Thought: Requirements for Revival, Renewal, and Contemporaneity* (Beirut, Lebanon: Dar Al-Tali'at, 2007) [in Arabic]; *Theological Essays in Service of Dialogue*, Christianity and Islam in Dialogue and Collaboration. Center for Research in Christian Muslim Dialogue. (Jounieh, Lebanon: Paulist Library, 1997) [in Arabic]; *Theological Foundations for Constructing Christian Muslim Dialogue*, Muslim Christian Studies and Documentation. University of St. Joseph, Beirut. Institute of Islamic and Christian Studies. (Beirut, Lebanon: Dar Al-Mashrik, 2003) [in Arabic].

27 On the need for a history of Arabic Christian theology, many manuscripts of theological writings from of the Abbasid era (750-1258), considered to be a formative period of Arabic theology, have been rediscovered and published over the past few decades. The publication of such writings constitutes an important step in the construction of the history of Arabic theology. In the opinion of some contemporary theologians, these writings could be a helpful resource for developing a contemporary theology of Islam. Both Samir Khalil Samir and Mouchir Aoun agree that there is potential in the writings of Yahya Bin 'Adi (893-974), for example, for articulating an Arabic Christian theology using terminology from the Islamic theological tradition that could be helpful for Arab Christian theologians today.

28 Aoun, *Toward A Christian, Arabic, Contemporary Theology*, 91. The new work by Antoine Fleyfel, *Theologie Contextuelle Arabe Modèle Libanais* (L'Harmattan, 2011), is a new, creative attempt at articulating a Lebanese contextual theology. But despite its creativity in engaging Western frameworks of contextual theology, it does not constitute a real break with the old pattern of translation and imitation.

tion. The works of theologians such as Naim Ateek and Mitri Raheb are among the best known in this area.[29] The recent ecumenical document "A moment of truth: a word of faith, hope and love from the heart of Palestinian suffering," is a clear example of a Palestinian contextual theology. Commonly known as *Kairos Palestine*, this document, which was issued in 2009 and endorsed by most Palestinian churches, is an example of collaborative, ecumenical theology that articulates an Arabic, Christian contextual theology of peace and reconciliation between Israel and Palestine from a Christian, Palestinian perspective.[30]

The Synod for the Middle East

In October 2010, a special synod of the (Catholic) Bishops of the Middle East was held in Rome. The theme of the synod was "The Catholic Church in the Middle East: Communion and Witness." The *Lineamenta*, circulated by the Vatican a year in advance, included a list of the challenges facing Christians in the Middle East that should be addressed at the synod. Many of these challenges were not new and had already been articulated in the pastoral letters of the Patriarchs, mentioned above. These concerns include political instability and conflicts, migration, religious freedom, poverty and unemployment, and, of course, relations with Islam and Judaism. The tone and language used in the *Lineamenta*, however, was not well received by several Middle Eastern theologians and bishops and was strongly critiqued. The critique that pertains to the main topic of this essay concerns the use of the concept of "rights of minorities," in reference to the Christian communities of the region. The Commission on Islamo-Christian Dialogue of the Lebanese Bishops Conference strongly rejected the use of such language, whether explicit or implied in the overall orientation of the *Lineamenta*. Many Christian communities in the Middle East today, emphasized the bishops' commission, reject the thesis and language describing them as persecuted minorities in constant need for help from Western Christians in order to defend their rights and identity in a majority Muslim world. What several new voices in the churches of the Middle

[29] See for example, Naim Stifan Ateek, *Justice and Only Justice: A Palestinian Theology of Liberation* (Orbis Books, 1989); *Faith and the Intifada: Palestinian Christian Voices* (Orbis Books, 1992); *A Palestinian Christian Cry for Reconciliation* (Orbis Books, 2008); Mitri Raheb, *I Am a Palestinian Christian* (Fortress Press, 1995).

[30] "Kairos Palestine: A Moment of Truth," www.kairospalestine.ps.

East seem to be strongly and repeatedly saying is that Middle Eastern Christians want to speak for themselves and not continue to be (mis)represented.[31]

The pastoral challenges and concerns from the perspective of the local churches are concrete issues such as how to end wars and occupations, and find a just resolution of the Israeli-Palestinian conflict that guarantees the right of self-determination to the Palestinian people; how to end the ongoing colonial interventions in the internal affairs of the countries of the Middle East and respect the new political movements and their aspirations, etc. Although the critiques to the *Lineamenta* were addressed in the *Instrumentum Laboris*, the working document for the synod prepared by the Vatican, the theme of "persecuted minorities in need of protection" was still present in the debates during the synod. From the debates during the synod, it appeared that there were several points of tension, both among the Eastern bishops themselves, and between the bishops and Rome on some of the above mentioned points, which is not unusual in a synod.

At a conference co-organized by the European Union at the University of the Holy Spirit, Kaslik, Lebanon in November 2011 on the theme "The Future of Christians in the Middle East," newly elected Maronite Patriarch Bechara Boutros Rai interpreted to the participants the main message of the Synod for the Middle East. Communion, the main theme of the Synod, noted Rai, extends beyond the internal life within the Christian communities to the other religious and cultural communities and embraces diversity. He cited the pastoral letter of the Patriarchs from 1991 mentioned above on the shared cultural identity of Christians and Muslims:

> Les chrétiens d'Orient sont une partie inséparable de l'identité culturelle des musulmans. De même, les musulmans en Orient sont une partie inséparable de l'identité culturelle des chrétiens. De ce fait, nous sommes responsables les uns des autres devant Dieu et devant l'histoire.[32]

On September 5, 2011, the French Senate received the newly elected Maronite Patriarch Rai, as has been the custom for several centuries. In his speech to the

---

[31] See the recent research paper by journalist Ghassan Shami, "Arab Christians in the Levant and Their Relationship with Muslims," published by the Conflicts Forum, Beirut-London-Washington, February 2009, www.conflictsforum.org. See also Boutros Labaki, "Questions and Facts about the Situation of Christians in Lebanon and the Levant," tayyar.org, October 28, 2011.

[32] Bechara Rai, Speech at the conference on "The Future of Christians in the Middle East," University of the Holy Spirit, Kaslik, November 18, 2011 (in French), www.bkerkelb.org/french/index.php?option=com_content&view=article&id=395:discours-de-sa-beatitude-a-kaslik&catid=71:divers&Itemid=119, May 25, 2012.

Senate, Rai emphasized respect for cultural and religious diversity and quoted Pope John Paul II's exhortation to the Christians of the Middle East to collaborate with Muslims for building a common future. This is a significant change from the above cited statements on Phoenicianism made by Maronite Patriarch Houayek at the Peace Conference of Versailles in France in 1919. Times have indeed changed!

Concluding Remarks

I would like to conclude by highlighting what I consider significant trends in two main areas. A growing number of Middle Eastern Christians today at all levels of leadership in the church and society are thinking of themselves and their churches as indigenous integrated communities among the other peoples of the Middle East, rather than as an "extension of the West" or a "minority in need of protection." This is a new development and I believe it will continue to grow. The Christian communities in the Middle East are no longer a battlefield of colonial powers and their interests. That historical moment is over. Some Christian communities in the area might be tempted to play the colonial power game again, and some certainly continue to think this way, but none of these groups has enough support to seriously move in that direction at the present moment. Establishing Christian mini-states along the lines of the Jewish State of Israel, besides the fact that it is a bad idea for any Christian community to do that, is simply not doable. In addition, the narrative of "the suffering Christians for their faith in the birthplace of Christ, and that their communities are dwindling toward extinction," other than the fact that it is not true, no longer appeals to Western Christians in any significant way.

The second trend I observe, which is related to the first one, is that many new Middle Eastern Christian theologians and scholars are thinking about Islam in a positive way and engaging Islamic thought and theology seriously. The discussion on contextual Arab theology mentioned above is just one example. Many theologians and religious leaders in this new movement, are convinced that Islam and Christianity in the Middle East drink from the same cultural and religious well and that together they form one civilization; not two different civilizations. The fact that a new generation of theologians is attempting to do Christian theology in dialogue with Islam, using a theological language understandable to Muslims, will in the future bring Christians closer to Muslims rather than away from them, as has been the case in the past. This growing phenomenon could potentially generate new movements of theological, religious and spiritual renewal with significant implications for the future.

Despite these positive developments and shifts in the official teaching of the churches on Islam, many Arab Christians today continue to have an attitude of religious and cultural superiority toward Islam and Arab culture. They continue to look at the East through "Western" eyes and mind and continue to think of themselves as an extension of the *mission civilisatrice* of the West.[33] I can relate to this attitude from my own personal experience and how I was socialized growing up in the Lebanese Christian cultural and religious context. Yet, at the same time, as indicated above, there is a growing realization among many other Christians and church leaders that the main challenge to the mission of the churches is not to "evangelize and civilize" Muslims, but rather to better understand and work together with the Muslim communities as people of faith committed to the common good, building a common future of justice and peace for all. In other words, the focus of the mission of the churches in the Middle East, in my opinion, is shifting from a "mission *to* the Muslim communities and Islam," as has been historically the case, to "mission *with* the Muslim communities," as many hope would be the future.

References

Aoun, Mouchir B. *Arab Christian Religious Thought: Requirements for Revival, Renewal, and Contemporaneity*. Beirut, Lebanon: Dar Al-Tali'at, 2007.

—. *Theological Essays in Service of Dialogue*. Christianity and Islam in Dialogue and Collaboration. Center for Research in Christian Muslim Dialogue (Harissa, Lebanon). No. 7. Jounieh, Lebanon: Paulist Library, 1997.

—. *Theological Foundations for Constructing Christian Muslim Dialogue*. Muslim Christian Studies and Document. University of St. Joseph, Beirut. Institute of Islamic and Christian Studies. 6. Beirut, Lebanon: Dar Al-Mashrik, 2003.

Ateek, Naim Stifan. *A Palestinian Christian Cry for Reconciliation*. Orbis Books, 2008.

—. *Faith and the Intifada: Palestinian Christian Voices*. Orbis Books, 1992.

—. *Justice and Only Justice: A Palestinian Theology of Liberation*. Orbis Books, 1989.

Fleyfel, Antoine. *Theologie Contextuelle Arabe Modèle Libanais*. L'Harmattan, 2011.

"Kairos Palestine: A Moment of Truth." http://www.kairospalestine.ps/.

Kaufman, Asher. "Phoenicianism: The Formation of an Identity in Lebanon in 1920." *Middle Eastern Studies* 37, no. 1 (January 2001): 173.

Labaki, Boutros. "Questions and Facts about the Situation of Christians in Lebanon and the Levant." October 28, 2011, tayyar.org.

Maïla, Joseph. "The Arab Christians: From the Eastern Question to the Recent Political Situation of the Minorities." In *Christian Communities in the Arab Middle East: The*

[33] See Habib C. Malik, *Islamism and the Future of the Christians of the Middle East* (Hoover Institution Press, 2010).

Challenge of the Future, edited by Andrea Pacini, 23-47. Oxford: Clarendon Press, 1998.

Makdisi, Ussama. *Artillery of Heaven: American Missionaries and the Failed Conversion of the Middle East*. Cornell University Press, 2009.

—. "Reconstructing the Nation-State: The Modernity of Sectarianism in Lebanon." *Middle East Report* (September 1996): 23-30.

Malik, Habib C. *Islamism and the Future of the Christians of the Middle East*. 1st ed. Hoover Institution Press, 2010.

Pour une théologie contemporaine du moyen-orient?: actes du Ier symposium interdisciplinaire, Institut Saint-Paul de philosophie et de théologie, Harissa, 15-18 octobre 1987. Beyrouth, Liban: Editions Saint Paul, 1988.

Raheb, Mitri. *I Am a Palestinian Christian*. Fortress Press, 1995.

Rai, Bechara. Speech at the conference on "The Future of Christians in the Middle East," University of the Holy Spirit, Kaslik, November 18, 2011 (in French). www.bkerkelb.org/french/index.php?option=com_content&view=article&id=395: discours-de-sa-beatitude-a-kaslik&catid=71:divers&Itemid=119.

Robson, Laura. *Colonialism and Christianity in Mandate Palestine*. Austin: University of Texas Press, 2011.

Salibi, Kamal. *A House of Many Mansions: The History of Lebanon Reconsidered*. University of California Press, 1990.

Sand, Shlomo. *The Invention of the Jewish People*. Translated by Yael Lotan. Verso, 2010.

Shamsuddin, Imam M.M. *Muslim Christian Dialogue: Toward a Project of Shared Struggle (in Arabic)*. Beirut, Lebanon, 2004.

Toward A Christian, Arabic, Contemporary Theology. Seminary of the Maronite Patriarchate, Lebanon, 2002.

12 Vatican II and Interreligious Dialogue: Its Impact on the World and the African Church

Michael MCCABE, SMA

Introduction

The Second Vatican Council was the first ecumenical council in the history of the Church to give serious consideration to the Church's relationship to the followers of other religions and to advocate interreligious dialogue as an integral dimension of her mission. Its positive statements about other faith traditions decisively shaped the Church's understanding of itself and its mission in ways from which there is no return, in spite of some current difficulties and set-backs. This chapter will attempt (a) to underline the significance of the Council's teaching on interreligious dialogue and draw out its implications for the understanding and practice of mission and, (b) to highlight some achievements, difficulties and challenges of interreligious dialogue, especially in the present African context.

The Significance of Vatican II

Over the past 50 years the Church's relationship to the followers of other religions has moved "from confrontation to dialogue," to quote from the title of a popular book by Belgian theologian, Jacques Dupuis.[1] Most missionary congregations were born at a time when the Church's relationship to non-Christian religions oscillated between hostility and neglect. It was not the purpose of mission to enter into dialogue with the followers of other religions but rather to convert them to Christ and make them members of the true Church.

The missionaries were the Church's frontier troops, leaving their home countries in a spirit of self-sacrificing love and service to proclaim the Gospel and establish the Church in pagan lands. They saw themselves as engaged in a one-way traffic.[2] It was they who had to bring the true faith, while the pagans were merely the recipients; it was they who had to convert, while the pagans were the

[1] *Christianity and the Religions: From Confrontation to Dialogue*, trans by Phillip Berryman, Orbis Books, Maryknoll, NY, 2002.

[2] Cf. Justin Ukpong, "Contemporary Theological Models of Mission: Analysis and Critique," *AFER*, June 1983, pp. 162-164.

ones to be converted. For the missionaries it was inconceivable that other religions apart from Christianity—or more precisely the form of Christianity found in the Catholic Church—could facilitate a saving encounter between God and people. Far from being "seeds of the Word" (*Ad Gentes* 11), other religions were viewed as "cocktails of idolatry or superstition,"[3] and works of the devil. This negative evaluation of other religions, which continued practically up to the time of the Second Vatican Council, found expression even in the language of Christian prayer. We prayed for 'the poor heathen,' for 'those steeped in superstition and ignorance.' In a Prayer for the Conversion of Africa, still in use up to 1964, when I entered the Society of African Missions, we prayed as follows:

> O my God, behold us humbly prostrate in thy presence beseeching thee through Jesus Christ, Thy Son, to have pity on infidel Africa. Change the hearts of its unhappy children and save their souls.[4]

In the light of this negative evaluation of other religions, the positive approach endorsed by Vatican II seemed like a revolution. Jacques Dupuis has termed the Council a "watershed"[5] in the Church's approach to other religions. Certainly no simple 'hermeneutic of continuity' can do justice to the newness of the Council's teaching. However, this positive approach did not just suddenly appear out of the blue, so to speak. It should be seen rather as the climax of a theological and pastoral movement around the middle of the 20th century that tried to develop a more positive approach to other cultures and religions and to promote dialogue as an important component of mission.

In Africa and Asia there were theologians and anthropologists who sought to find within the local cultures of 'non-Christians' what were called human and spiritual values that could serve as 'stepping stones' to the Gospel (*preparatio evangelii*). I should also add here that missionaries themselves played a significant role in bringing about this change of approach.[6] Their own positive experiences

3 Melchior de Marion Brésillac, *Faith, Hope, Charity (Spiritual Exercises given to Indian Seminarians),* translated from the French by John Flynn, SMA, Rome, 1988, p. 134.

4 *Directory of the African Missions*, Guy & Company Ltd., Cork, 1957, p. 44.

5 *Op. cit.*, p. 59.

6 In Africa the contribution of Placide Frans Temples, a Belgian Franciscan missionary who worked for over 20 years in the Congo and published an important study of what he termed *Bantu Philosophy* (*Philosophie Bantou*) in 1945 is widely acknowledged. Less well known is the contribution of Kevin Carroll, SMA, a missionary in Ghana and Nigeria for nearly 50 years, to the appreciation of African art and culture, especially among the Yoruba. That lacuna has now been rectified with a major Conference on his work, organised by the SMA, and held in the Dromantine Retreat and Conference Centre, Newry, N. Ireland on the 6th October, 2012.

often led them to question the negative theological evaluation of other religions they had received and to bring to light the many positive values they found in the cultures and religious traditions of the people among whom they worked.

Vatican II took this irenic approach to a new level with its recognition and affirmation of spiritual and moral values ("seeds of the Word") in non-Christian religions and cultures. This affirmation can be seen especially in the major documents of the Council: the Decree on the Church's Missionary Activity, *Ad Gentes* (*AG*); the Dogmatic Constitution on the Church, *Lumen Gentium* (*LG*); the Pastoral Constitution on the Church in the Modern World, *Gaudium et Spes* (*GS*); and the Declaration on the Relation of the Church to non-Christian Religions, *Nostra Aetate* (*NA*).[7]

The Spiritual Treasures planted by God Among the Nations

The acknowledgement of authentic human and spiritual values in other religions is expressed more forcefully in *AG* 9 & 11 and *NA* 2 than elsewhere in the Council documents. *AG* 9 states that "whatever truth and grace is already found among the nations is a sort of secret presence of God." *AG* 11 goes on to spell out the implications of this affirmation for the members of the Church and especially for missionaries, emphasizing the need for dialogue:

> In order to be able to witness to Christ fruitfully, Christians must be united to those people (*gentes*) in esteem and love. They must take part in their cultural and social life through the various dealings and occupations of human life. They must be familiar with their national and religious traditions; with joy and reverence they must discover the seeds of the word hidden in these traditions.... Just as Christ searched the hearts of people and led them to the divine by truly human contacts, so his disciples, deeply imbued with the Spirit of Christ, should know the human persons among whom they live and associate with. In this way, through sincere and patient dialogue, they will learn what treasures the bountiful God has distributed among the nations.

This positive approach receives even more emphatic expression in *Nostra Aetate*. In its first paragraph the Declaration situates its directives on the Church's relations to the followers of other religions in the broad context of the common origin

---

7 Other themes found in these documents, e.g., the broadening and deepening of the meaning of mission, and the acknowledgement of cultural diversity as a value to be cherished by missionaries, also give strong theological foundation for viewing interreligious dialogue as an integral dimension of mission. I have elaborated these themes at greater length in an article I wrote a few years back. Cf. "Mission as Dialogue" in the *Tangaza Journal of Theology and Mission*, 2010/1, pp. 31-46.

and destiny of all people in God, and of the search, common to all religious traditions, to answer ultimate question about the meaning of human life. It then goes on, in the second paragraph, to exhort the members of the Church

> prudently and lovingly, through dialogue and collaboration with the followers of other religions, and in witness to the Christian life and faith, to acknowledge, preserve and promote the spiritual and moral good, as well as the socio-cultural values found among them (*NA* 2).

Despite its expression of appreciation for the authentic human and spiritual values to be found in other religions and its exhortation to missionaries, and to all members of the Church, "to acknowledge, preserve and promote" these values, Vatican II did not offer, according to Dupuis, a definitive theological evaluation of non-Christian religions or spell out what role, if any, they may have in God's plan for the salvation of humanity. Be that as it may, there is more than sufficient evidence to support the conclusion that the Council viewed the spiritual and moral values found in other religions as part and parcel God's personal outreach to all peoples and not merely an expression of the human search for God.[8] This theological evaluation of other religions would later receive further support and affirmation in the writings and speeches of Pope John Paul II.

A major theme running through several of John Paul II's encyclical letters and speeches is that of the universal presence and action of God's Spirit in human history. His first encyclical, *Redemptor Hominis,* speaks of "the firm belief of the followers of other religions" as an effect of the Spirit of truth operating outside the visible confines of the Mystical Body" (*RH* 6). His strongest statement on the universal presence and action of the Holy Spirit is in his encyclical on the Permanent Relevance of the Church's Missionary Mandate, *Redemptoris Missio* (*RM*), published in 1990. *RM* 28 states unambiguously that the presence and action of the

---

[8] This seems to be the line adopted by Pope Paul VI in *Evangelii Nuntiandi* (1975), where non-Christian religions are termed "natural religious expressions, worthy of esteem" but incapable of establishing "an authentic and living relationship" with God (Cf. *EN* 53). The Congregation for the Doctrine of the Faith's *Dominus Iesus* (2000) seems altogether too niggardly in its theological evaluation of other religions as representing "the sum of experience and thought that constitutes the human treasury of wisdom and religious aspiration," but not to be considered in any way as belonging to the realm of revealed truth (*DI* 7). This, in turn, means that the followers of these religions cannot be said to have "theological faith" (*ibid.*). This position, it seems to me, is impossible to reconcile with *Ad Gentes* 9 which speaks of "elements of *truth* and *grace*" to be found among the nations and which "are, as it were, a hidden *presence of God*" (italics mine).

Holy Spirit, everywhere in the world, "affect not only individuals but also society and history, peoples, cultures and religions."

It is clear that, for Pope John Paul II, the many and varied religious traditions of humanity are much more than mere attempts by human beings to reach out to God. They are genuine, if always limited,[9] expressions of God's outreach to human beings beyond the boundaries of the Church and manifestations of the Spirit of God at work in the world. If, then, God's Spirit is present in, and works through, other religions, it is surely legitimate to speak of these religions as playing at least a participatory role (albeit dependent on the unique and definitive mediation of Christ) in the salvation of their followers.[10] And, if this is accepted, may we not also view these religions as integral elements in God's providential plan for the salvation of human beings? This is the line being followed by a number of highly respected Catholic theologians, notably Jacques Dupuis[11] and Claude Geffré,[12] and it provides, I submit, a strong case for attuning mission to the key of dialogue.[13]

Mission as Dialogue

The teaching of Vatican II on other religions has enormous implications for the understanding of the Church's mission, especially its mission *ad extra*. The Church and all its members are called to participate in a movement of self-giving love that comes from God and of which God's Spirit is the primary agent—and who is present and active among all peoples in and through their religions and cultures.

9 Christianity, too, as a socio-cultural phenomenon, is also a limited expression of God's loving self-donation in history.

10 *Redemptoris Missio* seems to allow for such a dependent but important mediatory role for non-Christian religions when it refers to "participated forms of mediation of different kinds and degrees" beyond the frontiers of Christianity. Cf., the final sentence of *RM* 5.

11 While Dupuis' views came under the scrutiny of the Congregation for the Doctrine of the Faith, its final judgement cleared Dupuis of any trace of doctrinal error.

12 See Geffré's article, "The Crisis of Religious Identity in an Age of Religious Pluralism" in *Concilium* (2005/3), pp. 13-26. Geffré argues that Christians need to de-absolutise Christianity as an historical religion and accord other religions a *de jure* role in God's plan of salvation.

13 The clearest official endorsement of this position is to be found in a 1984 Document of the then Vatican Secretariat for Non-Christians (later changed to The Pontifical Council for Interreligious Dialogue) on "The Attitude of the Church towards the Followers of Other Religions" which insists that mission and dialogue can never be separated: "Dialogue is the norm and necessary manner of every form and aspect of Christian mission" (no. 29). Cf. also in this regard the major contributions of Michael Barnes SJ (*Theology and the Dialogue of Religions*, Cambridge University Press, Cambridge, UK, 2002) and Paul F. Knitter (*Introducing Theologies of Religions*, Orbis Books, Maryknoll, NY, 2002).

As participants in God's mission, missionaries never begin from a *tabula rasa*. Rather they encounter human beings and a world in which God's Spirit is already operative. God is everywhere before them, and salvifically active in ways unknown to us. Mission thus means entering into the mystery of a missionary God whose love embraces the world and all its inhabitants: the mystery of the Spirit's power, present in unexpected places and unsuspected ways; the mystery of people's participation in the paschal mystery in ways we have neither known nor imagined (cf. *Gaudium et Spes*, no. 22). To encounter this mystery we need to look, to contemplate, to discern, to listen, to learn, to respond, to collaborate.

Engaging in mission in this more open and dialogic mode does not mean in any way bracketing, much less abandoning, the missionaries' core convictions, as disciples of Christ, about the unique and constitutive role of Christ in the salvation of humankind. Some advocates of religious pluralism, like Alan Race,[14] John Hick[15] and Paul Knitter[16] argue that in order to enter into genuine dialogue with the followers of other religions, Christians must abandon or radically revise their claims about Christ so as to accord other religions parity of esteem with Christianity. However, the parity of esteem required for genuine dialogue is to be accorded to the dialogue partners, not necessarily to the belief systems they espouse.[17] As Jacques Dupuis rightly points out, holding on to one's faith in Jesus Christ as unique Savior of all people need not undermine a commitment to mutual dialogue on equal terms.[18] What is essential in interreligious dialogue is that one is prepared to listen to the other, to allow oneself to be challenged by the other, and to believe and hope that through this dialogue one can come to a more adequate understanding of the faith of the other and of one's own faith as well. This is the approach taken by a number of Catholic theologians today, who are committed to exploring their own Christian faith in the context of dialogue with other religious traditions. For example, John Keenan and Joseph S. O'Leary are exploring Buddhism to gain

[14] Cf. *Christians and Religious Pluralism: Patterns in the Christian Theology of Religions*, Orbis Books, Maryknoll, New York, 1983.

[15] While Hick has written several books in support of the pluralist model of the relationship between the religions, the clearest exposition of his position is to be found in *God and the Universe of Faiths: Essays in the Philosophy of Religions*, Macmillan, London, 1973.

[16] Cf. Knitter's best known work is: *No Other Name? A critical survey of Christian Attitudes Towards World Religions*, Orbis Books, Maryknoll, New York, 1985.

[17] As the Declaration of the Congregation for the Doctrine of the Faith, *Dominus Iesus*, states: "Equality, which is the presupposition of interreligious dialogue, refers to the personal dignity of the parties in dialogue, not to doctrinal content" (no. 22).

[18] Cf. *Toward a Christian Theology of Religious Pluralism*, Orbis Books, Maryknoll, NY, 1997, pp. 387-389; cf. also"Relating to other faiths: how far can you go?" in *The Tablet*, 8 June 2002, p. 16.

a better understanding of aspects of their own Christian faith. Francis X. Clooney is doing something similar while comparing Christian and Hindu texts, and David Burrell finds it profitable to dialogue with Islamic thought so as to deepen his understanding of the Christian doctrine of God.[19]

In the encounter with others, the first task of missionaries is to seek out and discern where and how God's Spirit is present and active among them, in and through their religions and cultures. They must not impose their agendas on people. Rather they must try to discover God's agenda by entering into the already existing dialogue between God and people with the heart and mind of Christ. For this they need to develop a capacity to be surprised by God and to recognize the multiform presences of the infinitely resourceful Christ who "plays in ten thousand places,/ lovely in limbs, and lovely in eyes not his/ To the Father through the features of men's faces" (G. M. Hopkins), far beyond the boundaries of the institutional Church. Here I will quote what Pope John Paul II said to the SMA General Assembly delegates on 13 May, 1989:

> Keep your eyes and your hearts open to discern "the seeds of the Word" in those cultures where Christianity is still absent. Since every culture needs conversion, promote that conversion, in the hope and realization that God is already there. This presupposes a spirit of dialogue of the kind I tried to show at the Assisi meeting. Evangelization is a two-way street. The herald of the Good News invites non-Christian religions to discover Christ. But he himself is challenged, by the signs of God's presence in those religions, to welcome new light on differing ways to live a human life and, therefore, to live with God. The missionary has to invite people to conversion, but he is also invited to it himself.[20]

Achievements, Difficulties and Challenges of Interreligious Dialogue in the African Context

It must be acknowledged that the Council's teaching on interreligious dialogue as an essential dimension of the Church's mission was, for the most part, taken to heart by most missionary and religious congregations working in Africa as well as by the local Church. Catholics no longer speak in derogatory terms

---

[19] Cf. also, James L. Fredericks, *Faith among Faiths: Christian Theology and non-Christian Religions*, Paulist Press, New Jersey, 1999, pp. 139-180. This author also sees the positives to be gained from a comparative study of non-Christian religious traditions.

[20] This address can be found in Interreligious Dialogue: *The Official Teaching of the Catholic Church (1963-1995)*, ed. by Francesco Goia, Pauline Books & Media, Boston, U.S.A., 1997, p. 405.

about the followers of other religions as "infidels" or "pagans" but rather refer to them by name, e.g. Hindus, Buddhists, Muslims, or followers of traditional religion.[21] Courses in Islamic Studies, Interreligious Dialogue, African Traditional Religion,[22] the Christian Theology of Other faiths, are offered in many African seminaries (though not all), Universities and Theological Colleges throughout the continent.

Numerous seminars, Summer Schools and workshops have updated and deepened the understanding of priests, religious and some of the laity regarding the Council's teaching on interreligious dialogue and the new faces of mission.[23] Congregations like the Jesuits, the Dominicans, the Franciscans, the Passionists, the Combonis, the Missionaries of Africa, and indeed many others, have not only initiated specific projects of interreligious dialogue (especially with Muslims) but have also adopted a dialogic approach in their understanding and praxis of mission. I will illustrate this point with just two examples, the first taken from the revised *Constitutions and Laws of the Society of African Missions* and the Second from the *Constitutions of the Medical Missionaries of Mary*.

The *SMA Constitutions and Laws* (2004) article 1 states:

> Under the guidance of the Holy Spirit we aim to be a sign of communion and an instrument of dialogue among cultures, religions and churches, so that the Kingdom of justice and peace, love and truth, may become a reality.

Article 20 gives even clearer expression to the dialogic dimension of the Society's mission:

> In our mission we seek to be enriched by the cultures and religions of the people among whom we live and work. Thus with them we may be more fully evangelised by the Holy Spirit who works in all.

---

21 Unfortunately, as Bishop Peter Sarpong has stated, African traditional Religion is sometimes still referred to as a primal religion—a pejorative term used to distinguish it from the so-called great religions of the world. Cf. "Can Christianity dialogue with Traditional African Religion" at http://www.afrikaworld.net/afrel/sarpong.html. Accessed 15 August, 2012.

22 A lacuna in this context has been the religions of Asia which have received very little attention in most African theologates, seminaries or universities. Cf., Guido Oliana's "The Theological Challenges of Religious Pluralism: Towards a Christian Theology of Other Faiths" in the *Tangaza Journal of Theology and Mission*, 2010/1, pp. 9-30, at p. 17

23 However, as Albert de Jong had pointed out, religious and missionary Congregations were given many more opportunities for updating on the theological and pastoral orientations of Vatican II than were the pastoral agents of the local Church. Cf., his work, *The Challenge of Vatican II in East Africa*, Paulines Publications Africa, Nairobi, Kenya, 2004, pp. 186-192.

The revised Constitutions of the Medical Missionaries of Mary (2005), article 9:15, states that the members of the Congregation are "called to pray and to celebrate the liturgy with people of different national and religious traditions and beliefs and to search with them for the 'seeds of the Word' which lie hidden in their cultures." An earlier article, referring to the healing ministry of the Congregation, insists that its members should study the history, traditions and customs of those among whom they work and strive "to understand their interpretation of misfortune, sickness, suffering and death."

Setbacks, Difficulties and Challenges

Despite significant achievements and some outstanding efforts on the part of a number of missionary congregations, it must be admitted that interreligious dialogue, especially the dialogue with Islam and with traditional religion(s) is still in its infancy in Africa. Indeed, in some places and instances, it has gone into reverse mode.[24] Regarding the dialogue with Islam, following many decades of peaceful coexistence and collaboration between Christians and Muslims, the relatively recent emergence of a virulent stream of Islamic fundamentalism and an equally dangerous Islamophobia in some Christian circles, has given rise to new tensions and even open conflict in some countries. In the missionary society to which I belong (SMA), our 2007 General Assembly noted a significant lessening of enthusiasm for the dialogue with Islam in recent years.[25]

However, sometimes setbacks can prove to be a stimulus to fresh efforts. The recent clashes between Christians and Muslims in various parts of Africa have led to renewed efforts at dialogue and collaboration.[26] The contribution of Nigerian women to Christian-Muslim dialogue has been highlighted in an important

[24] Perhaps a sign that interreligious dialogue in Africa still has a long way to go is reflected in a recent book on African Theology. *African Theology Comes of Age. Revisiting Twenty Years of the Theology of the Ecumenical Symposium of Eastern Africa Theologians (ESEAT)*, ed. Laurenti Magesa, Paulines Publications Africa, Nairobi, 2010. Not one of the 14 articles contained in this book reflect on the challenge of interreligious dialogue. We still have a long way to go in implementing the teaching of Vatican II on the importance of interreligious dialogue.

[25] Cf. "The Official Texts of the 19th General Assembly of the Society of African Missions", *Bulletin*, no. 124 (May 2007), pp. 38-39.

[26] In recent years there have been several initiatives from religious groups working in Africa, as well as the local Church, to counteract existing tensions and conflicts between Christian and Muslim and promote peace through dialogue. E.g., The Damietta Peace Initiative, launched by the Franciscans in 2002 (an account of this initiative can be found at the following website: http://www.damiettapeace.org.za/page.php?p_id=149.) The efforts of the Catholic Archbishop of Abuja, John Onaiyekan, and the Sultan of Sokoto to foster peace and unity be-

study by Sr Kathleen McGarvey OLA.[27] Paradoxically, too, the debacle of Pope Benedict XVI's 2006 Regensburg Lecture,[28] where he cited a disparaging remark about Islam's violent tendencies, made by a medieval Byzantine Emperor, has led to a renewed and intensified dialogue between Muslims and Christians under the initiative known as "A Common Word".[29] It should be noted that this initiative was taken not by the Vatican but by 138 Muslim scholars who sent a document ("A Common Word") to the Pope, the Archbishop of Canterbury, and other Christian leaders, reminding them of what Muslims and Christians hold in common, namely, love of God and love of neighbor, and challenging all to search for mutual understanding in the cause of peace.[30] In spite of this progress, the dialogue with Islam remains an extremely difficult one, which, nevertheless, must be pursued with courage and patience for the sake of reconciliation, peace and religious freedom.[31]

If the dialogue with Islam is still in its infancy, this is even more true of the dialogue with the followers of traditional religions in Africa. I must confess disappointed that Pope John Paul II's post-synodal Exhortation, *Ecclesia in Africa* (1995) had so little to offer by way of orientation for this dialogue beyond saying that the followers of traditional religion should be treated with respect and

tween Muslims and Christians in Nigeria are well known. Perhaps less well know is an initiative launched by the SMA General Council: a two-week workshop on Christian-Muslim dialogue, held in Abuja in September 2011. Taking part in this workshop, facilitated by Fr Basil Soyoye, SMA, and Sr Kathleen McGarvey, OLA, were missionaries working in eight African countries. An account of the workshop can be found on the website of the SMA Irish Province at: http://www.sma.ie/index.php?option=com_content&view=article&id=903%3Achristian-muslim-dialogue-2011&catid=100%3Aministry&Itemid=101. In East Africa, the work of the Shalom Centre for Conflict Resolution and Reconciliation (SCCRR), based in Nairobi, also promotes dialogue and collaboration with Muslims. For information on the work of this Center, cf. the following website: http://www.shalomconflictcenter.org/home.html.

27 Cf., *Muslim and Christian Women in Dialogue: The Case of Northern Nigeria* (Religion and Discourse Series, vol. 42), Peter Lang, Wien, 2009.

28 An English translation of the Pope's lecture can be found at: http://www.zenit.org/article-16955?l=english.

29 Cf. David Burrell's engaging and insightful account of this initiative: "Dialogue between Muslims and Christians as Mutually Transformative Speech" in *Criteria of Discernment in Interreligious Dialogue*, ed. by Catherine Cornille (Interreligious Dialogue Series/1), Cascade Books, Oregon, USA, 2009, pp. 87-98.

30 Cf. David Burrell, *art. cit.*, pp. 88-89.

31 Cf. Pope Benedict XVI's Post-synodal Apostolic Exhortation, *Africae Munus*, Paulines Publications Africa, Nairobi, 2011, no. 94.

esteem and that courses on African traditional religion should be given in houses of formation for priests and religious (cf. *EA* 67).[32]

Pope Benedict XVI's *Africae Munus* (2011), his Exhortation following the Second African Synod (2009), has somewhat more to say but is rather guarded and more concerned about the dangers to be avoided than the potential to be developed in this dialogue. While acknowledging the need for dialogue with traditional African religions, the focus of *Africae Munus* is on the need for "guidance in gaining a deeper and more accurate knowledge of the traditions" in order "to identify points of real divergence" from the Gospel message, to "clarify the vital distinction between culture and cult and to discard those magical elements which cause division and ruin for families and societies" (*AM* 92).[33] The Exhortation also sounds a dire warning particularly about the "scourge" of witchcraft "currently experiencing a certain revival" (*AM* 93) in Africa.

The dialogue with traditional religion in Africa had been stalled by the enormous rift which developed between the Christian faith and traditional African cultures during the modern missionary era when the Church was implanted in Africa. This rift has been deepened more recently by the transportation to almost every part of Africa (especially through the mass media) of the secularized and materialistic Western culture with its attendant problems and negative influences.[34]

32 One might have expected more from the first Pope in history to have made direct contact with the followers of African Traditional Religion. He met and addressed representative of ATR when he visited the Benin Republic in 1993.

33 Following the publication of *Africae Munus*, the executive council of the Orisa Community Development Corporation (CDC), an American based group of Africans who practice Traditional Religion, wrote a letter to Pope Benedict accusing *Africae Munus* of "encouraging forms of cultural violence that re-inscribe Africans – and many other non-Christian and non-white peoples by extension – as backward and in need of a "civilization" that, purportedly, only Christianity can offer. Though couched in terms of God's divine love, the reality of your *Africae Munus* is that, in calling for the shunning of African Indigenous Religions and what you refer to as 'excessively African' forms of Christianity, it is essentially calling for the shunning of African cultures, as spiritual understandings are very deeply imbedded in the cultures of most African peoples" (This Letter can be found on the internet at: http://orisacdc.org/wp-content/uploads/2011/12/Open-Letter-to-Pope-Benedict-XVI.pdf (Accessed 20 July 2012).

34 One of today's leading African theologians, Laurenti Magesa, insists that the Church must help African peoples resist the forces of globalization and regain the ability and power of self-definition, thus affirming their dignity and self-respect. For Magesa, the issue of self-definition is critical, for this is precisely what globalization, following on the heels of colonization, is taking away from Africans. Cf., "Africa's Struggle for Self-Definition During a Time of Globalization" (*SEDOS BULLETIN*, August-September 1999). Available on the SEDOS website at: http://sedosmission.org/old/eng/magesa_1.htm. Accessed 12th August, 2012.

This situation surely calls for a deep healing and integration, which can be effected only through a painstaking and sustained dialogue with the local cultures, in which the traditional religions are embedded. Here is surely a major challenge for the African churches today.

Another difficulty which confronts the Church's dialogue with traditional religion is its heavy and heady emphasis on creeds and doctrines, whereas in traditional religions (not only in Africa but throughout the world), the emphasis is more on myth, ritual and celebration. Those who wish to engage in a fruitful dialogue with the followers of traditional religions have to get out of their intellectual grove and examine how the rituals of traditional religion function within the community and respond to human needs rather than to abstract or theoretical questions. To dialogue with the followers of traditional religion we need to attend to what we are feeling or experiencing than to what ideas come into our mind. Indeed, if we are open enough, this dialogue can awaken dimensions of our own experience (for example, greater awareness of our bodies) which we have forgotten or ignored—and may lead us to a more integrated or holistic practice of our own faith.

Personally I have found helpful a suggestion made by one of the participants at a Staff Colloquium on Interreligious Dialogue held in Kimmage (Dublin) in 2001. She said that instead of trying to search for answers given, or even for the questions being addressed, by other religions, it might be more fruitful to try and identify the core values of a religion. In this perspective, it is assumed that each religion has some key or core religious value or set of values which, while probably overlapping with those of other religions, can nevertheless be said to be distinctive to that religion. An Irish missionary and author, Donal Dorr, has identified the core value in traditional religion as "rootedness in nature and in the community."[35]

From my own experience missionaries who have worked in Africa can readily identify and name the key values of traditional religion. This was verified for me some years ago when I gave a three day seminar on the theme "Mission and the Challenge of Interreligious dialogue" to groups of African missionaries on a Renewal Course in Jerusalem. I asked them to identify the values they discovered in the local cultures of the people among whom they worked. The values they identified were: joy and celebration, the unity of all life, relationship and friendship, hospitality and solidarity, patience and endurance. These were not values they brought to the people, but values they found among them, religious values embedded in the cultures—values which they found had enriched and deepened

[35] *Mission in Today's World*, The Columba Press, Dublin, 2000, p. 40.

their living out of their own faith in Christ. From my own experience of working as a missionary in Liberia I would add the value of forgiveness. The capacity of so many Liberians to forgive those who have inflicted the most abominable atrocities upon them in the aftermath of the civil wars (1990-2005) is utterly extraordinary. As an Irishman I have never come across anything like it in my own country, where we have certainly been victims of criminal oppression by the British but find it so hard to let go of the past.

While focusing on the positive values to be found in traditional religions, we must be careful not to romanticize these religions (as was done in the movie, "the Emerald Forest", which hit the headlines some 25 years ago, and perhaps more recently in the film, "Avatar") and ignore negative and apparently destructive elements in them. Spirit possession is a striking feature of many traditional religions, where a group of people or a shaman deliberately set out to be possessed by a particular spirit. While such spirit possession may not always be for an evil purpose (in Zambia, for example, it is used to bring about healing), it is at least ambiguous.

Even more ambiguous is the practice of witchcraft, which, as *Africae Munus* acknowledges, still has an enormous impact on the everyday life not only of adherents of traditional religion but also of African Christians. There is here a dabbling in the forces of evil which creates an enormous amount of fear, even terror. We cannot ignore the presence of "witch camps" in some of the most developed countries of sub-Saharan Africa.[36] A fundamental Christian conviction is that Christ came to liberate people from this kind of fear. Dialogue with the followers of traditional religions surely requires that the oppressive elements in these religions are also identified and honestly named, and that people's fears are addressed and redressed. This is what I would see as the purifying or redeeming aspect of the dialogue between the Gospel and a particular culture.

Dialogue with Traditional Religions means dialogue with the followers of these religions and their cultures.[37] Mention of the dialogue with culture raises

---

[36] Kate Whitaker, of BBC World Service, gives a disturbing account of the horrific conditions under which these women now live in such camps in Northern Ghana. Her program, "No Country for Old Women", which was broadcast on 1st September, 2012, can be accessed on the website: http://www.bbc.co.uk/programmes/p00x8hm4

[37] Peter Sarpong expresses well the intimate relationship between religion and culture in the African context when he writes: "The role of traditional religion in determining the *modus vivendi* [of Africans] has been vital. African cultures are known for their religious orientation. In fact, African cultures are religious cultures. It is not possible to study African culture in isolation from religion. Religion permeates the ideal African from cradle to grave. African traditional religion, therefore, comes into play in the shaping of the African's future. We have to know the past in order to understand the present and be better equipped to plan the future.

another difficulty, namely, the sense that this dialogue, despite the many positive statements made in official and unofficial circles, is somehow stuck in a rut or deadlocked. The gap between the Christian world and the world of traditional religion in Africa has certainly not been bridged and hardly even lessened. Many reasons are advanced for this failure. The main ones are (a) that past and present inculturation projects are not sufficiently anchored in the everyday life of the people, and (b) that the process of inculturation was and remains mostly a dressing up with some local color of an essentially foreign (Western) product.

It is sometimes said that the New Religious Movements, offering healing, success, security, dignity and recognition to people, have stepped into the lacuna created by the failure of the mainstream Christian Churches to inculturate the Gospel message. True, the solutions these movements are offering are simplistic in the extreme. Yet, they are responding to real needs in the everyday lives of the people. I would suggest that a possible way out of the present deadlock in the Churches' dialogue with local cultures is to identify what Paulo Freire terms "the generative issues"[38] of a particular culture. There are the issues which respond to the deep, unmet needs and hungers of the community (or of significant sectors of the community). Then, instead of just adding an African, Indian or Caribbean flavor to existing rituals, the Church should develop new rituals in response to these issues. While this may be primarily a challenge for the local Church it is also a challenge to which religious and missionary congregations must respond and for which they have an important contribution to make.

Conclusion

Shortly before he died on 31 August, 2012, the well-known Italian Prelate and Scripture scholar, Cardinal Carlo Martini, gave a now widely circulated interview to *Corriere della Sera*, in which he criticized the institutional Church for its pomp and circumstance, its inability to relate to the world in which we live and to communicate the Word of God effectively to the men and women of our time, its lack of flexibility and courage.[39] As I read his remarks in the context of revising

We cannot know the past of the African if we neglect his [sic] religion. Traditional religion is part of the African's ethos and an understanding of it should go hand in hand with Christian evangelization" in "Can Christianity dialogue with Traditional African Religion" at website: http://www.afrikaworld.net/afrel/sarpong.html (Accessed 20 August 2012).

38 Cf. *Pedagogy of the Oppressed* (30th Anniversary Edition), translated by Mrya Bergman Ramos, Continuum, London, 2000.

39 The text of this interview translated into English on 4 September by John Allen Jr. can be found at: http://ncronline.org/blogs/ncr-today/translated-final-interview-martini.

this essay, I was struck by the relevance of interreligious dialogue not only to the Church's mission of creating truly inculturated Christian communities and of promoting peace in the world but for its own renewal and creative fidelity to the divine truth it bears but can never fully grasp. This idea is beautifully expressed by an Irish theologian teaching in Japan, Joseph S. O' Leary:

> Christian thought has to be fully open to the plurality of religious and secular voices that situate and relativise it as a contingent cultural history, which can be responsibly continued only in attentive response to these other voices. This imperative has begun to make itself strongly felt only in the recent past, and it has given rise to the most interesting religious thinking of today. Dialogue … saves Christianity from turning in on itself in an incestuous rehash of its traditions, lets in some fresh air, and restores a human, natural complexion to religious language.[40]

The dialogue with other religions is ultimate essential for the health and vitality of the Christian message itself.

Bibliography

Barnes, Michael, *Theology and the Dialogue of Religions*, Cambridge, UK: Cambridge University Press, 2002.

Benedict XVI, Post-synodal Apostolic Exhortation, *Africae Munus,* Nairobi: Paulines Publications Africa, 1995.

Burrell, David, "Dialogue between Muslims and Christians as Mutually Transformative Speech" in *Criteria of Discernment in Interreligious Dialogue*, ed. by Catherine Cornille (Interreligious Dialogue Series/1), Oregon: Cascade Books, 2009, pp. 87-98.

Congregation for the Doctrine of the Faith, *Dominus Iesus* (Declaration on the Unicity and Salvific Universality of Jesus Christ and the Church, 6 August 2000), Nairobi: Paulines Publications Africa, 2000.

De Jong, Albert, *The Challenge of Vatican II in East Africa*, Nairobi: Paulines Publications Africa, Kenya, 2004

De Marion Brésillac, Melchior, *Faith, Hope, Charity* (Spiritual Exercises given to Indian Seminarians), translated from the French by John Flynn, Rome: SMA, 1988.

Dorr, Donal, *Mission in Today's World*, Dublin: The Columba Press, 2000.

Dupuis, Jacques, *Toward a Christian Theology of Religious Pluralism*, Maryknoll, NY: Orbis Books, 1997.

—, *Christianity and the Religions: From Confrontation to Dialogue*, Maryknoll, NY: Orbis Books, 2002.

—, "Relating to other faiths: how far can you go?" in *The Tablet*, 8 June 2002, pp. 16-17.

40 Joseph Stephen O'Leary, *Religious Pluralism and Christian Truth*, Edinburgh University Press, Edinburgh, 1996, p. x.

Fredericks, James L., *Faith among Faiths: Christian Theology and non-Christian Religions*, Paulist Press, New Jersey, 1999.

Freire, Paulo, *Pedagogy of the Oppressed* (30th Anniversary Edition), translated by Mrya Bergman Ramos, London: Continuum, 2000.

Geffré, Claude, "The Crisis of Religious Identity in an Age of Religious Pluralism" in *Concilium* (2005/3), pp. 13-26.

John Paul II, Post-synodal Apostolic Exhortation, *Ecclesia in Africa*, Nairobi: Paulines Publications Africa, 2011.

—, Enclyclical Letter, *Redemptor Hominis* (4 March 1979), AAS 71, 1979, pp. 257-324.

—, Encyclical Letter, *Redemptoris Missio*, Nairobi: Paulines Publications Africa, 1991.

Knitter, Paul, *No Other Name? A critical survey of Christian Attitudes Towards World Religions*, Maryknoll, New York: Orbis Books, 1985.

—, *Introducing Theologies of Religions*, Maryknoll, NY: Orbis Books, 2002.

Magesa, Laurenti, "Africa's Struggle for Self-Definition During a Time of Globalization" (*SEDOS Bulletin*, August-September 1999). Available on the SEDOS website at: http://sedosmission.org/old/eng/magesa_1.htm.

—, (ed.), *African Theology Comes of Age. Revisiting Twenty Years of the Theology of the Ecumenical Symposium of Eastern Africa Theologians (ESEAT)*, Nairobi: Paulines Publications Africa, 2010.

McCabe, Michael A., "Mission as Dialogue" in the *Tangaza Journal of Theology and Mission*, 2010/1, pp. 31-46.

McGarvey, Kathleen, *Muslim and Christian Women in Dialogue: The Case of Northern Nigeria* (Religion and Discourse Series, vol. 42), Wien: Peter Lang, 2009.

O'Leary, Joseph S., *Religious Pluralism and Christian Truth*, Edinburgh: Edinburgh University Press, 1996

Paul VI, Post-synodal Apostolic Exhortation, *Evangelii Nuntiandi*, Nairobi: Paulines Publications Africa, 1992.

Race, Alan, *Christians and Religious Pluralism: Patterns in the Christian Theology of Religions*, Orbis Books, Maryknoll, New York, 1983.

Sarpong, Peter, "Can Christianity dialogue with Traditional African Religion" at website http://www.afrikaworld.net/afrel/sarpong.html.

The SMA General Assembly 2007, "The Official Texts of the 19th General Assembly of the Society of African Missions", *Bulletin*, no. 124 (May 2007).

The Society of African Missions, *Directory of the African Missions*, Cork: Guy & Company Ltd., 1957.

Vatican Secretariat for Non-Christians, *The Attitude of the Church towards the Followers of Other Relgions*, Rome: Vatican City, 1984.

Vatican II, *Nosta Aetate* (Declaration on the Relation of the Church to non-Christians, 28 October 1965) in *Documents of Vatican II*, ed. by Austin Flannery, Grand Rapids, Michigan: Eerdmans, 1984, pp. 738-742.

—, *Ad Gentes Divinitus* (Decree on the Church's Missionary Activity, 7 December 1965) in *Documents of Vatican II*, ed. by Austin Flannery, Grand Rapids, Michigan: Eerdmans, 1984, pp. 813-856.

Part IV:

Mission and Ministry

13 Vatican II and the Challenge of Marriage and Family in Africa[1]

Bénézet BUJO

It is generally known that the teaching of Catholic Moral Theology before Vatican II focused especially on the aim of marriage. It emphasized the three aims which St Augustine pointed out: *proles*, *fides*, *sacramentum*.[2] Love seemed to be secondary because children were seen as the highest good of the sacred bond between wife and husband. From this viewpoint the Constitution *Gaudium et spes* of Vatican II sounds revolutionary when it states:

> Marriage to be sure is not instituted solely for procreation; rather, its very nature as an unbreakable compact between persons, and the welfare of the children, both demand that the mutual love of the spouses be embodied in a rightly ordered manner, that it grow and ripen. Therefore, marriage persists as a whole manner and communion of life, and maintains its value and indissolubility, even when despite the often intense desire of the couple, offspring are lacking.[3]

This has played an important role in further discussions on the understanding of sexuality when we take for instance the whole debate on the encyclical *Humanae Vitae* into consideration. In Africa, however, this fresh impetus of *Gaudium et spes* might not have been decisive on the new reflections initiated concerning the inculturation of marriage. The text which highly influenced the theological reflections was rather that of the Decree *Ad Gentes*, no. 22, where the Council encourages young Churches to borrow from "the customs and traditions of their people, from their wisdom and their learning, from their arts and disciplines, all those things which can contribute to the glory of their Creator, or enhance the grace of their Savior, or dispose Christian life the way it should be."

In this Chapter we shall try to demonstrate how theology after Vatican II asked radically for a genuine African way of understanding the sacrament of marriage different from the Western understanding of family and sexuality.

---

1 The author, Bujo, did not have the opportunity to reply to the criticism of Ngong (see the next chapter).

2 Cf. P. Adnès, *Le mariage*, Tournai: Desclée, [2]1963, 55-58.

3 *Gaudium et spes*, no. 50. http://www.vatican.va/archive/hist_councils/ii_vatican_council/documents/vat-ii_cons_19651207_gaudium-et-spes_en.html (accessed, January 3, 2015).

Anthropological Foundation of Marriage and Family

African marriage cannot be correctly understood unless we pay attention to the African worldview which forms the basis of the *ubuntu* life. In this worldview the concept of family is not only very important but also very broad and cannot be reduced to that of the West which restrains the full depiction of the meaning accorded by this concept in African languages. How concretely, therefore, should the family be understood in the world of the African?

Family in its three dimensions

The African family never consists only in father, mother and children. It rather includes three dimensions, namely the living, the dead and the not-yet-born. Besides, it embraces all the relatives; and one can also become a family member by covenant and alliance, for instance by blood pact, the most known form of alliance.

The living cannot be seen independent from the two other partial but invisible communities. This means that the living, the dead and the not-yet-born are in a continuous interaction. The relationship between living and dead can be described as a continuous and mutual begetting and bearing. The dead members of the family rely on the living for their further growth in the life hereafter. Following the African rationality, the happiness of the deceased has not only something to do with God but without the *anamnestic* action of the living their *ubuntu* cannot reach its fulfilment. Vice versa, the survival of the terrestrial partial community is possible only when the bond with the dead is not disrupted. Indeed, the living members contribute to the happiness of the deceased; but, in return, the latter provide them with all the necessary gifts for their daily life. Sickness, hunger, barrenness and so on do not occur in the community when the ancestors are not forgotten. Hence, it becomes clear that life in these partial communities of the living and the dead consists in an interaction. The individuals exist because of their mutual relationship to each other and this has to go beyond the grave.

Furthermore, the two partial communities have to take into consideration the third dimension which consists of the not-yet-born. Even these are not passive towards the two other dimensions; they contribute to the begetting and bearing of the living and the dead. The living and the dead know that their existence is not guaranteed if they are deprived of descendants. But the not-yet-born, who are in their own world and are ready to join the terrestrial community, give hope to both the visible and the invisible communities. Through the children to come, the hope of posterity, the living are assured that their existence is not void of sense, and the ancestors are convinced of their survival. In other words, the not-yet-born contribute to keeping alive all who are awaiting them; hence they are involved in this process of mutual begetting and bearing. From this point of view, the eschatological fulfilment of the tridimensional community essentially depends on the not-yet-born children.

To understand correctly the African marriage and family, it is imperative to keep in mind this religious and anthropological conception.

Marriage and Sexuality as a Communitarian Action

From the very beginning it has to be emphasized that marriage, from the African point of view, is a bond between a man and a woman which involves the whole family from both sides of the spouses in the above illustrated sense. Any other form of marriage is unthinkable since one should not lose sight of the concept of bipolarity that Engelbert Mveng developed in his writings.[4] According to this thesis, the life of a *muntu*, the human being, consists in *monad*, *dyad*, *triad*, and these three, consequently, make him a *crowd* or *plurality*. It is in the rite of initiation that the *muntu* discovers the lack of the *ubuntu*-fullness which comes into being through the relationship between monad and dyad, and this is valid for both genders. The human being is at the beginning only a monad, but through the encounter with the dyad, which is different in gender, he/she becomes the *man-being* or *woman-being* and is capable of enrichment through triad and, lastly, by myriad (crowd, plurality).

To sum up: The person-being is to be accomplished by mutual relationship with a different gender. In the monad phase a *muntu* is only a "project" of becoming person and this project can be achieved and come about through the encounter with another sex.[5] Without respecting this process of monad and dyad there cannot be the triad, and no community of myriad (crowd) will start.

The community on the other hand is of necessity for the development of monad, dyad and triad because a full humanity, the *ubuntu*, is conditioned by

---

4 Cf. E. Mveng, *L'art d'Afrique noire. Liturgie cosmique et langage religieux*, Paris : Mame, 1964, 75-85 ; id., " Essai d'anthropologie négro-africaine ", *Bulletin de Théologie Africaine* 1 (1979) 229-239 ; id., *L'Afrique dans l'Eglise. Paroles d'un croyant*, Paris : L'Harmattan,1985, 13-18.

5 For details cf. Bujo, *Plea for Change of Models for Marriage*, Nairobi : Paulines Publications Africa, 2009, 151ff; Cf. the two articles of E. Mveng in *Bulletin de Théologie Africaine* 1 (1979), pp. 100-103 and 235-235; id, *L'Afrique dans l'Eglise* 14.

the interaction between all the members of the extended community and not only by the couple or the partnership between wife and husband with their children. This explains the African conviction that the whole community of both sides—of the man and of the woman—should be involved in the process of marriage. The two individuals, the future spouses, are the principal interested parties, but they alone cannot make the marriage which is intrinsically a communitarian act since it binds two families not by contract, but rather by alliance. Put differently, the African understanding of marriage is different from that of the West because it sees the bond between wife and husband as a covenant in which the families of both parties play a decisive and indispensable role. Just because of this covenantal character marriage cannot be concluded punctually, but it implies a process with many stages. At every stage both the family of the man and of the woman are present.

One of these stages is the sexual intercourse which is a very necessary step towards the validity of the ongoing marriage. As one can easily imagine, this is the most criticized and condemned point by the Christian Churches, especially, the Catholic Church. We touch here the problem of the inculturation of the sacrament of marriage in Africa. Indeed, the pastoral experience of many bishops and priests before, during and after Vatican II showed clearly that a marriage concluded as indicated by the classic Western theology and Church law does not last in the African milieu, as it does not take into account the way of thinking in other cultures of the world. Concretely, what is missing in the Sub-Saharan African context is the dynamism which should accompany marriage. This supposes that the Church should neither focus on a punctual (exact) "yes" to the climax of the sacrament of marriage nor exclude the traditional communitarian character of the whole procedure. As already observed, it is a long way that finally leads to the definitive conclusion of what marriage is in African understanding. Hence, Bishop John Njenga is right in speaking of marriage in successive stages.[6] He brings to the fore a five-stage model that can be found among several ethnic groups. According to this model, there are (1) the time of courtship; (2) the introduction of the girl to the boy's parents; (3) a reciprocal visit to the girl's parents by the boy's parents; (4) the payment of the dowry followed by feasting; (5) the wedding (customary, civil or Christian).

The third step opens the door for both, the boy and the girl, to live together, although the whole process is not yet closed.[7] The Church, however, considers

---

6 Cf. J. Njenga, "Marriage in Successive Stages," *African Ecclesial Review* 28 (1986) 198-207.

7 Cf. ibid. 201.

this as concubinage. This question has been discussed not only by theologians, but even by some bishops. At the Bishops' Synod on marriage and Christian family, Bishop André Kaseba of Zaire (Democratic Republic of the Congo) defended the position that the stage where the future spouses can already have the sexual relationship is not to be condemned as immoral, because it belongs essentially to the process which leads to the definitive consent and is an inseparable part of the whole. The lack of one single step would mean the invalidity of all stages. Therefore it is unacceptable to speak of premarital intercourse that should be forbidden, within the marriage process.[8]

This thesis of Bishop Kaseba has been agreed to and continued by Cardinal Joseph-Albert Malula who is of the opinion that marriage is a creation reality and God did not dictate to the human being in detail a concrete way to follow in getting married. According to Malula, marriage is not to be interpreted independently of various cultures in the world. That is to say that Jesus Christ did not determine exactly which elements belong to indissolubility or at which moment the marriage can be seen as such. Consequently, the principle of *"ratum et consummatum"* should be revised, for it originated in/from another culture and sounds strange to Africans. Cardinal Malula therefore appealed to theologians to go deeper in this discussion in order to work out a theology which can interpret correctly revelation in the African context.[9]

The theology our Cardinal is pleading for has already started and is being discussed very controversially. Although some theologians refuse to agree with those who are in favor of accepting the customary marriage by stages as a whole, many others support the idea of integrating the same marriage in the Christian conception. The Church should be involved in the marriage process from the very beginning or at least be present in one of the stages considered as a decisive step, although the final conclusion has not yet taken place.[10] Radically argued, one could say that the true problem for the Church to accept the customary marriage as a successive stage in the Christian marriage is the question of sexual intercourse before the final ceremony which is the crowning of all the steps. As known in the Catholic Church, the sexual intercourse is the act which seals or consummates the

8 Cf. A. Kaseba, " L'alliance matrimoniale s'élabore au cours d'un processus par étapes dynamiques, " in: Conférence épiscopale du Zaire (ed.), *Fonctions et tâches de la famille chrétienne dans le monde contemporain*, Kinshasa 1984, 55.

9 Cf. Card. J.-A. Malula, " Mariage et famille en Afrique, " in: *Oeuvres complètes du Cardinal Malula*, rassemblées et présentées par Léon de Saint Moulin, Vol. 7, Kinshasa 1997, 135-144.

10 Cf. J. Njenga, " Marriage in Successive Stages ", 203; V. Mulago, *Mariage traditionnel africain et mariage chrétien*, Kinshasa 1981, 84-91.

marriage and makes it indissoluble. In history, however, it is known that there was a long discussion about "concubitus" and "consensus". At the end, it was agreed to say that the essence of marriage is not in the sexual act (*concubitus*) but in the consent (*consensus*): *"nuptias consensus non concubitus facit"*.[11] The Catholic Church until the present day accepts this theory mainly defended by Peter Lombard. The Church, however, added the thesis of Gratian saying that the *copula* is the fulfilment of the sacrament of marriage showing clearly the union between Christ and his Church.

It is at this point that African marriage has some critical questions. If it is true that consent makes the essence of marriage, the African understanding is in accordance with the teaching of the Church. However, it goes beyond this teaching, for, consent involves a holistic dimension. Not only a single punctual/exact moment is of importance, but the definitive consent embraces the consents at all the steps constituting the marriage. The *copula* itself is one of these steps and can be, according to this rationality, integrated into the process before the final stage. Actually, the *consummatio* is not a physical reality, but it is rooted in the *ubuntu*, expressed by the will of both the spouses and their communities.[12] Finally, the *minister of the sacrament of marriage* is not the married couple alone but the whole tridimensional community.

Consequences for the Traditional African Understanding of Sexuality

We have insisted on the communitarian dimension of marriage in Sub-Saharan Africa. This conception shapes also the understanding of sexuality in its various aspects. In the following we shall give a panorama of the problem and in a second step highlight this by a concrete example related to the problem of pedophilia and homosexuality.

Sexuality and Its Anamnestic Dimension

Sexuality is not an individualistic matter but involves, as in the case of marriage, the whole three-dimensional community of the living, the dead and the not-yet-born. Actually, the final goal of sexuality is eschatological, for it directly leads to

[11] For the discussion and history of this question cf. N. H. Mitendo, *Vers une sacramentalité du système matrimonial négro-africain. Une analyse des concepts de contrat-alliance appliqué au mariage*, Fribourg : Academic Press, 2003, 184-194 ; P. Adnès, *Le mariage,* Tournai : 1963, 77-82 ; E. Schillebeeckx, *Le mariage. Réalité terrestre et mystère de salut*, Paris : Cerf, 1966, 253-266.

[12] On the whole cf. B. Bujo, *Plea for Change of Models* 117-120.

the survival of the tripartite community. At this point the most important aspect to be considered is that related to the ancestors.

Sexuality is not simply an act of self-realization but, ultimately, a remembrance of the forbears who have entrusted the sexual act to the descendants in order to keep alive their memory. Hence, sexual activity in the marriage between man and woman is a *poiesis* nobody should avoid without endangering the *memoria* of the forbears and the existence of the three-fold community as a whole. The reason is that the goal of sexuality in marriage is procreation and, thereby, the assurance of the future of the human being. Furthermore, sexuality is not only an obligation or a duty to fulfill, it is also, and much more, a *gift* of God and of the forbears so that one must learn a correct and respectful attitude towards it. The reason for this attitude is that sexuality is the channel of life. Such a rich conception can be explicitly found for instance among the Dogon of Mali.[13] As Louis-Vincent Thomas reports, this conception seems to be confirmed by the *diola* of Senegal when one of them states that among the things which are of importance for a man who is happy and pleasing to God the body of a woman should not be overlooked because it is the highest organ which is transforming the male seed into a new life.[14]

Given that sexuality embodies such a high value, the African communities pay a special attention to the education of children in this area. Children and especially young people have to learn to take sexuality seriously and to look at it in relationship to life, void of any kind of egoistic interest. One could say, according to the African rationality, that every sexual act which is destined to raise life and to take care of it is morally good and justified. However, this act should not be carried out without the cooperation of the community in its three dimensions. With respect to this, various ethnic communities have established precise rules to regulate the sexual life of their children and young people. Initiation is the time when the youth learn a lifelong discipline not only in sexuality but in everything in order to become a true *muntu* able to give the *ubuntu* to others.

The understanding of sexuality from the life and anamnestic perspective throws light on other problems like *pedophilia* and *homosexuality* in Africa.

---

[13] See especially the study of L.-V. Thomas, "Corps et société. Le cas négro-africain, " in: *L'Afrique et ses formes de vie spirituelle*, Kinshasa ^{2}1990, 193-214.

[14] Cf. ibid. 203.

The Judgement Concerning Pedophilia

When we emphasized the connection between sexuality and life, it should be added that this understanding is not to be related exclusively to the biological life, for in many African traditions sexuality in its bipolarity of man and woman can be practiced without intending for offspring. In fact, what is then essential is that, it should not lose sight of the communitarian dimension. Hence, sexuality in marriage can be expressed for instance at the occasion of great events in a clan's life such as the celebration of the wedding of a child, on the occasion of a funeral or the cutting of the first tooth of a new born, and so on. All these acts, however, are limited to the adults. The children are not mature and cannot be involved in these practices. Maturity is something that has to gradually come about and for the Africans it reaches its summit through the rite of initiation. In other words: The actuation of sexuality is acceptable only after young people have gone through the rite of initiation which enables them to participate fully in the life of adults. Of course, the child is not void of sexuality, yet it needs to be organized, developed, oriented and cultivated before it can become responsible and properly desirous. In this connection Buakasa Tulu Kia Mpansu speaking of some ethnic groups points out that for instance a young girl before the initiation belongs to the invisible world and is wife of the genius-spirits. She ceases to be it and is supposed to be mature, enabled to become wife of a man only after the initiation.[15] More clearly expressed: According to this African rationality, to misuse a child as a sexual object is a destruction of life because the adult who is keen only on his sexual desire does not promote the growth of *Ubuntu;* he/she rather is a murderer to an immature child.[16] It is however worthy to be stressed that, even after the initiation as the attainment of sexual maturity, the right place for sexuality remains within marriage.[17]

When nowadays it is spoken everywhere of child abuse, in Africa we should call to mind our traditions, though they sometimes are expressed as taboos or transmitted through tales and myths. Their goal is always to teach the community and to lead to the ethical norms for the growth of *ubuntu*.[18] The child is the future

[15] Cf. Buakasa T. K. M., *Le Zaire face au développement du sous-développement. Essai d'analyse des écarts d'une société africaine : Economie – Religion – Famille et Sexualité – Enseignement et Techno-Science*, Kinsahas/Libreville/Munich 1988, 134.

[16] Cf. ibid. 135.

[17] Cf. ibid. 136. Buakasa is quoting Mweze Baguma, " Le mariage chez les Bashi et ses transformations récentes. " Résumé de la thèse en français, Université de Paris V, Sorbonne 1987 (unpublished).

[18] For this see B. Bujo, "Funktion von Sprichwörtern, Erzählungen, Tabus und anderen Praktiken

of the ancestors and of the living as well. This future, as already emphasized, goes through sexuality connected with the mystery of life which is unthinkable without any relation to the invisible world of the ancestors and genius-spirits.[19] Therefore, pedophilia is the opposite of bearing/begetting the child as a gift of the invisible world including God, given that according to the African rationality only a witch can practice child abuse because he or she is by his or her very nature the enemy of life. This misuse of sexuality does not concern only pedophilia but also the problem of homosexuality which seems to contradict the fundamental African conception of human being as we shall show in the following paragraph.

What about the homosexuality?

It has already been pointed out how the African anthropology is based on monad, dyad, triad and plurality. The personality reaches its fullness only in the discovering of another gender, which is the encounter between monad and dyad. Stated in a different way, it means that the man as monad discovers his man-being through the woman and vice versa. The latter becomes conscious of her female being through the man. Both, man and woman, discover that they are complementary and that there is "masculinity" in the woman and "femininity" in the man. Only in discovering and accepting this double dimension can the achievement of self-realization as *muntu* be possible, because it means a going from "project" onto *ubuntu*. This process of becoming a full *muntu* opens the door to the community, as already observed: The bipolarity monad-dyad or man-woman generates the tripolarity monad-dyad-triad or man-woman-child which leads to "myriad" or community.

It is thus in the difference of gender that the tripartite community of the living, dead and not-yet-born comes about. A sexual relationship man-man or woman-woman from the perspective of this conception seems to be not only "an egoistic isolationism which dares not take the step to full human existence; it also leads to sexist discrimination against part of the human race and shows an unwillingness to accept the enrichment that comes from heterogenity."[20] We can go on to

---

für die Normbildung in der afrikanischen Ethik", in: Elisabeth Zwick (ed.), *Pädagogik als Dialog der Kulturen. Grundlagen und Diskursfelder der interkulturellen Pädagogik,* Münster/Berlin 2009, 163-182.

[19] See Buakasa T. K. M./H. Didillon, " Le khiita. Une technique yaka de guérison de la stérilité, " in : A. Ngindu M. (ed.), *Combats pour un christianisme africain.* Mélanges en l'honneur du Professeur V. Mulago, Kinshasa : Faculté de théologie catholique, 1981, 243-258.

[20] B. Bujo, *Foundations of an African Ethic. Beyond the Universal Claims of Western Morality,* New York: Crossroad, 2001, 6.

say that homosexuality understood in this way is not to be seen in the light of the traditional Western natural law, but the ethical judgement on it is based on the community understanding. The one who limits himself or herself to practice sexual action within the same gender (monad-monad) is compromising the whole tripartite community and destroying the eschatological destiny of it. In doing so he or she cannot realize him/herself, because a *muntu* cannot reach the *ubuntu* unless there is a contributive action to increase the life-force of the integral whole of community.

All this does in no way mean that there are no cases of homosexuality in traditional Africa. We only emphasize the fact that the cases of homosexuality that might have occurred in the tradition were neither accepted nor institutionalized. Considered from the perspective of bipolar-tripolar and communitarian dimension of the sexual act, the foundation of heterosexuality and the rejection of homosexuality in the tradition were not a matter of natural law. The highest norm was and is still the protection and promotion of life in its holistic dimension, and, consequently, heterosexuality alone can be seen as an acceptable way.

Conclusion

Our extremely rapid overview on African marriage does not intend to discuss the very complex problem of sexuality and family in detail. As shown all along in the whole text above the most important problem related to marriage in Sub-Saharan Africa is not the question of love as this occurs in the Western world. All focuses rather on the family understood as a tripartite community. Until Vatican II many studies had been written on marriage but they mostly dealt with seemingly negative aspects like polygamy, levirate or widow inheritance and so on. It is the merit of the Second Vatican Council to have opened the door for all cultures to raise their voices within the Church in order to enrich Christianity. If the Westerners can claim this openness of the Council for a better understanding of love and marriage, for the Africans it is rather the liberty granted to introduce a new way of dealing with the values of their ancestors. Paul VI encouraged Africans in this way by calling on them to be their own missionaries, because they can and must develop an African Christianity considering the values embodied in their culture.[21] The encouragement of Paul VI continuing the teaching of Vatican II goes back to the whole Church tradition that seemed no more to be remembered, although it

[21] Cf. Pope Paul VI, Discours aux évêques africains in Kampala 1969. See also id., *Africae terrarum* (1967).

was sometimes recalled. However, the Church after the encounter with the Jewish and Greek cultures did nowhere become truly familiar with another local culture.

Many theologians, not only in the recent time but already in the patristic period and in the middle ages, were conscious of the necessity of integrating culture into their interpretation of the Gospel. It may be surprising; but a thinker like Thomas Aquinas pleaded for the use of such a method in the proclamation of the Good News of Christ. He says that the transmission of faith can require the inclusion of the truth found in any science or any wisdom outside the Scripture.[22] This has been confirmed and called to mind by the Decree *Ad gentes*, n. 22. It is therefore legitimate to claim and to repeat that African Christianity can become genuinely African, as Paul VI asked for, only if the Church of the Black Continent continues to consider its culture as a valid instrument for the Gospel which does not remain superficial but addresses the whole *muntu* in his or her *ubuntu*.

22 See the commentary of Thomas Aquinas in Letter to the Galatians, Gal., c. 3, lect. 6, n.154: "Here, indeed, we have an argument to show that in discussions bearing on faith, we may use any truth of any science: 'If thou seest in the number of the captives a beautiful woman and lovest her and wilt have her to wife, thou shalt bring her into thy house," i.e., if you are pleased with worldly wisdom and science, bring it within your boundaries, "and she shall shave her hair, and pare her nails,' i.e., you shall cut away all erroneous opinions (Deut 21:11). This is why in many places in his epistles the Apostle uses the authority of the Gentiles; for example: 'Evil communications corrupt good manners" (1 Cor 15:33), and "The Cretans are always liars, evil beasts, slothful bellies' (Tit. 1: 12)." See, http://dhspriory.org/thomas/SSGalatians.htm (accessed 1/17/2015).

14 Christianity as Fertility Religion: A Response to Prof. Bénézet Bujo

David T. NGONG

Introduction

My original intention for this chapter was to critique the immanent understanding of fertility that has come to characterize much of African Christianity. I intended to appropriate the debate on the difference between Baalism and Yahwism in twentieth century German biblical and theological studies and the recent consensus on the perception of God as a fertile God, to call for a deeper and more nuanced understanding of fertility. This deeper and more nuanced understanding of fertility went beyond the biological and immanent view of the subject. This biological and immanent view of fertility, I think, dominates the understanding of marriage in both African Christianity and a significant document of Vatican II, *Gaudium et Spes* (Pastoral Constitution of the Church, 46-50). It seems to me that this immanent understanding of fertility and fruitfulness has negatively affected married life in Africa, especially for those couples who have not been able to bear children. The point of the paper was to argue that there is a crying need for a pastoral theology that engages infertile couples so that they may not be regarded by church and society as some kind of sub-human beings, as is currently the case in much of Africa. This was the goal of my essay before I was asked to respond to Prof. Bujo's essay. It remains the goal of this chapter after I read Prof. Bujo's presentation. I have tailored my thoughts to respond to some of the specific issues which Prof. Bujo has raised. The overall tenor of my essay will be to question Prof. Bujo's methodological move, which is the theology of inculturation, in terms of the theological and practical viability of some of the positions taken in the previous chapter. My conclusion is that an expansive and nuanced view of fertility is needed to supplement the view of marriage found in both *Gaudium et Spes* and the work of Prof. Bujo. I will begin by giving a brief description of fertility religion.

What is Fertility Religion?

Fertility religions are based on the birth, death, and rebirth or rejuvenation of creation. This process generates a cycle that especially ensures the fertility of the land, thus guaranteeing bountiful harvest. It also guarantees human fertility, thus ensuring the continuation of community. In fertility religions, the fertility of the land and human beings is critical and deity or deities are perceived as singularly concerned with this process. The critical nature of fertility as manifested in fertility religions is understandable: without the fertility of the land there will be no food to sustain the population and famine may lead to the extinction of the people. Also, without human fertility the people will go extinct. Seeing the gods or god as concerned with issues of fertility is therefore quite logical. The religion of the Canaanites, whose land the Israelites seized, has been described as a fertility religion because Baal, the Canaanite God, was pictured primarily as a God who ensured fertility. According to twentieth century German biblical studies, a significant difference between Canaanite religion and the religion of the Hebrew people was that the Canaanite God was a fertility God while the God of the Hebrews was a God who was primarily interested in history. Thus, Baalism, the religion of the Canaanites, was pitted against Yahwism, the religion of Israel, by the portrayal of Baalism as a fertility religion and Yahwism as a historical religion. This distinction between Baalism and Yahwism no longer appears to be apposite because it is now acknowledged that the issue of fertility is critical to both Yahwism and Baalism. In fact, it has been pointed out that a robust doctrine of creation entails taking biblical notions of fertility seriously. As Walter Brueggemann points out, God, as creator, is the one who freely grants fertility to land, humans, and the rest of creation.[1] The importance of fertility can be seen in the critical role births play in biblical religions. From the births of Ishmael and Isaac to the birth of Jesus the Christ, cardinal points in the story of God and creation are marked by births. The importance of birth to the Christian story partly accounts for why Vatican II discussed marriage within the context of procreation, as found in *Gaudium et Spes*. Vatican II also uses language that is reminiscent of procreation when it discusses celibacy in terms of "spiritual fruitfulness" in *Presbyterorum Ordinis* (Decree on the Ministry and Life of Priests, 16). Prof. Bujo's thoughts on the centrality of procreation in the married life also conceptualize Christianity, especially Christianity in Africa, as a fertility religion.

The questions about perceiving Christianity as a fertility religion raised in this chapter are therefore not based on the notion that the Christian faith does not or should not prize fertility. From a theological perspective, fertility is critical to a creative God. From a practical perspective, human beings and other animals

[1] Walter Brueggemann, *Reverberations of Faith: A Theological Handbook of Old Testament Themes* (Louisville, KY: Westminster John Knox Press, 2002), 80–83.

would perish if the land is not fertile and if children are not born. The questions raised here are rather based on how the Christian faith should be conceptualized as a fertility religion. Is fertility decreed by church and society or is it the gift of a transcendent God in whom we live and move and have our being? In other words, does human relationship with God ultimately transcend fertility? Is fertility ultimately theocentric or should it be conceived anthropocentrically, as seems to be the case with the work of Prof. Bujo? What role should fertility, especially human fertility, play in Christian life? We begin answering these questions by looking at the context in which the question of human fertility has often been discussed—the context of the married life. Prof. Bujo's view of marriage in Africa has been influential in the discussion of marriage in Africa.

Crafting an African Theology of Marriage

Prof. Bujo situates his theology of marriage within the context of the development of the theology of inculturation in Africa authorized by Vatican II in *Ad Gentes*. This theology, as is now well known, endeavored to give an African color or face to Christianity, as the titles of some important reflections on the subject, such as that of Mulago and Tshibangu, suggest.[2] Prof. Bujo has been one of the leading voices in this endeavor.[3] The importance of ensuring that the Christian faith speaks to the questions which Africans are asking cannot be overemphasized. One of these issues is, of course, marriage.

The issue of the complexity of African marriages has been raised by Prof. Adrian Hastings in his book *African Catholicism*. This book called for the regularizing of African Catholic marriages.[4] The notion of regularizing African Catholic marriages speaks to one of the central concerns of Prof. Bujo's, namely, that Christianity has delegitimized elements of African marriages. Leaving aside the thorny issue of polygamy, even monogamous marriages still suffer the spite of the church

2 Vincent Mulago, *Un visage Africaine du christianisme: L'Union vitale bantu face à l' Unité vitale ecclésiale* (Paris: Présence Africaine, 1965); T. Tshibangu, "Vers une théologie de couleur Africaine?" *Revue du Clergé Africain* (juillet 1960): 333–346.

3 Bénézet Bujo, *African Theology in Its Social Context* (Maryknoll, NY: Orbis Books, 1992); Idem., Bujo, *Foundations of an African Ethic: Beyond the Universal Claims of Western Morality*, Translated by Brian McNeil (New York, NY: Crossroad, 2001). Also see Wilson Muoha Maina, "African Communitarian Ethics in the Theological Work of Bénézet Bujo" *Pacifica* 21 (June 2008): 192–209.

4 Adrian Hastings, *African Catholicism: Essays in Discovery* (London: SCM Press, 1989). For a history of Christian engagement with African marriages, see Adrian Hastings, "The Church's Response to African Marriage," *African Ecclesiastical Review* XIII no. 3 (1971): 193–203.

which despises carefully constituted marriages in African societies. Prof. Bujo's work holds tremendous insights into how the church may approach marriage in Africa. His call that marriage in Africa be viewed as a communal process rather than a punctiliar event is quite apposite. To this very eloquent call, I would like to state that one of the problems with the punctiliar view of marriage is not mainly that it is Western; rather, the main problem is that it is deeply elitist and casts the lot of the church with the elite rather than with the common people. In my experience, the punctiliar view of marriage has been the preserve of the rich who can afford enough resources to foot the bills that accompany church weddings. Growing up in the village in Cameroon, I never saw a wedding ceremony in the church because the church was made up of poor people who cannot afford the cost of getting married in the church. Men usually followed the process of getting married in the village and brought their wives home without much fanfare. Protestant churches in my village accepted these marriages but the Roman Catholic Church called it irregular. I knew of Christians who were refused the Eucharist because the church deemed their marriages irregular. Such state of affairs demonstrates a continuous devaluation of salutary elements of African cultures in spite of the call by *Ad Gentes* that Africans glorify God within the context of their cultures. Prof. Bujo's work thus carries continued urgency.

My central contention with Prof. Bujo's work is the anthropological framework that undergirds his view of African marriage.

Marriage, Anthropological and Theological Eschatologies

Prof. Bujo's broader framework of marriage is located in African anthropology. This is an anthropology in which human well-being is found in community that includes, first, the living, the dead, and the yet to be born[5] and, second, in the interaction among what he calls the monad, the dyad, and the triad, making up the plurality of the community. In this context, marriage is meant to ensure the continuity of this community because the life of each group or individual in the community is intertwined with the other. First, the life of the dead or what John Mbiti calls the living-dead is not placed only in a theological context in which the

[5] Actually Bujo does not use the concept "yet to be born", but rather "not-yet-born." For Bujo the "yet to be born" could mean that the children will be necessarily born. However, the "not-yet-born" means that some may be born and some others not! Bujo incorporates "pre-existence" in his reading of the African anthropology: in many areas, the children, before coming into this world, have their own world, and as Christians we say they are in the mind of God, according to Jer. 1: 5! (Editor).

dead are expected to spend eternity with God; rather, the life of the dead is also sustained through *anamnesis*, the memory accorded them by the living. Thus, the dead have a vested interest in seeing to it that the living continue to procreate so that there would continue to be members of the community who would keep the memory of the dead alive. It is only when the living foster the memory of the dead that the immortality of the dead is ensured. On the other hand, for the living to have a sense of holistic well-being, they need to maintain cordial relations with the dead.

In this framework, marriage serves as the context in which both the physical and spiritual futures of the community are preserved. A tremendous and even awesome task is thus placed on the living— they are responsible for bringing forth the yet to be born so as to ensure the survival of the dead and the living. In this task, they are of course not alone—the living-dead bestows spiritual blessings that ensure fertility. As Prof. Bujo points out "the living members contribute to the happiness of the deceased, but, in return, the latter provide them with all the necessary gifts for their daily life. Sickness, hunger, barrenness and so on don't occur in the community when the ancestors are not forgotten". One may wonder whether the sickness, hunger, and death found in many African societies are due to the fact that the ancestors have been forgotten. The answer to this question would at best be ambiguous. That question aside, in Prof. Bujo's eschatology, there is a mixture of what one might call African ancestral eschatology with a Christian theological anthropology. The accent is placed on African ancestral eschatology in which the life of the dead depend not so much on God as it does on the living. In short, this eschatology says that our future in the spiritual world is in our own hands.

If the argument were that humans need to procreate because the survival of the human community depends on it, that would be less controversial. The difficulty here is not that human survival depends on procreation; it is rather that the survival of the life of the dead depends on such procreation. And here is where the difficulty lies—what becomes of those married or even unmarried people who do not procreate? African societies have generally shunned those people and Prof. Bujo's anamnestic ancestral eschatology provides no respite for these people. Prof. Bujo's sentiments are echoed by one of the most influential scholars in African Traditional Religions, John Mbiti, when he writes:

> marriage and procreation in African communities are a unity: without procreation marriage is incomplete ... A person who, therefore, has no descendants quenches the fire of life, and becomes forever dead since his line of physical continuation is blocked if he does not get married and bear children ... Unfortunate, therefore, is the man or

> woman who has nobody to 'remember' him (her), after physical death. To lack someone close who keeps the departed in their personal immortality is the worst misfortune and punishment that any person could suffer. To die without getting married and without children is to be completely cut off from the human society, to become disconnected, to become an outcast and to lose all links with mankind.[6]

This ancestral eschatology has caused tremendous grief to countless men and women in Africa, one of whom is a foremost African theologian, the Ghanaian, Mercy Amba Oduyoye. In a very revealing article, she grieves the spite with which she was treated by her in-laws because she was unable to conceive a child. In spite of the fact that she has raised many of the children in her extended family to adulthood, she was still treated with scorn because she could not have her own child. She writes of awkward conversations with people who simply assumed that as a married woman she should have children. She reports of embracing biblical stories of women and men who had children even when they were past their childbearing age. She writes of how Christian men who were friends of her husband's proposed to make her pregnant if her husband was the problem (that is, was infertile). She underwent both traditional and Western medical treatment, some of them in very humiliating circumstances, before finally accepting her lot as an infertile woman destined to be remembered in other ways.[7] If she were the one who was infertile, such was ground for her husband to get married to a second wife so as to have a child by her. Oduyoye even talks of men, some of them pastors, who had children out of wedlock if their wife could not have a child. Because these men were not allowed to marry a second wife because of their position in the church, they preferred to have children out of wedlock. She mused how the marital vow and the injunction against adultery do not mean much if there aren't children in some African Christian marriages. In this context, the important issue is not so much faithfulness and companionship in marriage but the ability to procreate. In all her struggles, both church and society in Nigeria and Ghana, the two African countries where she lives and works, hardly had a soothing word for her.

Oduyoye's forlornness in the African Christian scene has led her to symbolically disavow her marital status by opting to reclaim her maiden name. This symbolic move was preceded by her request to divorce her husband given that she

---

6 John S. Mbiti, *African Religions and Philosophy* (New York: Praeger Publishers, 1969), 133–134.

7 See Mercy Amba Oduyoye, "A Coming Home to Myself: The Childless Woman in the West African Space," in *Liberating Eschatology: Essays in Honor of Letty M. Russell*, ed. Margaret A. Farley and Serene Jones (Louisville, Kentucky: Westminster John Knox Press, 1999), 105–120.

could not be the kind of wife society wanted her to be. A successful marriage, according to this African anthropological eschatology, is one teaming with children. Oduyoye's marital experience as a childless wife made her to feel that nothing else mattered in this African universe. Thus, she symbolically disavowed her marital status by reclaiming her maiden name, Amba Ewudziwa, the name she was given on the eighth day after she was born. This is how, she says, she "would like to come home to herself" as a childless wife, a "woman alone," in the West African space.[8] Oduyoye's disavowal of her marital status because it offers her no fulfillment as a childless wife is a stinging indictment of the African anthropological eschatology and the African church that uncritically espouses it. In addition to symbolically disavowing her marital status as a coping mechanism against the "child factor" in the West African space, Oduyoye also draws from her Christian spirituality characterized by a deep prayer life and the recognition of various spiritual gifts. She then makes the following recommendation for African theology:

> For me childlessness in the West African space has been a challenge—to my womanhood, my humanity, and my faith ... It is for the church to acknowledge and raise up the diversity of God's gifts and to celebrate all the ways of bringing forth life. My concern is for a theology of procreation that responds to this challenge, a theology and eschatology that will speak to both those who reproduce themselves biologically and those who do not, a theology that embraces forms of fruitfulness, biological and beyond.[9]

African theology has, however, not heeded her call for there is a dearth of theological treatment of infertility in African theology. The ancestral eschatology that is based on procreation has rather been carried over into Pentecostal churches in which infertility is interpreted as a curse that needs to be broken. Infertile couples are made to see infertility as an evil which can only be relieved through having their own children. Even adoption, they are told, is no substitute for having their own children.[10] *Gaudium et Spes* does not relieve this grief when it states that "[b]y its very nature the institution of marriage and married love are ordered to the procreation and education of the offspring and it is in them that it finds its crowning glory." This being the case, it does not sound quite revolutionary when the same document later states that "[e]ven in cases where despite the intense desire of the spouses there are no children, marriage still retains its character of

---

8 Oduyoye, "A Coming Home to Myself," 107.

9 Oduyoye, "A Coming Home to Myself," 119.

10 Kwabena Asamoah-Gyadu, "Broken Calabashes and Covenants of Fruitfulness: Cursing Barrenness in Contemporary African Christianity," *Journal of Religion in Africa* 37 no 4 (2007): 437–460.

being a whole manner and communion of life and preserves its value and indissolubility."[11] This concession, while rooted in the theology of creation, fits into the narrative of African ancestral eschatology and worsens the plight of the childless in Africa. In all this, a central question that keeps coming to mind is: where is the theology in this eschatology? Does the human journey into divine life ultimately depend on human beings? Is African ancestral eschatology a sufficient Christian theological eschatology? Should it not rather serve as the raw material from which a viable African Christian theological eschatology is crafted?

A related context in which Prof. Bujo's understanding of African marriage is situated is that of the relation among the monad, the dyad, and the triad that leads to plurality. The monad is the individual person who is an incomplete version of the notion of *ubuntu* (I am because you are; you are because I am). Since the monad is the incomplete version of the notion of *ubuntu*, part of the being of the monad is found by finding the other, particularly the other of the opposite sex. In this case, part of the being of the male is found by finding a female and vice versa. By finding each other, the two unite to produce a third, the triad. It is the various connections among the monad, the dyad and the triad that form the multitude of the community. The main point here is that a person is incomplete if they remain a monad or single. They are still incomplete even if they become a dyad by finding each other of the opposite sex but without conceiving a triad. Completion comes only if they procreate and thus form a triad that gives rise to the plurality of community. While the emphasis on community which this conception entails has much to be said for it, it is still not clear how individuality works within this framework. It is clear from this conception that an individual is an incomplete being who can only find wholeness in being immersed in a community that encompasses the physical and the spiritual. Since this is the case, is there any place for individuality that may invite dissent with this community? Can an individual be allowed to hold views that are ultimately radically incompatible with that of their community? This appears to be impossible as Prof. Bujo has intimated elsewhere that in the African communal context, the individual "has no individual conscience but that of the community."[12] Does this view not necessarily demand the kind of consensus that came to characterize the dictatorship of many African countries?

A related question has to do with how Prof. Bujo conceptualizes celibacy. Since it is the case that monads are by nature incomplete versions of the *ubuntu*,

[11] *Gaudium et Spes*, 48, 50.

[12] Benezet Bujo, *The Ethical Dimension of Community: The African Model and the Dialogue Between North and South* (Nairobi: Paulines Publication Africa, 1998), 28, 75.

are celibates therefore subhuman? This question becomes urgent when we consider that celibates are not only those who will never become a dyad by meeting members of the opposite sex, they are also those who have taken vows to never procreate and so will never form a triad, unless they break their vows. The question becomes even more urgent when we take into consideration the fact of African ancestral eschatology. Who will remember these people when they die, given that they have no offspring to keep alive their memory? A trajectory that has developed in this regard is for the community as a whole to make ancestors of celibates, as it happened in Cameroon in the case of the late African theologian, Prof. Jean-Marc Éla who died in 2008. Considering that he was a Roman Catholic priest who did not have offspring to remember him and that he was perceived as someone who had lived a life that made significant contributions to his people, his village community made him an ancestor. This shows that it is possible to make someone an ancestor in African anthropological eschatology even if that person does not have a child. However, this method of making someone an ancestor is still centered on human achievement, albeit an achievement different from biological procreation. This eschatology, notwithstanding, is still significantly different from a Christian theological eschatology. It makes no place for grace.

A Christian theological eschatology is an eschatology that is not based on procreation, notwithstanding the claim in 1Timothy 2:15 that women will be saved through procreation. Christian eschatology is based on the life, death, and resurrection of Christ and how this singular event draws wayward human beings into the triune divine life. Taking the life of Jesus Christ seriously, it becomes clear that our life with God finally does not rest on the offspring we have but on our single-minded desire to do the will of God. Jesus Christ himself did not have any children and we remember him today not because of his offspring but because he draws us into the life of the triune God. In fact, some African theologians such as Charles Nyamiti and Professor Bujo have even described Jesus Christ as the ancestor.[13] That Jesus is the proto-ancestor of some Africans is clearly not based on any claim that these Africans are his biological offspring. It is rather a declaration that these Africans have come to accept Jesus Christ as their savior. Accepting a childless person as an ancestor and savior of Africans should serve to redefine what it means to be an ancestor in African Christian theology because Jesus Christ does not fit the ordinary definition of an ancestor in Africa. The life, death, and resurrection of Jesus Christ should therefore transform the anthropological escha-

[13] See Ludovic Lado, "The Roman Catholic Church and African Religions: A Problematic Encounter," *The Way* vol. 45 no. 3 (July 2006): 7–21, especially p. 14. Available online. Also see Robert J. Schreiter, ed., *Faces of Jesus in Africa* (Maryknoll, NY: Orbis Books, 1991).

tology of ATRs that seem to inform some forms of African theology today to a theocentric eschatology that takes up the human into divine life, valorizing the biological in the spiritual life of God. This view of salvation is one that takes up the material into divine life so that all material forms of life are transformed in God. In this scheme of things, having children is a good thing but it is ultimately not decisive for the Christian life with God. As Christians, our goal is to participate, eternally, in the life of God rather than to become ancestors. Becoming an ancestor is a worthy goal that needs to be pursued by Africans who cherish that goal. However, African Christians should be enabled to come to the realization that becoming an ancestor is not the critical issue in a Christian eschatology; participating eternally in divine life is the goal. In this case, the continuation of life is not based on human memory but on divine memory. And divine memory is not based on the number of offspring people have.

A final issue which Prof. Bujo's essay raises is that of homosexuality. Homosexuality, as Prof. Bujo sees it, is effectively ruled out by the nature of *ubuntu*. Homosexuals, like infertile people, kill the creative impulse that generates the community of both the living and the dead. Homosexuals, in the African scheme of things, will never form a dyad because they will never meet the opposite sex. Because they will never form a dyad, it follows that they will also never form a triad and a plurality. Thus, homosexuality is rejected in Africa not on any biblical or theological ground but on the ground of African anthropology which finds its ultimate end in ancestral eschatology. In spite of this rejection of homosexuality, Prof. Bujo acknowledges that there have been homosexuals in Africa. One must hasten to add that there continue to be homosexuals in Africa. Thus, the pressing question that needs to be raised is what to do with these people? The widespread homophobia in much of Africa is well known. In some cases, homosexuals have been killed and some have sought asylum in foreign lands. Is this the fate which African Christian theologians expect to befall homosexuals in our continent? Does portraying homosexuals as enemies of a holistic life not put their lives in danger even more? Why would African theologians want to be remembered as people who have taken up the cudgel against homosexuals?[14] More importantly, where is God in all this?

---

[14] Adriaan S. Van Klinken and Masiiwa Ragies Gunda, "Taking up the Cudgel Against Gay Rights? Trends and Trajectories in African Christian Theologies on Homosexuality," *Journal of Homosexuality* 59 (2012): 114–138. Also see Marc Epprecht, "Religion and Same Sex Relations in Africa," in *The Wiley-Blackwell Companion to African Religions*, ed. Elias Kifon Bongmba (Oxford: Oxford University Press, 2012), 515–528.

Conclusion

This essay has argued that although situating Christian marriage in the African cultural context may have some value, it is also very problematic in other respects. The African anthropological or ancestral eschatological context poses difficulty because human worth and memory is finally not located in the life of God but rather in human biological fertility. From a Christian theological perspective, humans are created in the image of God and their final destiny is to find their ultimate rest in God. This does not depend on biological procreation but rather on many different ways of participating in divine creativity. While Christianity can and should clearly be seen as a fertility religion because the Christian God is a fertile God, it is theologically very problematic to situate human worth and ultimate destiny mainly within the context of biological procreation. For African cultures that seem to prize human holistic well-being, situating human well-being mainly within the context of procreation causes grief to many. Any culture that inscribes such grief in its central salvific narrative needs to be rethought. The African church is still to construct a viable theology that shows that human worth and ultimate destiny rests in divine life rather than in human procreation.

15 Africa, Priorities of Mission: The Second Special Assembly of the Synod of Bishops for Africa and *Africae Munus*

James Chukwuma OKOYE, C.S.SP.

Introduction

The second Special Assembly of the Synod of Bishops for Africa met in Rome, October 4-25, 2009. The synod fathers handed over to the pope the whole documentation of the synod, including fifty-five propositions (henceforth Prop). On November 19, 2011, in Ouidah, Benin Republic, His Holiness, Benedict XVI presented to the bishops of Africa the Post-Synodal Apostolic Exhortation *Africae Munus* (henceforth *AfrM*), On the Church in Africa in Service to Reconciliation, Justice and Peace.[1]

A Snap Shot of the Synod

There are positive signs in the situation of Africa today. They include the rebirth of a dynamic Christianity, the growing number of African missionaries inside and outside, the advent of peace in some African countries, a growing commitment to human rights, especially to the empowerment of women (Lineamenta[2], 6-7). But the continent continues to resemble the paralytic of Mark 2:1-12, paralyzed in different ways and in great distress (AfrM, 98). Though rich in human and natural resources, she suffers "through a tragic complicity and criminal conspiracy of local leaders and foreign interests" (Message[3], 5). The burden of international debt cripples many countries. Under the pretext of reducing poverty an unjust order has

1 The first Special Assembly of the Synod of Bishops for Africa took place in Rome, April 10 to May 8, 1994. On September 14, 1995 in Yaoundé, Cameroun, John Paul II issued the Apostolic Exhortation *Ecclesia in Africa* On the Church in Africa and its Evangelizing Mission towards the Year 2000. The five priorities of mission discussed by that synod were: The Proclamation of the Good News, Inculturation, Dialogue, Justice and Peace, and the Means of Social Communication.

2 Lineamenta. Synod of Bishops, II Special Assembly for Africa. The Church in Africa in Service to Reconciliation, Justice and Peace. "You are the salt of the earth... You are the light of the world" (Matt 5:13-14).

3 Message to the People of God of the Second Special Assembly for Africa of the Synod of Bishops.

often helped to aggravate it (AfrM, 79). The result is widespread deterioration in the standard of living and insufficient means for educating the young or providing elementary health; the infant mortality rate continues to grow (Lineamenta, 8). The situation is made worse by fratricidal wars and conflicts leading to the record number of fifteen million refugees and migrants, who often suffer discriminatory migration policies and laws (Prop 28).

The Church's Engagement

The Church is fully engaged in improving the situation. She is resolutely committed to the fight against infirmities, disease and the great pandemics (*AfrM*, 139; *Message*, 31). In many parts of Africa the Church is the last standing institution that functions well, able and willing to speak truth to power and influence the political process for good. She has been ready, when called upon, to act as artisans of peace and reconciliation, for example in Mali, the Republic of the Congo, Burkina Faso, Senegal and Niger (*Message*, 18). Through her Justice and Peace Commissions, the Church in Africa has initiated programs for the civic formation of citizens; she assists in the electoral process in a number of countries (*AfrM*, 23). However, "the first and most specific contribution of the Church to the people of Africa is to proclaim the Gospel of Christ" (*Message*, 15). The Church lives this witness to the gospel in the public domain, yet must avoid both immediate engagement in politics and withdrawal or evasion (*AfrM*, 17). For Christ does not propose a revolution of a social or political kind, but a revolution of love (*AfrM*, 26). This revolution calls for a genuine conversion of heart for all, and in this conversion is the good of humanity. To promote such conversion within the household of the Church, the first assembly of the synod of bishops for Africa (1994) proposed a pastoral based on the "Church as Family of God." To promote it in the body politic, the Church in Africa must be more proactive in proclaiming and bringing to bear the social doctrine of the Church, a necessary dimension of the proclamation of the gospel (*AfrM*, 22). One value to inculcate in both Church and society is commitment to solidarity. Solidarity calls for that *justice of love* which goes beyond distributive justice to give itself to the utmost (*AfrM*, 25), so that "the abundance of some compensates for the want of others (*AfrM*, 24, *Lineamenta*, 44). The Church works eagerly for the "globalization of solidarity" so as to inscribe "in commercial relations the principle of gratuitousness and the logic of gift as an expression of fraternity" (*AfrM*, 86; Benedict XVI, *Caritas in Veritate*[4], 36). For in the Family of God all peoples are brothers and sisters.

Paths towards Reconciliation, Justice and Peace: Church, Family of God

"Evangelization today takes the name of reconciliation" (*AfrM*, 174). It is God's grace that gives us a new heart and reconciles us with him and with one another (*AfrM*, 20). All Christians are admonished to welcome the grace of the Holy Spirit and to "be reconciled to God" (2 Cor 5:20). The Church, Family of God in Africa, is called to model a reconciled and just national institution (*Message*, 18). As befits the family of God, she is to witness to care for others, solidarity, warmth in human relationships, acceptance, dialogue and trust (*AfrM*, 7; *Ecclesia in Africa*, 63). To accomplish this, catechesis must be lived catechesis and lead to permanent conversion of life (*AfrM*, 32; Prop 43), so that reconciliation becomes a way of life and a mission. This demands that the Church use the graces of the sacrament of reconciliation more effectively, in its dual aspects of ongoing personal and communal *metanoia* (Prop 5). That way, "being disciples of Jesus supersedes all other forms of allegiance to clan or political party" (Prop 5). For the good of the continent, bishops are to promote intra-ecclesial solidarity at all levels, in personnel and finances, especially as regards SECAM (Symposium of the Episcopal Conferences of Africa and Madagascar) and COMSAC (Confederation of Conferences of Major Superiors of Africa and Madagascar) (*AfrM*, 106-7). Bishops are to incorporate the values of traditional reconciliation procedures in so far as these help to transform the people's psyche (*AfrM*, 33; Prop 8). African experiences of the faith need be internalized in an African theology (*AfrM*, 136; *Ecclesia in Africa*, 103), and the phenomenon of "dual affiliation" (*AfrM*, 93) addressed. Priests affirm reconciliation brought by the gospel when they live and work across tribal and racial lines (*Message,* 19), just as religious community living where brothers and sisters coming from different ethnic or racial backgrounds live and work together in love (*AfrM*, 117). All Christians, no matter the denomination, must set the example of ecumenical working together for unity and mutual reconciliation. All who believe in God must banish every form of discrimination, intolerance and religious fundamentalism that easily has recourse to violence (*AfrM*, 94). Each country is to celebrate a day or week of reconciliation, particularly during Advent

[4] Encyclical Letter *Caritas in Veritate*, June 29, 2009.

or Lent. In union with the Holy See, SECAM could promote a continental Year of Reconciliation as an extraordinary Jubilee Year (*AfrM*, 157; Prop 8).

Paths towards Reconciliation, Justice and Peace: The Body Politic

The social doctrine of the Church is founded on the dignity of the human person made in the image of God. It therefore calls for the defense of life and of marriage and family, seeing that the family is the first setting for a culture of forgiveness, peace and reconciliation (*AfrM*, 43). The defense of life also entails the elimination of ignorance. Illiteracy is not only a scourge on a par with that of the pandemics, but is also one of the principal obstacles to development (*AfrM*, 76). Catholic schools are a precious resource for learning; enabling children of the proper age to receive schooling is a matter of justice for each child and for the future of Africa (*AfrM*, 134). Bishops are to promote the formation of women so they assume "their proper share of responsibility and participation in the community life of the society and … of the Church" (*AfrM,* 57; *Ecclesia in Africa*[5], 121). Every effort needs be made to eliminate the death penalty, also to reform the penal system to ensure respect for prisoners' human dignity. The study and use of *restorative justice*[6] as a means and process for promoting reconciliation, justice and peace is encouraged (Prop 54). Victims have a right to truth and justice; it is thus important for the present and future to purify memories and so build a better society where tragedies do not repeat (*AfrM*, 21). All members of the Church are to work for and speak out in favor of an economy that cares for the poor and is resolutely opposed to the unjust order (*AfrM*, 79). The Church is to encourage politicians to protect such fundamental goods as land and water for present and future generations and for peace between peoples (*AfrM*, 80; Prop 30).

Permanent formation programs offered to laity and above all the political and economic leaders must insist on conversion as a necessary condition for the transformation of the world (*AfrM*, 103). A necessary part of such programs must be the Church's social doctrine (*AfrM, 128*), so that Christian laity and professionals can have a transforming presence in the public arena and in arts and culture (*AfrM*, 131). Prop 37 (not explicitly taken up by the pope) mentions leadership training for transformative action as part of such programs.

---

5 John Paul II, Post-Synodal Apostolic Exhortation *Ecclesia in Africa*, September 1995.

6 "Restorative justice is a process to involve, to the extent possible, those who have a stake in a specific offense and to collectively identify and address harms, needs, and obligations, in order to heal and put things as right as possible." Howard Zehr, *The Little Book of Restorative Justice* (Intercourse: Good Books, 2002) 37.

Two fundamental values are to be at the center of all human, political, economic or social activity: the human person and the common good (*AfrM*, 129). It is indispensable that students be taught the Church's social doctrine (*AfrM*, 137). Ways in which such formation could be given (though not explicitly taken up by the pope) are the following: Catechetical materials could be revised at every level to include appropriate elements of the church's social doctrine (Prop 18); the bishops could gather collections of their own social teaching in pastorals and other messages; a team of researchers could draw up a syllabus for social and Christian values from primary school to university level; the church's social doctrine could become mandatory in all seminary and ongoing formation for priests, religious and laity (ibid), and peace and conflict resolution could be integrated into courses for seminary formators (Prop 21). Bishops are to establish new Catholic universities wherever these do not yet exist. These can shed both the light of the gospel and the light that Africa needs (*AfrM*, 135). Catholic cultural centers give the Church presence and action in the field of cultural exchange (*AfrM*, 136).

Conclusion

Some propositions, not explicitly taken up by the pope but which lie within the competence of the bishops, are the following:

1. On justice and poverty—the Church in Africa is to develop internal systems for taking care of the poor, orphans and the marginalized, perhaps experiment with micro-finance in function of this. She could sponsor educational programs that are more production-oriented (Prop 17). She could invest in career counseling, entrepreneurial training and creation of jobs for youth (Prop 48).
2. In view of conflicts all over Africa, the Church could establish a permanent organization for inter-ethnic dialogue (Prop 21). The picture is that of a Church not closed up in herself and her liturgies, but committed to Africa precisely because of her commitment to the Lord and his gospel. Christians, though "not of this world" (John 17:14, 16) must so love the world as give all their energy for its reconciliation and peace (cf. John 3:16). Nevertheless, she must bear in mind that the Lord has not assigned her competence in the secular arena, so clergy must shun the temptation of becoming political leaders or social agents (*AfrM*, 108).

I conclude with two messages. First the bishops of Africa (*Message*, 42):

> Africa is already moving; and the Church is moving with her, offering her the light of the Gospel. The waters may be turbulent. But with our gaze on Christ the Lord (cf. Matt 14:28-32), we shall make it safely to the port of reconciliation, justice and peace.

Finally, His Holiness, Benedict XVI:

> Get up, the Church in Africa … because you are being called by the heavenly Father, whom your ancestors invoked as Creator even before knowing his merciful closeness revealed in his only-begotten Son, Jesus Christ. Set out on the path of a new evangelization with the courage that comes to you from the Holy Spirit (*AfrM*, 173).

16 Relational Theologies of Ministry and Implications for Plural, Missional Identities

Maureen R. O'BRIEN

Introduction

This Chapter will focus on a particularly "local," United States contextual phenomenon that I see as having broader significance for mission: the emergence of new ministries and ministers and the resulting theological reflection. As the numbers of ordained priests and vowed religious shrink, laity and, in many dioceses, permanent deacons have assumed significant ministerial roles in a variety of settings: not only parishes, but healthcare facilities, prisons, social service agencies and other venues. Considerable resources and energy are being invested in the formation and oversight of these ministers in order that they become faithful and effective representatives of the church.

So-called "relational" theologies of ministry, developed in response to and recognition of these new configurations, propose ecclesiological models emphasizing both Trinitarian communion and hierarchical differentiation. Church documents, notably the United States Bishops' *Co-Workers in the Vineyard of the Lord*, published in 2005, seek to articulate such a model for lay ecclesial ministers vis-à-vis ordained ministers.[1] Concurrently, professional ministers' organizations, local churches and the US Conference of Catholic Bishops are developing common standards for formation and, in the case of lay ministers, certification and authorization.

These attempts are laudable and represent significant efforts to move from a stark clergy/laity division to one of genuine collaboration in ministry, with all ministers operating in organic, dynamic mutuality. However, as I will argue, such approaches are not fully cognizant of the ambiguities inherent in the lived realities of ministers, which often do not easily conform to the emerging ecclesial "ordering" of their roles. I believe that North American relational theologies of ministry need to be informed by emerging global perspectives on marginality and hybridity in order to become truly contextualized and to foster effective mission today. Such informing will, in turn, raise new insights for how ministries may be configured in global mission in diverse contexts.

[1] United States Conference of Catholic Bishops, *Co-Workers in the Vineyard of the Lord* (Washington, D.C.: USCCB, 2005).

Accordingly, I will proceed in this essay to summarize the central elements of current relational theologies of ministry in the United States Catholic Church. Then, focusing on the newly delineated category of "lay ecclesial ministers," I will point to ways in which their experiences challenge these theologies, highlighting the ministers' movements among ecclesial and communal margins and their own reflections on this marginality. Finally, I will suggest how various global approaches to mission may inform and be formed through engagement with relational theologies.

Relational Theologies of Ministry

Edward Hahnenberg, a young US theologian, has become one of the most prominent proponents of this method, especially as presented in his book, *Ministries: A Relational Approach.*[2] He also was an influential consultant to the US bishops as they drafted *Co-Workers in the Vineyard of the Lord*. He finds in Trinitarian communion the basis for a viable relational theology of ministry. "Thinking about God as Trinity leads us into the mystery of relationships. Talking about ministry in the language of Trinitarian doctrine leads us to a relational approach to ministry."[3] This approach naturally emerges, of course, from the presentation in *Lumen Gentium's* Chapter 1 of the church as drawing its life from the communion of the Trinity and thus basing its identity and mission on communion. The bishops' *Co-Workers* document, as well, develops its theological foundations for lay ecclesial ministry through grounding these in the Triune God. All the baptized are drawn into relationship with this relational God, gifted with the Spirit's diverse charisms for the transformation of the world.

As in *Lumen Gentium*, so in this USCCB document, once the essential unity of the church in communion with the Triune God is established, hierarchical roles are delineated. *Co-Workers* uses the phrase "right relationships" to characterize the importance of the proper ordering of the ecclesial body's gifts and consequent mission (*CVL,* 21). The document maintains the necessity of distinctions so that the church's nature is properly illuminated (*CVL*, 13), and goes on to discuss the

2 Edward P. Hahnenberg, *Ministries: A Relational Approach* (New York: Crossroad, 2003). Others include the authors in the collection edited by Susan K. Wood, *Ordering the Baptismal Priesthood: Theologies of Lay and Ordained Ministry* (Collegeville, Minn.: Liturgical Press, 2003), and the collection edited by William J. Cahoy, *In the Name of the Church: Vocation and Authorization of Lay Ecclesial Ministry* (Collegeville, Minn.: Liturgical Press, 2012).

3 Hahnenberg, *Ministries: A Relational Approach,* 76.

relationship of the lay ecclesial minister to the bishop, the priest, the deacon and the lay faithful.

Hahnenberg takes a somewhat different tack in outlining a set of relationships that seeks to hold together both the status and the tasks of the minister. He explicitly places himself in the trajectory of Yves Congar and Thomas P. O'Meara, who worked in response to Vatican II to lay out new constructs for how clergy and laity are related within the conciliar vision of the church.[4] Like them, he rejects a sharply demarcated or pyramidal division between clergy and laity, opting instead for a schema of concentric circles. Here he places in the center circle those with the most permanent calling and/or most central responsibilities for community leadership: bishops, pastors and canonically installed "parish life coordinators."[5] In the next circle are found "full-time leaders of important areas of ministry within the community"[6]—generally lay ecclesial ministers or perhaps deacons with functions such as director of religious education or parish pastoral associate. Next are Christians who serve in more part-time, occasional ministries such as lectors and Eucharistic ministers. In the outer circle are all who "serve the church and the Reign of God in witness, charity and service."[7]

Hahnenberg maintains that such a model is most adequate both to include the ancient ordained ministries and to incorporate the contemporary realities of the non-ordained ministers, especially those whose ministries require extensive training and a relatively stable commitment. By his own admission, he is focusing primarily on "ecclesial," rather than what he calls "interpersonal," relationships in his theology.[8] However, I believe that we need to probe the interpersonal, experiential realities of today's ministers to illuminate his theoretical construct and increase its adequacy. Such investigation reveals that even his more flexibly ordered relationships—not to mention the more dogmatically presented ones in *Co-Workers*—are altered by the fluidity and ambiguity of ministerial experience. Thus we turn to the next section.

---

4 See, for example, Yves Congar, "My Path-Findings in the Theology of Laity and Ministries," *The Jurist* 32 (1972): 169-88; and Thomas P. O'Meara, O.P. *Theology of Ministry* (New York/Mahwah: Paulist Press, 1999).

5 Cf. Canon 517.2.

6 Hahnenberg, *Ministries: A Relational Approach,* 127.

7 Ibid.

8 Ibid., 94-95.

Lay Ecclesial Ministers: Hybrid and Marginal Identities

Certainly the Catholic Church is at pains in its teachings—if not always in practice—to acknowledge and celebrate the diversity of its people, and to affirm the right of all to develop and maintain their distinctive cultures. In the United States, concerted attention is given to such diversity in the formation of Catholic ministers, lay and ordained.

However, the relational theologies represented thus far fail to consider adequately the blurring of identities and sense of plural selves increasingly characteristic of our global contexts and, indeed, characteristic of many lay ministers.[9] In my research with them I am struck by their frequent expression of finding themselves "betwixt and between" in their identities and functions—to use a phrase from an essay by Peter Phan.[10] Not ordained, yet exercising ministerial leadership in ways different from other laity, they find themselves in a kind of hybrid existence that can be fraught with conflicting expectations and demands. Here I will draw upon the voices of these ministers in dialogue with other theological writers to illuminate aspects of this ambiguous identity.[11]

In an insightful article, Michele Saracino discusses what she calls the "borders" that exist both *between* and *within* people, places and things in our globalized context. Persons have "multiple borders" and hybrid identities, and "each of us, rather than being any essential core, is an aggregate of many stories."[12] Being this way highlights the vital role of story, memory and "the affective ambiguity or the emotional turmoil of borders."[13] People who are embodied as racially and culturally blended or "hyphenated" carry such ambiguity in an especially pointed manner. Writing from his own experience of hybrid identity, Korean-American theologian Jung Young Lee stated that "To be in-between two worlds means to

---

9 Friedrich Schweitzer provides a helpful treatment of postmodernity's effects on the human life cycle in Northern cultures in *The Postmodern Life Cycle: Challenges for Church and Theology* (St. Louis, MO: Chalice Press, 2004).

10 See Peter C. Phan, "Betwixt and Between: Doing Theology with Memory and Imagination," in *Journeys at the Margin: Towards an Autobiographical Theology in Asian-American Perspective*, ed. Phan and Jung Young Lee (Collegeville, Minn., Liturgical Press, 1999), 113-134.

11 All quotations from lay ministers in this essay derive from my research project, "A Collaborative Theological Research and Writing Project with Catholic Lay Ministers," funded by the Faculty Development Fund of Duquesne University. The project is further described in Maureen R. O'Brien and Susan Yanos, eds., *Emerging from the Vineyard: Essays by Lay Ecclesial Ministers* (Fortuity Press, 2014).

12 Michele Saracino, "Hybridity and Trespass: With Jesus at the Borders of Identity," *Horizons 33/2 (2006):* 223.

13 Ibid., 224.

be fully in neither. The marginal person who is placed between this two-world boundary feels like a non-being."[14]

As reflected in statistical studies, US lay ecclesial ministers generally do not embody hybridity so starkly—most are white and female. Yet, while relational theologies promote a harmonious interplay between the concentric circles or organizational lines of ecclesial ministry, these become problematic when compared with the everyday dilemmas of lay ecclesial ministers. They readily name conflicts among their various roles (for example, as minister, wife and mother), degrees of authority, and other factors as occasioning turmoil that affects the stability of their identity construction and ministerial effectiveness. For example, when invited to discuss the topic of ecclesial marginality in their own life narratives, some lay ecclesial ministers acknowledged the pain of having, on one hand, experiences of being recognized for their expertise and credentials, and on the other, being marginalized from the centers of ecclesial power, especially in pastor-to-lay interactions. One, after being verbally abused by her pastor, compared it to the employer-employee relationships between white and African American women in the recent movie, *The Help*:

> ... In some ways I couldn't help but think as lay ecclesial ministers, in many cases, we are "the help."... I lament the lack of integrity and truth telling that is allowed to creep into parish work. And I often fear because this is my livelihood, that I too may feed into it at times.[15]

Another, who holds a position designed to support lay ministers in her diocese, finds herself regularly in positions of both "centrality" and "marginality"—categories developed by Lee—in the exercise of authority:

> I am on the margins in many ways: when I minister in a liturgy, when I try to advocate for one of my youth ministers with a pastor who is canonically in charge of the parish, when I try to get funding for my programs. Although it looks like I have the power to make changes, I often can't.... But I move to the center in ministry as well. Youth and parish ministers in the field look to me as a leader. Sometimes, people defer to me in meetings. There are public events in which I speak, teach and help present policy. There are times when I represent Church.

Saracino points to the sense of "homelessness" engendered by such conflicts.[16]

---

[14] Jung Young Lee, *Marginality: The Key to Multicultural Theology* (Minneapolis: Fortress Press, 1995), 45.

[15] All quotations from lay ecclesial ministers come from my own research, funded by a grant from the Faculty Development Fund of Duquesne University, 2010-12.

[16] Saracino, "Hybridity and Trespass: With Jesus at the Borders of Identity," 229.

With this brief survey of themes and narratives, let us move to some implications for mission.

Claiming Insights for Transformed Ministerial and Missional Practices

In *The New Catholicity,* Robert Schreiter has argued that a truly "catholic" church will seek to hold together many tensions raised by the dissipating and conflictual effects of globalization on people's identity and agency.[17] This disposition is hard-won and difficult to maintain, especially if ecclesial energies are being spent on shoring up the distinctions between clergy and lay. While the relational theologies I outlined briefly in my first section undoubtedly have their merits in helping to order the diverse ministries of Christians, such efforts primarily address only one of the *tria munera* of Christ, that of the "kingly" or governing mission. I maintain that lay ecclesial ministers, in dialogue with theologies of border crossings and marginality, are well positioned to contribute to a necessary, corresponding focus on the "priestly" and "prophetic" dimensions of Christian mission. Thus I will conclude with two implications, drawing for support on the voices of lay ecclesial ministers and those of theologians who treat hybridity and marginality.[18]

The Need To Highlight Priestly And Prophetic Missions As Interwoven In The Agency Of Ministers As They Move Between "Margins" And "Centers."

To be priestly is to mediate between human and divine, to sanctify and transform one's everyday world through holy practice. When the marginal are *priestly*, though, they are also necessarily *prophetic*, for they speak and act in ways that challenge the prevailing "order," however well-intentioned its relational construals may be. Jung Young Lee names this as the creation of new centers *at* the margins, where the Spirit's power is manifested in new and creative ways.[19]

---

17 Robert J. Schreiter, *The New Catholicity: Theology between the Global and the Local* (Maryknoll, N.Y.: Orbis, 1997), 128.

18 I am not denying, of course, that ordained ministers will also likely experience hybridity and marginality.

19 See Lee, for example: "the core or new center is also the margin at the same time. However, in new marginality, the margin is no longer the margin of centrality, the margin defined by dominant groups, but the new margin, the margin of marginality. Thus, in new marginality, the creative core is also the margin. In this margin of marginality, the conflict between the margin and the center disappears, and a reconciliation between marginality and centrality takes place" (60-61).

Another lay minister recounted how she, her pastor and a lay parishioner were invited to make a presentation on their teamwork model for a large conference of clergy and lay parish council members. She described her role in literally standing between the voluble pastor and shy parishioner for as they received audience questions:

> [As a lay ecclesial minister] I have been granted the authority to gently wrest the microphone from my pastor's hand and deliver it to my parishioner, when the question was better answered there; and then hand it back to the clergy, when appropriate. I even provided a few answers myself.
>
> The spirituality of the lay ecclesial minister: helping lay people to speak their voice and to better appreciate their need for the Church; and vice versa.

To me this action vividly conveyed her "priestly" mediation in balancing the voices of pastor and parishioner and honoring what both could communicate of the workings of the Holy in their lives. She also was "prophetic" in claiming this role at the ecclesial "borders" and exercising it effectively as a layperson.

Another lay ecclesial minister created a new "center" at the margins, to use Lee's terms, in a manner both priestly and prophetic. Angered by his pastor's refusal to allow a local homeless man to sleep in the parish's empty convent during a frigid winter, he invited the man to stay in his own home with his young family. This happened in Advent, and the minister also decided to invite several parishioners to join the family and their homeless guest in a home ritual and shared meal during each Sunday of the season. He spoke of his strong sense of calling to create and take on leadership in this liturgical space—a "priestly" function in the domestic church—and simultaneously witnessed to the official exclusion of the economically and socially marginalized in his parish—a "prophetic" function. He named these Sunday experiences as "epicenters of grace."

The Importance Of Drawing Wisely Upon Christian Narratives And Metaphors That Speak To The Fluidity Of Margins And Centers In Mission And Ministry.

Those in global mission, like those in US lay ecclesial ministry, will move between margins and centers if they are committed in discipleship to Jesus. Border crossings will be required of them. A variety of narratives and metaphors will be needed to speak to the variety of experiences and others whom they encounter in their changing roles.

Lee and Saracino both highlight the marginality of incarnation to show how Jesus moves from divine center to human margin in his kenotic and hybrid existence. The diocesan-employed lay ecclesial minister cited above stated:

> When I am in the center, images that are helpful in ministry are Jesus coming in humility to serve, healing, showing compassion and empowering others through teaching and prayer. When I am at the margin, I think of Jesus praying, speaking truth in love, leading through powerlessness. In the center, I think of Jesus feeding the 5000. On the margins it's the cross.
>
> I don't mind moving between margin and center. Our tradition teaches that mobility is a path to holiness. Traveling is what Jesus did.... I feel [my ministry] is both action and contemplation, and that God is dynamic and always moving....

Again, relational theologies of ministry in themselves are inadequate for fully plumbing the Christian tradition in search of the metaphors needed amid experiences that pull one between marginal and central standpoints. One Gospel account, one strand of the tradition, may be more appropriate when marginality is highlighted, and another for situations in which the minister wields authority. God is, indeed, "dynamic and always moving," and so are we if truly in mission to a world of border crossings and all their consequences.

Contributors

Victor Anderson is the Oberlin Theological School Professor of Ethics and Society at Vanderbilt Divinity School and the Program in African American and Diaspora Studies in the College of Arts and Sciences. A member of the Vanderbilt faculty since 1992, he is author of three books: *Beyond Ontological Blackness: An Essay on African American Religious and Cultural Criticism* (1995), *Pragmatic Theology: Negotiating the Intersections of an American Philosophy of Religion and Public Theology* (1998), and *Creative Exchange: A Constructive Theology of African American Religious Experience* (2008). Professor Anderson received his Ph.D. in Religion, Ethics and Politics from Princeton University. He teaches courses in religion and cultural studies, ethics, and social theory.

Michel Elias Andraos is Associate Professor Catholic Theological Union, Chicago, Department of Intercultural Studies and Ministry. Professor Michel Andraos' areas of research and teaching in theology include religion, violence and peace, and theologies of religious pluralism and interreligious dialogue. His current research projects focus on the encounter of the church and Indigenous peoples of the Americas and reconciliation, and the relation between the Christian communities in the Levant and Western Christianity during the European colonial period.

Gerald M. Boodoo, Ph.D., a native of Trinidad & Tobago, specializes in world theologies with emphasis on the Caribbean. He explores appropriate ways to enable multiple and varied voices to be heard to enhance contemporary theological endeavor. He has published on theology in the Caribbean and immigrant Caribbean communities, as well as on transgressive and liberation theologies. Dr. Boodoo currently directs the Center for African Studies at Duquesne University and is a member of the theology department. He serves as methodological coordinator of the World Forum on Theology and Liberation, editorial coordinator of EATWOT's VOICES, on the executive board of the Conference of Theology in the Caribbean Today.

Bénézet Bujo is a diocesan priest from the Democratic Republic of the Congo, professor emeritus of moral theology and social ethics at the University of Fribourg, Switzerland. He is the author of *African Theology in Its Social*

Context (2006). Other influential books by Bujo include *Foundations of an African Ethic: Beyond the Universal Claims of Western Morality* (2001). *The ethical dimension of Community: the African Model and the Dialogue between North and South* (1998). He also edited with Juvénal Ilunga Muya *African Theology – the Contribution of the Pioneers* (2 volumes, 2005). *Introduction à la théologie africaine* (2008). *African Theology in 21st Century - the Contribution of the Pioneers* (vol. 3, 2013).

Michael S. Driscoll is a priest of the Helena Diocese and since 1994 has been on the faculty at the University of Notre Dame Indiana where he teaches sacramental theology and liturgy. He is actively involved in pastoral practice, having worked as Choir Director of the Helena Cathedral and liturgical consultant around the United States. He is the founding director of the Notre Dame graduate program in Sacred Music and the undergraduate minor in Liturgical Music Ministry. He has served as president of the North American Academy of Liturgy (2002) and the Catholic Academy of Liturgy (2013) and was twice elected to the Council of the Societas Liturgica, an international ecumenical learned society.

Kenneth R. Himes is Associate Professor and former chairman of the Department of Theology at Boston College. He received his Ph.D. from Duke University in religion and public policy. A member of the Order of Friars Minor the Franciscans, Professor Himes is also an ordained Catholic priest. He has a special interest in the area of Catholic social teaching and the role of the church in American public life. A past president of the Catholic Theological Society of America, Fr. Himes is author of three books and co-editor of two others. His latest book, *The Ethics of Targeted Killing and Drones* will be published in 2015.

Laurenti Magesa teaches African Theology and Ethics at Hekima College Jesuit School of Theology, Tangaza University College, and the Maryknoll Institute of African Studies in Nairobi, Kenya. Some of his influential books include *African Religion. The Moral Traditions of Abundant Life* (1997); and *Anatomy of Inculturation – Transforming the Church in Africa* (2004). His latest book is *What Is Not Sacred? African Spirituality* (NY: Orbis Books, 2013 and Nairobi: Acton Publishers, 2014).

Michael McCabe is a member of the Irish Province of the SMA, and their current Provincial Leader. He worked as a missionary in Zambia and Liberia; lectured in Mission Studies at the Kimmage Mission Institute, Dublin (1996-2001), and was President of that Institute (1999–2000). He served as a member of the SMA General Council (1989–1995; 2001–2006). He was President of the Executive Committee of the Africa/Europe Faith and Justice Network (2002-2004). He taught courses in Mission Theology at Tangaza College, Nairobi (2008–2013). He is the author of several articles in the areas of Mission Theology, Interreligious-Dialogue and JPIC commitment.

David T. Ngong (Ph.D., Systematic Theology, Baylor University), is originally from Cameroon, Africa, and currently is Assistant Professor of Religion and Theology at Stillman College, Tuscaloosa, Alabama. His research focuses on the religious and theological constructions of African identity in the modern world. Among his publications are *The Holy Spirit and Salvation in African Theology* (2010) and *Theology as Construction of Piety* (2013).

Maureen R. O'Brien, PhD, is Associate Professor of Theology at Duquesne University. Her primary research and teaching commitments focus on practical theology, religious education and the education of ministers, especially Catholic lay ministers. She has published articles in *The International Journal of Practical Theology, Religious Education, Horizons* and others. She co-edited with Susan Yanos a collection of essays by lay ministers, *Emerging from the Vineyard* (2014).

James Chukwuma Okoye, C.S.Sp., is the Director of the Center for Spiritan Studies at Duquesne University and Editor of *Spiritan Horizons*. He taught (1996-2012) at the Catholic Theological Union, Chicago, where as full professor (2008), he held the Carroll Stuhlmueller Chair of Old Testament Studies. Prior to that, he served as Provincial Superior of the Spiritan Province of Nigeria, general councilor in Rome (1986-1992), and a *peritus* at the first Synod of Bishops for Africa (1992-1994). His recent books are *Israel and the Nations: A Mission Theology of the Old Testament* (2006); *Scripture in the Church. The Synod on the Word of God and the Post-Synodal Exhortation Verbum Domini* (2011).

Peter Cho Phan is Ignacio Ellacuría, S.J. Chair of Catholic Social Thought, Department of Theology Georgetown University. He is General Editor of the "Theology in Global Perspective" — 25 volumes (Orbis Books); General Editor of the "Pastoral Spirituality Series" — 12 volumes

(Paulist Press); General Editor of *Studies of Christianities in the World* (Palgrave/Macmillan). His influential publications include: *In Our Own Tongues: Perspectives from Asia on Mission and Inculturation* (2003); *Being Religious Interreligiously: Asian Perspectives on Interfaith Dialogue in Postmodernity* (2004); *Vietnamese-American Catholics* (2005); *Living into Death, Dying into Life: Death and the Afterlife.* (2014); *Catholic Christianities of Asia: History and Theologies* (2015, forthcoming).

Robert Schreiter, C.PP.S. is Vatican Council II Professor of Theology at the Catholic Theological Union in Chicago. He is past president of the American Society of Missiology and of the Catholic Theological Society of America. He has written extensively on inculturation, world mission, reconciliation, and religious life. Among his influential books are *Constructing Local Theologies* (1985), *The New Catholicity: Theology between the Global and the Local* (1997), and *Mission in the Third Millennium* (2001).

Cardinal Peter Kodwo Appiah Turkson, Archbishop emeritus of Cape Coast (Ghana), is President, Pontifical Council for Justice and Peace. He was General Relator of the 2nd Special Assembly for Africa of the Synod of Bishops (October 2009). He served as president of the Ghana Catholic Bishops' Conference (1997-2004), a member of the Governing Council of the University of Ghana, Legon (2001-2006) and of the Board of Directors of Central Region Development Commission (2002-2006). He served as President of the Regional Episcopal Conference of West Africa (2007-2010), and serves as Vice President of the Association of Episcopal Conferences of Anglophone West Africa. He was awarded honorary doctorate degree by Duquesne University (2012).